Survival

GLOBAL POLITICS AND STRATEGY

Volume 63 Number 2 | April–May 2021

'We should not conclude that Russia is in any way the master of the internet, or that it outclasses the US at cyber operations.'

Marcus Willett, Lessons of the SolarWinds Hack, p. 12.

'Reformists would do well to pave over their differences and collectively push for those limited reforms that are feasible, rather than insisting on maximal demands. Permanent members, for their part, should bear in mind that ultimately the council is useful to them only if UN member states believe in its legitimacy and are willing to heed its decisions.'

Martin Binder and Monika Heupel, The Intricacies of UN Security Council Reform, p. 66.

'This was the era in which Richard Nixon and Henry Kissinger had deputised Iran as the linchpin of America's strategy in the Persian Gulf. They ignored all the warnings and kept selling weapons to the shah even though his army could not use them and his economy could not afford them.'

Ray Takeyh, Did the US Intelligence Community Lose Iran?, p. 158.

T0144509

Survival
GLOBAL POLITICS AND STRATEGY
Volume 63 Number 2 | April–May 2021

Contents

Cover: Alexander Nemenov/AFP via Getty Images

On the cover
The headquarters of Russia's Federal Security Service overlooks Lubyanka Square in central Moscow on a snowy day in February 2021.

On the web
Visit www.iiss.org/ publications/survival for brief notices on new books on the Environment and Resources, the Middle East and the United States.

***Survival* editors' blog**
For ideas and commentary from *Survival* editors and contributors, visit www.iiss.org/blogs/ survival-blog.

Survival
GLOBAL POLITICS AND STRATEGY

The International Institute for Strategic Studies

2121 K Street, NW | Suite 600 | Washington DC 20037 | USA
Tel +1 202 659 1490   Fax +1 202 659 1499   E-mail survival@iiss.org   Web www.iiss.org

Arundel House | 6 Temple Place | London | WC2R 2PG | UK
Tel +44 (0)20 7379 7676   Fax +44 (0)20 7836 3108   E-mail iiss@iiss.org

14th Floor, GBCorp Tower | Bahrain Financial Harbour | Manama | Kingdom of Bahrain
Tel +973 1718 1155   Fax +973 1710 0155   E-mail iiss-middleeast@iiss.org

9 Raffles Place | #49-01 Republic Plaza | Singapore 048619
Tel +65 6499 0055   Fax +65 6499 0059   E-mail iiss-asia@iiss.org

Survival Online www.tandfonline.com/survival and www.iiss.org/publications/survival

Aims and Scope *Survival* is one of the world's leading forums for analysis and debate of international and strategic affairs. Shaped by its editors to be both timely and forward thinking, the journal encourages writers to challenge conventional wisdom and bring fresh, often controversial, perspectives to bear on the strategic issues of the moment. With a diverse range of authors, *Survival* aims to be scholarly in depth while vivid, well written and policy-relevant in approach. Through commentary, analytical articles, case studies, forums, review essays, reviews and letters to the editor, the journal promotes lively, critical debate on issues of international politics and strategy.

Editor **Dana Allin**
Managing Editor **Jonathan Stevenson**
Associate Editor **Carolyn West**
Assistant Editor **Jessica Watson**
Production and Cartography **John Buck, Kelly Verity**

Contributing Editors

Ian Bremmer	**Toby Dodge**	**John L. Harper**	**Jeffrey Mazo**	**Angela Stent**
Rosa Brooks	**Bill Emmott**	**Matthew Harries**	**'Funmi Olonisakin**	**Ray Takeyh**
David P. Calleo	**Mark Fitzpatrick**	**Erik Jones**	**Teresita C. Schaffer**	**David C. Unger**
Russell Crandall	**John A. Gans, Jr**	**Hanns W. Maull**	**Steven Simon**	**Lanxin Xiang**

Published for the IISS by
Routledge Journals, an imprint of Taylor & Francis, an Informa business.

About the IISS The IISS, a registered charity with offices in Washington, London, Manama and Singapore, is the world's leading authority on political–military conflict. It is the primary independent source of accurate, objective information on international strategic issues. Publications include *The Military Balance*, an annual reference work on each nation's defence capabilities; *Strategic Survey*, an annual review of world affairs; *Survival*, a bimonthly journal on international affairs; *Strategic Comments*, an online analysis of topical issues in international affairs; and the *Adelphi* series of books on issues of international security.

SUBMISSIONS

To submit an article, authors are advised to follow these guidelines:

- *Survival* articles are around 4,000–10,000 words long including endnotes. A word count should be included with a draft.
- All text, including endnotes, should be double-spaced with wide margins.
- Any tables or artwork should be supplied in separate files, ideally not embedded in the document or linked to text around it.
- All *Survival* articles are expected to include endnote references. These should be complete and include first and last names of authors, titles of articles (even from newspapers), place of publication, publisher, exact publication dates, volume and issue number (if from a journal) and page numbers. Web sources should include complete URLs and DOIs if available.
- A summary of up to 150 words should be included with the article. The summary should state the main argument clearly and concisely, not simply say what the article is about.

- A short author's biography of one or two lines should also be included. This information will appear at the foot of the first page of the article.

Please note that *Survival* has a strict policy of listing multiple authors in alphabetical order.

Submissions should be made by email, in Microsoft Word format, to survival@iiss.org. Alternatively, hard copies may be sent to *Survival*, IISS–US, 2121 K Street NW, Suite 801, Washington, DC 20037, USA.

The editorial review process can take up to three months. *Survival*'s acceptance rate for unsolicited manuscripts is less than 20%. *Survival* does not normally provide referees' comments in the event of rejection. Authors are permitted to submit simultaneously elsewhere so long as this is consistent with the policy of the other publication and the Editors of *Survival* are informed of the dual submission.

Readers are encouraged to comment on articles from the previous issue. Letters should be concise, no longer than 750 words and relate directly to the argument or points made in the original article.

ADVERTISING AND PERMISSIONS

For advertising rates and schedules

USA/Canada: The Advertising Manager, Taylor & Francis Inc., 530 Walnut Street, Suite 850, Philadelphia, PA 19106, USA Tel +1 (800) 354 1420 Fax +1 (215) 207 0050.

UK/Europe/Rest of World: The Advertising Manager, Routledge Journals, Taylor & Francis, 4 Park Square, Milton Park, Abingdon, Oxfordshire OX14 4RN, UK Tel +44 (0) 207 017 6000 Fax +44 (0) 207 017 6336.

SUBSCRIPTIONS

Survival is published bimonthly in February, April, June, August, October and December by Routledge Journals, an imprint of Taylor & Francis, an Informa Business.

Annual Subscription 2021

	UK, RoI	US, Canada Mexico	Europe	Rest of world
Individual	£172	$290	€ 233	$290
Institution (print and online)	£620	$1,085	€ 909	$1,142
Institution (online only)	£527	$922	€ 773	$971

Taylor & Francis has a flexible approach to subscriptions, enabling us to match individual libraries' requirements. This journal is available via a traditional institutional subscription (either print with online access, or online only at a discount) or as part of our libraries, subject collections or archives. For more information on our sales packages please visit http://www. tandfonline.com/page/librarians.

All current institutional subscriptions include online access for any number of concurrent users across a local area network to the currently available backfile and articles posted online ahead of publication.

Subscriptions purchased at the personal rate are strictly for personal, non-commercial use only. The reselling of personal subscriptions is prohibited. Personal subscriptions must be purchased with a personal cheque or credit card. Proof of personal status may be requested.

Dollar rates apply to all subscribers outside Europe. Euro rates apply to all subscribers in Europe, except the UK and the Republic of Ireland where the pound sterling rate applies. If you are unsure which rate applies to you please contact Customer Services in the UK. All subscriptions are payable in advance and all rates include postage. Journals are sent by air to the USA, Canada, Mexico, India, Japan and Australasia. Subscriptions are entered on an annual basis, i.e. January to December. Payment may be made by sterling cheque, dollar cheque, euro cheque, international money order, National Giro or credit cards (Amex, Visa and Mastercard).

Survival (USPS 013095) is published bimonthly (in Feb, Apr, Jun, Aug, Oct and Dec) by Routledge Journals, Taylor & Francis, 4 Park Square, Milton Park, Abingdon, OX14 4RN, United Kingdom.

The US annual subscription price is $1,023. Airfreight and mailing in the USA by agent named WN Shipping USA, 156-15, 146th Avenue, 2nd Floor, Jamaica, NY 11434, USA. Periodicals postage paid at Jamaica NY 11431.

US Postmaster: Send address changes to Survival, C/O Air Business Ltd / 156-15 146th Avenue, Jamaica, New York, NY11434.

Subscription records are maintained at Taylor & Francis Group, 4 Park Square, Milton Park, Abingdon, OX14 4RN, United Kingdom.

ORDERING INFORMATION

Please contact your local Customer Service Department to take out a subscription to the Journal: **USA, Canada:** Taylor & Francis, Inc., 530 Walnut Street, Suite 850, Philadelphia, PA 19106, USA. Tel: +1 800 354 1420; Fax: +1 215 207 0050. **UK/ Europe/Rest of World:** T&F Customer Services, Informa UK Ltd, Sheepen Place, Colchester, Essex, CO3 3LP, United Kingdom. Tel: +44 (0) 20 7017 5544; Fax: +44 (0) 20 7017 5198; Email: subscriptions@tandf.co.uk.

Back issues: Taylor & Francis retains a two-year back issue stock of journals. Older volumes are held by our official stockists: Periodicals Service Company, 351 Fairview Ave., Suite 300, Hudson, New York 12534, USA to whom all orders and enquiries should be addressed. *Tel* +1 518 537 4700 *Fax* +1 518 537 5899 *e-mail* psc@periodicals.com *web* http://www.periodicals. com/tandf.html.

The International Institute for Strategic Studies (IISS) and our publisher Taylor & Francis make every effort to ensure the accuracy of all the information (the "Content") contained in our publications. However, the IISS and our publisher Taylor & Francis, our agents, and our licensors make no representations or warranties whatsoever as to the accuracy, completeness, or suitability for any purpose of the Content. Any opinions and views expressed in this publication are the opinions and views of the authors, and are not the views of or endorsed by the IISS and our publisher Taylor & Francis. The accuracy of the Content should not be relied upon and should be independently verified with primary sources of information. The IISS and our publisher Taylor & Francis shall not be liable for any losses, actions, claims, proceedings, demands, costs, expenses, damages, and other liabilities whatsoever or howsoever caused arising directly or indirectly in connection with, in relation to or arising out of the use of the Content. Terms & Conditions of access and use can be found at http://www.tandfonline.com/page/terms-and-conditions.

The issue date is April–May 2021.

The print edition of this journal is printed on ANSI-conforming acid-free paper.

Lessons of the SolarWinds Hack

Marcus Willett

In late 2020, the American cyber-security community discovered a widespread breach of private-sector and government networks. A primary vector for the breach appeared to be the hacking of software provided by the US information-technology company SolarWinds. The United States government identified the likely perpetrator as a Russian intelligence agency. Ever since, complex and painstaking technical investigations have been under way into the precise nature and extent of the breach. At the same time, debate has raged about the intent behind the hack and the implications for the cyber policies of the US, and states in general, including whether some form of retaliation is justified. This article examines issues raised by the SolarWinds hack with respect to the cyber-security, offensive-cyber and broader national-security policies of the US and its allies.

What we know

The story first broke when FireEye, a top US cyber-security company involved in many major investigations and responsible for publicly identifying the perpetrators of numerous attacks (including the Russian intelligence services), announced in December 2020 that it had been hacked by a state with 'top tier' capabilities. Its own 'red-team' tools – developed by FireEye to test client defences based on previously detected capabilities – had been

Marcus Willett is IISS Senior Adviser for Cyber. During his previous career in GCHQ, he helped design UK cyber strategy, and initiated and led a number of national cyber programmes.

Survival | vol. 63 no. 2 | April–May 2021 | pp. 7–26   https://doi.org/10.1080/00396338.2021.1906001

accessed. FireEye further discovered that the vector used by the hackers was the IT company SolarWinds and that there were many other victims.

SolarWinds is a Texas-based company that supports its clients by supplying software called Orion to monitor and manage IT networks, including by aggregating, analysing and visualising large amounts of data. Investigations following FireEye's initial discovery showed that the hackers had infected SolarWinds' Orion software as early as October 2019, allowing them to use a routine software security update from SolarWinds in March 2020 to install malicious software in the company's clients' networks. The hackers may have taken advantage of lax security practices to penetrate SolarWinds in the first instance and, by hiding within that security update, evaded the clients' cyber-security defences. In that sense, it was an ingenious attack, with Microsoft suggesting that it might have taken '1,000 very skilled, very capable engineers' to design and execute it.[1] According to SolarWinds, 18,000 of its clients downloaded the infected software.

In February 2021, while acknowledging that the full extent of the breach was still under investigation, the US government stated that, as a result of a 'broad and indiscriminate effort', the hackers had gained access to the data and emails of at least nine US federal agencies, including the Department of the Treasury and the Department of Justice, and about 100 private companies.[2] These companies included major digital-technology outfits such as Cisco, Intel, Nvidia and Microsoft, as well as cyber-security companies like FireEye. There were also indications that the hackers may have hidden inside US cloud services (such as Microsoft's and Amazon's) to further exploit the results of their initial hack. As of mid-February, cyber-security experts also discovered that 30% of the identified victims of the hack had no direct connection with SolarWinds itself, with the possibility therefore remaining that SolarWinds was not the hackers' only initial launch point. Nevertheless, the infection has become widely known as the 'SolarWinds hack'.[3]

The US government attributed the hack to an 'advanced, persistent threat actor likely of Russian origin', meaning a Russian intelligence agency.[4] Some in the US have described it as one of the most significant attacks ever carried out against the US, arguably an act of war.[5] The extent to which it may have spread to other countries is unclear. Although experts believe the hack had a

US focus, clients of SolarWinds in Canada, Mexico, Europe, the Middle East and elsewhere may also have downloaded the infected software.

Given that the investigations are still under way, a great deal remains unknown about the hack. The information thus far publicly released about how the hack was detected may not tell the full story. It cannot be ruled out that secret US capabilities played a role behind the scenes. The use of sensitive government intelligence capabilities can be concealed behind other, less sensitive means of detection and attribution. Furthermore, classic counter-espionage operations can involve letting hostile activity continue and observing it to find out more, before potentially subverting it or revealing its detection. It is unclear whether there is sufficient coordination between private cyber-security companies and government agencies in the US to ensure that the right strategic decisions can be made about how and when to publicly reveal knowledge of such compromises.

In early March, the US revealed that further large-scale breaches unrelated to the Russian SolarWinds hack had been discovered. Attributed by Microsoft to a state-sponsored Chinese group and exploiting vulnerabilities in Microsoft's email servers, this new hack had apparently infected up to 30,000 public and private entities, mainly small businesses and local government. Other state and non-state cyber actors may have begun trying to exploit the initial hack in a race to beat installation of patches provided by Microsoft. Some speculated that this Chinese attack could turn out to be even more widespread than the Russian SolarWinds one. While the Chinese activity is not specifically analysed here, it is likely to have many of the same implications for US policy.

The hackers' intent

Although the SolarWinds hack has been labelled a cyber 'attack', initial analysis indicates that it was intended not to damage, disrupt or destroy networks, but rather to gain intelligence. Known as a 'supply-chain operation' since it used suppliers of IT services to get inside their clients' networks, and using clever techniques to evade detection, the SolarWinds hack appeared designed to infect multiple networks to gain broad access to potentially interesting data and emails. Thus, it does not appear to have the hallmarks of being targeted, surgical espionage. Furthermore, there seems to be no evidence thus far that it infected classified US networks. In that regard, it is not as serious as a widely reported Russian hack in 2008, which used an infected USB stick to leap the air gap onto US Department of Defense classified networks. Overall, therefore, the SolarWinds hack looks like an intelligence 'fishing trip' or reconnaissance operation unleashed on open networks, similar in intent to many other state cyber operations, such as the Chinese hack of the US Office of Personnel Management that occurred from 2013 to 2015.

It is perhaps equally instructive to compare the SolarWinds hack with a 2017 Russian operation that used malware called 'NotPetya' to target networks in Ukraine. NotPetya was a 'worm': self-replicating malware that spreads through networks in a fundamentally uncontrolled way. The SolarWinds hack was also designed to gain an initial presence on a large number of networks. Strictly speaking, though, it was not a worm, with the Russians appearing to retain sufficient control to be able to deactivate selected operations. Both were supply-chain operations, with NotPetya delivered via a back door in an automatic update to some popular Ukrainian tax-preparation software supplied by the company Intellect Services. But NotPetya appeared specifically designed to infect Ukraine's critical national infrastructure (its energy companies, power grid, transport sector and banks) and to damage devices rather than just collect intelligence. This highlights the difference between a large-scale offensive cyber attack, like NotPetya, and large-scale cyber espionage, like the SolarWinds hack.

There are other potentially relevant differences between the two operations. While the use of the tax software as the vector for the NotPetya attack clearly targeted Ukraine, the operation also made some use of a leaked tool developed by the US National Security Agency and sold for auction by the mysterious 'Shadow Brokers' group in April 2017. The tool exploited a widespread vulnerability in a Microsoft Windows protocol, which allowed hackers to remotely run code on unpatched machines. The Russian use of a worm in combination with such a widespread IT vulnerability meant that an attack targeting Ukrainian critical infrastructure infected many unintended networks the world over, including those used by the Danish shipping line Maersk and the US delivery company FedEx. An alternative interpretation of the SolarWinds hack is that, among the many unintended victims, the Russians likewise had specific targets in mind. For example, given that they accessed FireEye's red-team hacking tools, one aim could have been to penetrate the US cyber-security community or US cloud-service providers to bolster Russia's own arsenal of offensive tools, and to develop new supply-chain opportunities for potentially even more valuable operations in the future.

Whether intended as broad-gauge reconnaissance or with specific targets in mind, the result of the SolarWinds hack is that the Russians are present on a range of US governmental networks and, potentially, parts of the United States' critical national infrastructure. While the intent seems to have been to gather intelligence, the operations could be technically repurposed by the Russians at a time of their choosing to deliver a destructive effect. Their operations could also be hijacked by others with hostile intent, or could malfunction, causing an unintended accident. Furthermore, with such reconnaissance operations by states occurring every day in cyberspace, any one of them could be misinterpreted by the victim as an actual attack. Ultimately, though, it is the broad vulnerability caused to a state by an attack like the SolarWinds hack, regardless of intent and the actual damage that results, that could lead that state to conclude that a penetration of its networks went unacceptably beyond the routine daily attrition of state-on-state cyber operations and therefore called for retaliation. Broader escalation could easily follow. As Microsoft president Brad Smith put it, the SolarWinds operation is like a 'burglar who wants to break into a single apartment but manages to turn off the alarm systems for every home and every building in the entire city. Everybody's safety is put at risk.'[6] Such considerations raise the question of how the US might legitimately be able to respond if it were to discover that the Russians had penetrated, say, its power grids, irrespective of original intent.

How to respond

US private-sector companies have detected and are disrupting a large-scale Russian cyber-espionage operation. There is plenty of evidence in material leaked from the US government that the US engages in similar cyber-espionage operations, including using supply chains. So we should not conclude that Russia is in any way the master of the internet, or that it outclasses the US at cyber operations. Far from it – Russia is so worried about what it has learned about US and allied cyber capabilities from US intelligence leaks (especially Edward Snowden's) and by US commercial dominance of internet technology (exemplified by US pressure on the Chinese IT company Huawei) that the Russian government is seeking ways to isolate Russia physically from the global internet, despite the economic and social disadvantages of doing so.[7] Like China, Russia seems to recognise serious deficiencies in its own cyber security, with its low ranking in the relevant international cyber-security indices an indicator.[8]

SolarWinds was not an act of war

Given that the SolarWinds hack therefore appears to constitute reconnaissance and espionage of the sort that the US itself excels at, it is neither accurate nor sensible for US commentators to characterise it as an act of war requiring warlike retaliation.[9] If using spy planes, satellites and double agents to gather intelligence from inside the Soviet Union was normal business during the Cold War, the same is true of an operation like SolarWinds in the digital age.[10] The US would not have invoked Article V of the North Atlantic Treaty if it thought an adversary might have been able to blow up the Twin Towers on account of having hacked the power supply, for example; it invoked Article V because of the death and destruction caused by an actual attack.

The US did agree to a bilateral treaty with China in 2015 intended to limit cyber-espionage operations, but it was designed specifically to put large-scale commercial espionage off limits, not to stop other types of cyber espionage. Attempts to steal state secrets in peacetime are internationally tolerated because, among other things, they can reduce the chance of a misunderstanding that could lead to a real conflict. Broadly accepted retaliatory protocols for such activities have developed over time. When a state is caught spying in the physical (as opposed to virtual) world, the result is normally a tit-for-tat expulsion of diplomats and intelligence officers, nothing more.

More could be done to develop equivalent protocols for cyber espionage. One tactic employed by the US and its allies over the last five years has been to work together to publicly name individual perpetrators of cyber attacks. In some cases, the US has also indicted them, effectively barring them from travelling to relevant jurisdictions, with an eye to deterring similar conduct in future. These remedies demonstrate the ability of democratic governments not only to detect and attribute attacks, but also to operate in close alliance, with extensive sharing of cyber intelligence and, in some cases, integrated capabilities.[11] China, Iran, North Korea and Russia have nothing equivalent.

Internationally agreed protocols are also useful. One of the original 11 cyber norms of behaviour agreed under the auspices of the United Nations in 2015 encourages states to consider all relevant information, including the wider context and the nature and extent of the consequence of any cyber intrusion, before reacting.[12] The same norm, however, implies that it is difficult to attribute cyber operations, which might encourage some states to execute operations in the belief that they can avoid blame. Such a rationale seriously misconceives the nature of attribution.[13] Cyber-capable states have for some time been able to confidently identify perpetrators of attacks, though they have often hesitated to make those attributions public due to worries about protecting sensitive intelligence sources and methods. As cyber-security ecosystems have matured, particularly in terms of private-sector intelligence gathering and cooperation between governments and companies, the public attribution of cyber operations has become more commonplace. SolarWinds is a case in point, clearly signalling that, once detected, state cyber operations are likely to be firmly attributed.

Of course, the 11 original cyber norms of behaviour agreed in 2015, and those added subsequently by the Global Commission on the Stability of Cyberspace and other bodies, are voluntary and non-binding, and include various national-security exceptions. They are honoured more in the breach than in the observance, and are not enforceable. For example, one of the original 11 holds that states should take responsible steps to ensure the integrity of the supply chain for information- and communication-technology (ICT) products by seeking to prevent the proliferation of malicious ICT tools and techniques, and the use of 'hidden functions'. The NotPetya and SolarWinds hacks, as well as the US espionage operations exposed by Snowden and the Shadow Brokers, clearly contravene this guideline. Another norm advises that states should not intentionally damage or impair the use and operation of critical infrastructure, which the Russians did with NotPetya though not, it would seem, with SolarWinds.

Such guidelines need to be more tightly and realistically framed. For example, states will inevitably consider a potential adversary's critical networks a legitimate wartime target, and need to gain a technical presence on such networks during peacetime to prepare for that eventuality. There is little point in pretending that they won't try to do so. Also, the term 'critical national infrastructure' is too open to interpretation. Accordingly, it would be useful to establish a norm of behaviour that specifically identifies those networks that no nation should consider sensible to target for reconnaissance, espionage or attack in war or peace. Examples include hospitals, emergency services and nuclear command-and-control systems. Rather than unrealistically attempting to exclude an array of other aspects of 'critical infrastructure', an overarching norm of behaviour could broadly define as unacceptable the reckless use of indiscriminate techniques likely to undermine the day-to-day use of the internet by unintended victims. Given the potentially dangerous nature of their effects, the careless protection and reckless use of such capabilities would then deserve the same sort of international opprobrium given to carpet bombing, cluster munitions and chemical weapons. In the wake of the SolarWinds hack, President Joseph Biden has specifically highlighted the 'recklessness' of Russian behaviour and made cyber diplomacy and international cyber norms foreign-policy priorities. It would also help if the US community ceased labelling the SolarWinds hack 'sophisticated' – it is technically far more challenging to be surgical than to be indiscriminate – and instead reserved that description for attacks that so qualify.

Legal and diplomatic clarifications are required to give such voluntary norms sufficient teeth. In particular, states should be pressed to acknowledge that existing international law applies to cyber operations, emphasising that it is the effect rather than the specific means of a hostile operation that matters from a legal standpoint. In turn, states could agree on penalties that could be imposed on states caught behaving recklessly and imperilling the general safety of populations during peacetime, making clear that mere indignation over an operation's technical audacity and success – à la SolarWinds – would not trigger such penalties. These could range from exclusions from international forums to diplomatic expulsions to economic reprisals. Of note, work is under way at the International Committee of the Red Cross to better define the responsible use of cyber capabilities, including how international humanitarian law applies to cyber operations.

Implications for cyber security

Perhaps most importantly, the SolarWinds hack should focus attention on what adjustments are needed to the internal cyber-security strategies and capabilities of the US and its allies. This has been the central concern of expert testimony to the US Congress, which has called for increasing the powers of and funding for the US Cybersecurity and Infrastructure Security Agency (CISA); improving coordination between the US government and the corporate sector; grants to state and local government to enhance their cyber security; and accelerating IT modernisation across the federal government. Notably, most experts are not suggesting that all networks can be technically shielded from all attacks, or advocating that increased investment should be reserved solely for more and bigger technical solutions.

To be sure, protecting networks remains crucial for preventing the vast majority of attacks, especially those conducted by cyber criminals. The rapid growth in the criminal use of ransomware – whereby an organisation's data is encrypted and held to ransom – is arguably more strategically damaging than state cyber-spying. Ransomware attacks increased by approximately 40% during 2020 compared with 2019, as perpetrators took advantage of the COVID-19 pandemic, with the average payout more than doubling.[14] Criminals have also shifted towards soft targets, prioritising poorly defended sectors such as education, health and local government, as well as smaller companies. Even before the recent hike in ransomware attacks, the overall global loss to financially motivated cyber crime has been assessed to be 1–2% of global GDP.[15]

It would therefore be a mistake to let concerns about a complex state attack like the SolarWinds hack obfuscate the need for a concerted effort across all sectors to improve basic cyber hygiene.[16] The majority of cyber-criminal capabilities are not as sophisticated as those available to cyber-capable states, and do not involve the level of ingenuity employed in the SolarWinds hack. Instead, they rely on lapses in fundamental protections, as indeed do most state attacks. Many exploit human weakness: poor password discipline, poor awareness and training (particularly against phishing), failure to keep the routine patching of software up to date and failure to audit. Reinforcing basic cyber hygiene with new laws establishing disincentives to pay ransoms to cyber criminals – it is currently too convenient for companies simply to use their insurance to pay up – and stronger incentives for companies to report all breaches would make sense. Organisations that implement basic cyber hygiene can stop 90% of potential breaches.

Good cyber hygiene is part of a 'whole of society' approach to cyber security. This is, appropriately, the declared aim of cyber-capable democracies and requires central government to facilitate close public–private collaboration, develop appropriate upskilling and educational schemes, and heighten public awareness. For the US and some of its key allies, this approach is underpinned by a burgeoning cyber-security industrial sector, capable of detecting, attributing and preventing sophisticated hacks. In liberal democracies, where for good reason there are extensive restrictions on the ability of the intelligence community to monitor private networks (including those providing the cloud services that appeared to feature in the SolarWinds hack), this young industry has become a fundamental element of the overall cyber-security ecosystem. Russia and China have nothing of an equivalent scale, and therefore often try to copy Western technical cyber-security solutions. Notwithstanding SolarWinds, it would be a mistake to lose confidence in the cyber-security industry and the suppliers of secure IT solutions in general (including cloud providers), and certainly nobody would advocate increasing the government's internal surveillance powers. The fact that the US private sector detected and disrupted a complex Russian espionage operation is evidence that the liberal-democratic cyber-security model works.

That said, the US model was not nearly efficient or effective enough, given the time it seems to have taken to uncover the Russian hack. Having advised their clients repeatedly about the 'supply-chain' threat, cyber-security and IT companies should recognise that they themselves are prize targets for potential supply-chain operations and therefore need to rigorously follow their own security advice. This should include applying extra protections to their most valuable data which, for cyber-security companies, includes their own red-team hacking tools and stored threat intelligence. More generally, cyber-security experts in governments and companies are advocating the development of a 'zero-trust architecture' approach to security. This includes the requirement that users, devices and services be continuously authorised and authenticated once they are inside the network, not just when joining it.[17] There have also been calls in congressional testimony for major IT companies to modernise some of their key security-related processes, including authentication systems. Furthermore, debate has intensified over how the storage of critical data should be spread between the cloud and 'on-premise' solutions. The recently uncovered Chinese hacking of Microsoft email servers intensifies these concerns.

The psychology of security needs to change

Regardless of how much the security of cyber-security and IT services can be improved through regulation or corporate initiatives, their customers cannot afford to be complacent. It is still their data, the compromise of which is their reputational, legal and financial risk. They should therefore hold those selling them services closer to account for the security provided. How many of SolarWinds' many clients asked the company to provide proof of a recent, externally validated audit of SolarWinds' own security practices? The psychology of security in most companies still needs to change. In major companies, junior officials report security issues to boards primarily concerned with the implications for the company's legal compliance. Instead, the boards themselves should include a mandatory, permanent, full-time executive in charge of security, which should be treated on a par with legal and financial risk.

A further weakness in the cyber-security ecosystem is that a good deal of security consulting is done by the same companies that sell the services and technology. Objective appraisal may clash with sales goals, which raises a potential conflict of interest. Of course, some independent advice is already available through government organisations such as the National Institute of Standards and Technology and CISA in the US, and the National Cyber Security Centre in the UK. Nevertheless, the development of a stronger stable of independent private-sector consultancy firms with no technical solutions and only expertise and advice to sell, approved by government, would strengthen the overall system.

All of the aforementioned safeguards might have led to quicker detection or even prevention of the SolarWinds hack, or significantly limited its spread, raising the cost to Russia of successful espionage. But the balance of power would still remain with the capable state attacker. It still only needs to find one way around or through the defences, whereas the defender has to detect and stop every attack. While good cyber hygiene might prevent 90% of attacks, and more sophisticated layers of defence might take that to 95–99%, the most capable actors will still eventually get through. Perhaps the key lesson of SolarWinds for cyber security, and more broadly of ransomware attacks for those who cannot afford the best defence, is that greater priority should be given to improving resilience. Networks should be designed and constructed, and data stored, to lessen the impact of compromise by ensuring that the best protections and redundancy are applied to the most valuable subset of data. This could involve introducing a data-classification system and storing the most valuable data in several independent places, and in some instances even air-gapping its storage from the internet. In addition, processes for crisis management and response and disaster recovery should be regularly exercised, in preparation for the almost inevitable breach.

Finally, it is worth noting that the SolarWinds hack exploited software and equipment supplied by US companies. It had nothing to do with any Russian-owned or -supplied equipment. Neither did the recently discovered Chinese hack of Microsoft email servers involve Chinese equipment. Indeed, this is true of most state cyber-espionage operations, which might otherwise jeopardise the state's own companies and their exports. In this light, the inclination of the US government to ban Chinese equipment from national networks on account of an espionage risk appears somewhat overblown. The more formidable technological challenge to cyber security will arise with the Internet of Things: household appliances, cars, roads, healthcare systems and even whole cities connected to the internet so as to become 'smart'. This development portends a massive increase in the number of internet-connected devices, and a far wider vulnerability to disruption. Devising a security ecosystem, technical protections and even basic cyber hygiene to protect the Internet of Things involves far more complex tasks. In this instance, foreign ownership of key components inside national networks does present a major risk – not of espionage in peacetime, but rather sabotage in periods of heightened tension or war. Diversifying next-generation mobile networks by using open architectures to integrate equipment from multiple vendors, while placing restrictions on high-risk vendors, looks like one way to manage such risks in the future.

The implications for offensive cyber

The development and application of offensive cyber doctrine have been under way in the United States for almost as long as the internet it invented has existed.[18] Its notably successful use of sophisticated cyber capabilities between 2008 and 2010 to disrupt Iranian nuclear enrichment occurred only halfway through that short history.

The 2018 US National Cyber Strategy announced a Cyber Deterrence Initiative that aimed to impose 'consequences' on malign cyber actors. While the national strategy makes it clear that there are many ways to do this, the US Department of Defense's 2018 Cyber Strategy sets out the role aggressive US cyber operations are intended to play. The strategy contemplates using cyber operations for an assertive defence of national interests, defending 'forward' (that is, on adversary networks), pre-empting attack and competing daily by way of 'persistent engagement'.[19] As a result of the SolarWinds hack, some are questioning whether such use of cyber operations is working or could ever work, and whether the investment should instead be diverted to national cyber security.

If the intent of SolarWinds was espionage and reconnaissance, it should be no surprise that US offensive cyber capabilities did not deter it, as that is manifestly not their purpose. During the Cold War, the threat of retaliatory conventional and nuclear attack was to stop war, not to deter state-on-state espionage, reconnaissance, pre-positioning or even covert action; indeed, it incentivised such activities. We should not view actions taken in cyberspace differently. The United States' defend-forward strategy is intended to deter (and retaliate against) a state whose goal is to use cyber or other means to disrupt, damage or destroy rather than to spy. By contrast, in dealing with cyber espionage, a state's strategy should be to incorporate protective measures that make espionage against it as difficult as possible, and to detect, dissect and disrupt it when it occurs. It should not expect to prevent it completely, especially given that it is an accepted part of international behaviour. Indeed, the only publicly avowed US cyber operations to have taken place against a state actor under the Cyber Deterrence Initiative were conducted by US Cyber Command before the US mid-term elections in 2018 against a Russian group that attempted to disrupt – not merely spy on – the 2016 US presidential election. While there were probably many reasons the Russians did not attempt to disrupt the 2020 presidential election in the same way, the US operation may have contributed. Furthermore, the fact that in 2019 the US considered the use of cyber operations to retaliate against the shooting down of a US drone by the Iranians is a reminder that, ultimately, the development of offensive cyber capabilities is also for when deterrence fails. As the Pentagon's 2018 Cyber Strategy acknowledges, such capabilities are also needed for war.[20] Doctrinally, cyber-capable states recognise that they cannot just build cyber fortresses ('Maginot Lines') but also need to be able to manoeuvre in cyberspace.

Clearly, therefore, the SolarWinds hack does not detract from the need to invest in and develop offensive cyber. But the short history of cyber operations starkly shows how carefully this must be done. As noted, to attack Ukraine, the Russians used a worm in combination with highly sensitive capabilities that the US had developed for espionage, failed to protect and lost. The same leaked US capabilities also played a role in North Korea's worldwide use of a worm in the WannaCry ransomware attack of 2017 that infected 200,000 computers across 150 countries, and claimed the UK National Health Service as an unintended victim. Even if the US intent behind creating the original capabilities was to use them purely for espionage, and even if the Russian intent behind the SolarWinds hack was the same, the release of such capabilities 'in the wild' opens them up to reuse and repurposing by other states (and non-state actors, for that matter) to destructive effect.

Like their adversaries, though, liberal democracies still need to reconnoitre networks and position capabilities in peacetime to have any chance of success during war. As noted, the risks of miscalculation need to be carefully managed. In this connection, the United States' persistent engagement during peacetime with state adversaries on their networks appears risky. Such skirmishing can be easily justified when conducted to disrupt the state, or state-directed organisations, responsible for hostile cyber attacks. But if used to interfere with, or perceived to interfere with, the more general networks of state adversaries, it could become problematic. An adversary might use it to justify retaliatory interference in internal US networks, including, for example, those relating to the US electoral process. In that case, the intended deterrence would have failed. Defenders of persistent engagement might argue, of course, that operations demonstrating the potential to cause disruption on adversary networks could have precisely the deterrent effect the United States seeks. The point is that these are fine lines, and the history of offensive cyber is too short to support firm conclusions either way.[21]

Generally, there is not enough that is properly understood about the realities of offensive cyber to allow for informed public debate about its utility and the risks entailed. It is salutary that, without so far having had such a debate, some were quick to question the need to invest in offensive cyber at all. Given the US Cyber Deterrence Initiative and, for example, the UK's recent creation of a National Cyber Force, it is all the more urgent to have that informed debate.

*　　*　　*

The extent of the SolarWinds hack, and the vulnerabilities it has created, are extremely serious. Nevertheless, given that its intent was probably merely reconnaissance or espionage, direct retaliatory measures may be hard to justify. The priority instead is for the US to review and renew its approach to national cyber security, while at the same time working with allies and partners to redefine the boundaries of responsible cyber behaviour. In particular, the indiscriminate use of widespread IT vulnerabilities should be recognised as beyond the pale for a responsible state. Protocols for retaliatory and de-escalatory measures should be further developed, noting a key lesson from SolarWinds: that some informed US officials and analysts came close to construing Russian cyber espionage as an act of war.

At the same time, the US should not let the SolarWinds hack dislodge the basic tenets of its current strategy, including a 'whole of society' approach, greater attention to cyber hygiene, improving cooperation between government and the private sector, tackling as a priority the use of ransomware, and deterring destructive attacks by states. The US should maintain confidence in the key advantages that liberal democracies have over their adversaries: a strong and innovative private cyber-security sector, and the ability to act in concert with international allies. Companies in the IT-services and cyber-security sectors should still take a more rigorous approach to ensuring their own security; all organisations should plan for maximum resiliency; and perhaps new domestic regulations mandating the notification of breaches and discouraging the payment of ransoms to cyber criminals are needed.

More broadly, there needs to be a better understanding of the purpose of offensive cyber operations in a liberal democracy: when they are intended for deterrence or retaliation; how they are used in actual conflict; how they can be used in peacetime; and how the risks should be managed. The use of such capabilities to compete persistently on the networks of adversary states in peacetime warrants careful review, to weigh intended effects against attendant risks. Most importantly, liberal democracies need to tell the story publicly of how they, in contrast with their adversaries, develop, protect and use cyber capabilities responsibly. In that vein, both the US and UK governments have revealed publicly how they make decisions about releasing any 'zero day' computer-security vulnerabilities they discover, each announcing a default position to disclose them for patching rather than to retain them for exploitation.[22] This is a good first step, but more is needed.

Ultimately, while the US cannot afford to be complacent, it still needs to keep its assessment of the implications of the SolarWinds hack set in its wider context. Based on the relevant criteria – strategy, governance, cyber security, cyber intelligence, digital industrial capacity and innovation, diplomacy and international alliances, and offensive cyber – the US remains the world's most powerful cyber state by some margin.[23] The SolarWinds hack holds painful lessons for the US, requiring action, but it is unlikely to alter that reality.

Notes

1 Quoted in Kari Paul et al., 'SolarWinds Hack Was Work of "At Least 1,000 Engineers", Tech Executives Tell Senate', *Guardian*, 24 February 2021, https://www.theguardian.com/technology/2021/feb/23/solarwinds-hack-senate-hearing-microsoft.

2 See, for example, White House, 'Press Briefing by Press Secretary Jen Psaki and Deputy National Security Advisor for Cyber and Emerging Technology Anne Neuberger', 17 February 2021, https://www.whitehouse.gov/briefing-room/press-briefings/2021/02/17/press-briefing-by-press-secretary-jen-psaki-and-deputy-national-security-advisor-for-cyber-and-emerging-technology-anne-neuberger-february-17-2021/.

3 To add a further complication, there are apparently ongoing FBI investigations into a hack into SolarWinds, suspected to have been perpetrated by the Chinese state, which led to a breach of a federal payroll agency within the US Department of Agriculture. This used a different software flaw and was on a much smaller scale than the Russian operation. See Christopher Bing et al., 'Exclusive: Suspected Chinese Hackers Used SolarWinds Bug to Spy on U.S. Payroll Agency – Sources', Reuters, 2 February 2021, https://www.reuters.com/article/us-cyber-solarwinds-china-exclusive-idUSKBN2A22K8.

4 White House, 'Press Briefing by Press Secretary Jen Psaki and Deputy National Security Advisor for Cyber and Emerging Technology Anne Neuberger'.

5 See, for example, Yevgeny Vindman, 'Is the SolarWinds Cyberattack an Act of War? It Is, if the United States Says It Is', *Lawfare*, 26 January 2021, https://www.lawfareblog.com/solarwinds-cyberattack-act-war-it-if-united-states-says-it.

6 Quoted in Paul et al., 'SolarWinds Hack Was Work of "At Least 1,000 Engineers", Tech Executives Tell Senate'.

7 See 'Russia's Communications Ministry Plans to Isolate the RuNet by 2020', *Meduza*, 13 May 2016, https://

meduza.io/en/news/2016/05/13/
communications-ministry-plans-
to-isolate-runet-by-2020; and Justin
Sherman, 'Russia's Domestic Internet
Is a Threat to the Global Internet',
Slate, 24 October 2019, https://slate.
com/technology/2019/10/russia-runet-
disconnection-domestic-internet.html.

8   See, for example, International
Telecommunications Union, 'Global
Cybersecurity Index 2018', p. 62,
https://www.itu.int/dms_pub/itu-d/
opb/str/D-STR-GCI.01-2018-PDF-E.pdf.

9   See Tarah Wheeler, 'The Danger in
Calling the SolarWinds Breach an
"Act of War"', Brookings Institution, 4
March 2021, https://www.brookings.
edu/techstream/the-danger-in-calling-
the-solarwinds-breach-an-act-of-war/.

10   See Henrik Breitenbauch and Niels
Byrjalsen, 'Subversion, Statecraft and
Liberal Democracy', *Survival*, vol. 61, no.
4, August–September 2019, pp. 31–41.

11   This dispensation was enshrined in
the United States' 2018 National Cyber
Strategy as the Cyber Deterrence
Initiative: 'The United States will work
with like-minded states to coordinate
and support each other's responses
to significant malicious cyber inci-
dents, including through intelligence
sharing, buttressing of attribution
claims, public statements of support
for responsive actions taken, and joint
imposition of consequences against
malign actors.' See White House,
'National Cyber Strategy of the United
States of America', September 2018, p.
21, https://trumpwhitehouse.archives.
gov/wp-content/uploads/2018/09/
National-Cyber-Strategy.pdf.

12   See UN General Assembly, 'Report
of the Group of Government

Experts on Developments in
the Field of Information and
Telecommunications in the Context
of International Security', A/70/174,
22 July 2015, https://undocs.org/
pdf?symbol=en/A/70/174. A further
eight norms are set out in Global
Commission on the Stability of
Cyberspace, 'Advancing Cyber
Stability: Final Report', November
2019, https://cyberstability.org/report/.

13   See David Blagden, 'Deterring Cyber
Coercion: The Exaggerated Problem
of Attribution', *Survival*, vol. 62, no. 1,
February–March 2020, pp. 131–48.

14   See 'Former US Cybersecurity Chief
Calls for Military to Attack Hackers',
Financial Times, 5 February 2021,
https://www.ft.com/content/27c09769-
ceb5-46dd-824f-40b684d681ae.

15   See, for instance, Sarah Coble,
'Cybercrime Costs World Economy
Over 1% of Global GDP', *Infosecurity
Magazine*, 7 December 2020, https://
www.infosecurity-magazine.com/
news/cybercrime-costs-1trillion/;
and Zhanna Malekos Smith and
Eugenia Lostri, 'The Hidden Costs of
Cybercrime', McAfee, December 2020,
https://www.mcafee.com/enterprise/
en-us/assets/reports/rp-hidden-costs-
of-cybercrime.pdf.

16   The Global Commission on the
Stability of Cyberspace's 'Advancing
Cyber Stability' contains a discus-
sion of 'Basic Cyber Hygiene as
Foundational Defence'.

17   This requirement is advocated
by, for example, the UK National
Cyber Security Centre. See National
Cyber Security Centre, 'Zero Trust
Architecture Design Principles',
20 November 2019, https://www.

ncsc.gov.uk/blog-post/zero-trust-architecture-design-principles. Companies such as Microsoft and CrowdStrike also support it.

18 The term 'offensive cyber' here covers the full range of active cyber operations – from those designed to influence or for disruptive effect in peacetime, to those designed for destructive effect in war, and all variations in between – regardless of whether the operations are run by civilians or the military, or whether their intended purpose is military or non-military. The definition includes all the various conventional terms, including computer-network attack, computer-network operations, cyber effects, online covert action and cyber-enabled information operations and warfare.

19 See US Department of Defense, 'Summary of US Department of Defence Cyber Strategy', September 2018, https://media.defense.gov/2018/Sep/18/2002041658/-1/-1/1/CYBER_STRATEGY_SUMMARY_FINAL.PDF.

20 *Ibid.*, p. 4.

21 The use of offensive cyber operations for disruptive or destructive effect in peacetime is less controversial against non-state actors, such as terrorists and organised criminals, who are more difficult to deter than states. Nevertheless, such operations still need to avoid the indiscriminate exploitation of widespread IT vulnerabilities.

22 See White House, 'Vulnerabilities Equities Policy and Process for the United States Government', 15 November 2017, https://trumpwhitehouse.archives.gov/sites/whitehouse.gov/files/images/External%20-%20Unclassified%20VEP%20Charter%20FINAL.PDF; and GCHQ, 'The Equities Process', 29 November 2018, https://www.gchq.gov.uk/information/equities-process. A norm of behaviour set out in the Global Commission on the Stability of Cyberspace's 'Advancing Cyber Stability' is as follows: 'States should create procedurally transparent frameworks to assess whether and when to disclose not publicly known vulnerabilities or flaws they are aware of in information systems and technologies. The default presumption should be in favour of disclosure.'

23 See Nigel Inkster, 'Measuring Military Cyber Power', *Survival*, vol. 59, no. 4, August–September 2017, pp. 27–34; Marcus Willett, 'Assessing Cyber Power', *Survival*, vol. 51, no. 1, February–March 2019, pp. 85–90; and Julia Voo et al., 'National Cyber Power Index 2020: Methodology and Analytical Considerations', China Cyber Policy Initiative, Belfer Center for Science and International Affairs, Harvard Kennedy School, September 2020, pp. 11–12, https://www.belfercenter.org/sites/default/files/2020-09/NCPI_2020.pdf.

Eastern Exposure: Germany Looks at Russia

Aaron M. Zack

In the aftermath of a great conflict, the prospects for a functional international order often require the 'assimilation' of the defeated powers into a revised, stable relationship with the victors. Successful assimilation requires that the victors guarantee the core national interests of the vanquished, who, in turn, must renounce their earlier pretensions and accept a diminished, although respectable, status. Subsequent to their narrow victory in the First Punic War, the Romans failed to assimilate Carthage and thus faced a resurgent power preparing for a second trial of strength. At the Congress of Vienna, France was successfully assimilated into the Concert of Europe, and despite Napoleon Bonaparte's Hundred Days and defeat at Waterloo, the Vienna settlement essentially held. France never again attempted a revolutionary attack on the broad European peace. The Versailles Treaty of 1919 failed to assimilate Germany, which renewed its assault on the European order 14 years later. The Americans, having learned the lessons of that failure, successfully assimilated both West Germany and Japan after the Second World War; this success was a necessary condition for America's Cold War victory over its Soviet enemy.[1]

Complete and crushing victories provide the victors with latitude and scope to assimilate the defeated power. Partial or ambiguous victories limit the victors' ability to powerfully impose a durable and legitimate settlement,

Aaron M. Zack is Adjunct Associate Professor of Political Science and Public Affairs at John Jay College and Baruch College, of the City University of New York. He may be contacted at azack@jjay.cuny.edu.

Survival | vol. 63 no. 2 | April–May 2021 | pp. 27–40   https://doi.org/10.1080/00396338.2021.1905987

and place a premium on their ability to reconcile the quasi-defeated peoples' residual self-image and interests with the reality of their loss. The Soviets imploded from within and gave up their empire without firing a shot; they were not defeated in war or occupied by a victorious enemy. Therefore, assimilating Russia into a durable international order governed by liberal norms and de facto American pre-eminence was a difficult challenge, although the final decision would be determined by the Russians themselves. If Russia had liberalised and 'normalised', joining the Western order largely on Western terms and reconciling itself to a loss of power and status compared with its American former adversary, the American-led order would have been massively strengthened in the face of rising challenges from China and other revisionist or revolutionary powers, as well as the emerging challenges of ecological decay and terrorism. But it was not to be. The failure to assimilate Russia has weakened the entire liberal order's position and prospects, with the greatest consequences in Europe itself.

Here, the attitude and policy of Germany is of particular importance. Otto von Bismarck's adroit diplomacy and 'balance of tensions' bound Russia to Germany and restrained the rising Austrian–Russian rivalry in the Balkans and southeast Europe.[2] Bismarck's turn to protectionism and mercantilism in his latter years curtailed the burgeoning exchange between a capital-intensive Germany and resource-rich Russia, and undermined the economic rationale for close partnership.[3] When Bismarck's successors cut Russia loose, Europe was on the road to opposing coalitions and systemic war. Soviet Russia's exclusion from the Versailles settlement gave Germany room to manoeuvre between east and west, and hope that a path to renewed power and supremacy was still possible. The Soviet manipulation of German–Western hostility was the final factor which precipitated Adolf Hitler's destruction of the old European order in 1939–40.[4] When, after the war, Konrad Adenauer firmly anchored West Germany within the American-led Western Alliance, the Soviets were unable to detach the *Bundesrepublik* or manipulate it, and this inability to undermine the assimilation of the West Germans helped preserve the peace. The Western failure to assimilate Russia (or, Russia's own failure to liberalise), and a liberal Germany's latent and actual strength, raise a question of European and global importance: what is the likely trajectory of Russo-German relations? How do these powers view each other, and how are they likely to interact in the near future?

This article addresses German views of Russia. The 'other side of the hill' (that is, the Russian view of Germany), although alluded to, is a subject for another day.[5] The following represents the thoughts of German policy experts, academics and high-level government officials, all of whom deal with or focus on Russo-German relations. The author interviewed these experts and officials in Berlin, and the topics discussed ranged from broad German views of Russia, to the Ukraine conflict, German domestic politics, and transatlantic relations.[6]

The German debate over Russia

German views of Russia are in flux. On the one hand, the Germans assert that their security is impossible absent reasonable relations with a stable Russia. A purely antagonistic relationship with an unstable or disintegrating Russia is not a good, long-term German option. So Germany hasn't completely given up on Russia – it is too big, too close, too important and too powerful. The country is traditionally seen by the Germans as their natural economic partner. They have difficulty accepting that Russia is resistant to cooperation and help with modernising. However, the Germans are now digesting the fact that Russia is not normalising. There is a mental shift towards viewing Russia as an adversary. The talk now is about simultaneous deterrence and engagement: a more transactional, less hopeful relationship, due to Russian obduracy and aggression. There is a debate within Germany about whether Russia is weak or strong. But there is a consensus that Russia is corrupt and cannot reform, and that nothing can be done about this by the European Union and Germany. The Germans are not concerned that Russia will collapse or implode, but rather expect that it will simply muddle through.

German officials and policy experts were shocked by Russia's turn away from liberal normalisation towards autocracy and antagonism, but are now adjusting to this new reality. Parenthetically, German officials were also shocked by Donald Trump's election and hostility towards America's European commitments; but the Germans are now, incrementally, adjusting to American unreliability. The Germans cannot quickly shift their basic policies in response to such events, because of their mentality and history. Their policy shifts are incremental and gradual, and often occur within the cumbersome EU framework. They are not yet capable of thinking creatively in broad strategic or geopolitical terms, and still instinctively rely upon America, psychologically as well as materially, for their security.[7] The German public is split about whether Germany should even be a serious military power. However, German officials are highly capable and increasingly aware of the challenges their country faces in the east, and elsewhere. Awareness will gradually, eventually, be translated into action.

Two camps

The foregoing analysis presents the dominant views of the German foreign-policy elite. In domestic debates, however, the Germans have conflicting views about both the nature of the Russian regime and how Germany should respond to it. Broadly speaking, the Germans are split into two camps: the *Atlantiker* and *Russlandversteher*.[8] The former includes the foreign-policy elite in the Christian Democratic Union (CDU) party (but not the Christian Social Union – CSU), the foreign ministry, elite research institutes and major newspapers, as well as German journalists and foundations in Moscow. The *Atlantiker* – those who consider the transatlantic Alliance with the United States central to German security and interests – were concerned by American unpredictability and the Trump administration's hostility to the Alliance's traditional terms, but are less critical of America than the *Russlandversteher*.

Essentially, the *Atlantiker* reject the Russian regime's narrative that the antagonism between Russia and the West was caused by NATO expansion. The current Russian regime asserts that NATO is an 'alliance' of a hegemonic America with its European vassals, including Germany. Russian military doctrine distinguishes between 'dangers' (less severe) and 'threats' (more severe.) Once NATO – that is, America and its vassals – expanded eastward to the Russian border, the Russians no longer considered it merely a 'danger' but rather a 'threat'. The *Atlantiker* counter that, rather than a legitimate response to a real, external military danger, Russia's antagonism is a function of its own atrophied and corrupt internal politics. President Vladimir Putin and the Russian ruling elite are not especially fearful of Western military aggression, but rather of a domestic 'colour revolution' such as those in Belarus, Ukraine and elsewhere, which threatens the grip of corrupt elites. The Russian elite primarily fear regime change from within.

During the Duma elections in December 2011 and the presidential elections in March 2012, protests broke out against Putin as well as the Duma, characterising these rulers as rogues and thieves. In contrast with previous years, middle-class youth in cities were far more involved; tens of thousands protested against the ruling class. The protesters' slogan was 'Russia without Putin … and Russia without the Putin system'. These youth had hoped that during the 'tender' period of 2008–12, Dmitry Medvedev and other 'liberals' were developing an alternative to the 'Putin system': rather than pure military–industrial modernisation led by the state, Medvedev wanted social and legal modernisation. That is, he wanted Russia to normalise. Medvedev travelled to Silicon Valley and supported the Medvedev–Steinmeier 'modernisation partnership' and a Russian–EU modernisation project. The hope in both Russia and the West was that Medvedev would run for president on this platform against the Putin system of state-dominated corruption. When Medvedev declared that 'Russia is a country of legal nihilism', this was seen as an attack on Putin.[9] Then, in September 2011, Putin announced that he and Medvedev had agreed that Medvedev would not run for president; the response was international disappointment and, as noted, domestic demonstrations.

The *Atlantiker* therefore concluded that the crux of Russo-Western antagonism was the Russian power-elites' fear of their own people (an old story in Russia), whose aspirations would have strengthened as the country further opened to Western investment, norms, culture and influence. The Russian *siloviki* (strongmen from the security services) and military–industrial complex had recovered their power, because they wanted money and power for themselves. This required the rejection of normalisation and liberalism, a shift back towards national–patriotic mobilisation against the West, and the integration of a Eurasian space dominated by Russia. Whatever the Western policy, to justify their own power and maintain it against the protests of domestic liberals, Russia's rulers had to 'construct' the West as an enemy, and therefore 'antagonism' towards the West was a necessary condition for the continued power of the Russian regime. Good relations with the West are a threat to that regime's justifications for its domination, so reasons will be constructed by the Russian regime to maintain antagonism.

For the *Atlantiker*, then, the question is how to respond to this structural Russian antagonism. Social Democratic Party (SPD) elites (some of whom are *Atlantiker*, and others not) support a lenient response, and label a firmer response as confrontational and warmongering. Chancellor Angela Merkel, the CDU and Germany's dominant foreign-policy elite support a firmer response including limited, practical measures that will deter Russian opportunism. The CSU – the CDU's Bavarian partner – is opposed to a firm response and has been shifting towards the position of the *Russlandversteher*.

The *Russlandversteher*, on the other hand, accept the Russian regime's narrative that, in Thucydidean terms, the true cause of the conflict is the movement of American–NATO power eastward and the fear this caused in Russia. The far right, including the Alternative für Deutschland (AfD), and the far-left Linke party are both in the *Russlandversteher* camp. Their pro-Russian sympathies are the flip side of their anti-American, 'anti-imperialism' stance; they are enamoured with Putin's resistance to American hegemony but don't care as much about internal developments in Russia. The AfD in particular has extensive contacts in Russia, and is rumoured to have received Russian financing.

Some elements of the German business community are also in the *Russlandversteher* camp. Some scholars have argued that German foreign policy is essentially economic policy – 'geo-economics'.[10] Likewise, some business leaders certainly want good relations with Russia, a stance that can be traced back at least as far as the Cold War Ostpolitik conducted by business in conjunction with the SPD. In addition to commercial considerations, these Germans hoped that increased business contacts would spill over into the political sphere. However, weighing against such a development is the opposition by Russia's elites, for reasons already noted, to such a spillover. Others in the German business community have a more nuanced position; they want to see Russia develop into a *Rechtsstaat* – a legal state – since that accords with German values as well as long-term commercial interests. Thus the 'values vs interests' opposition, in which German business asserts its (supposedly) unqualified support of 'economic interests', might be overstated, and not all of German business falls within the unqualified *Russlandversteher* camp.

Ukraine and sanctions

Following the logic of the *Atlantiker* position, the Germans will not accept, *de jure*, the annexation of Crimea. However, the sanctions imposed in response to the annexation were more symbolic than substantial. Sanctions within the EU framework are a signal to Russia that its actions abroad are unacceptable, but the EU, while less divided about Russia than in 2014, is still divided about sanctions on Russia – some EU nations are economically impacted more than others. Germany never intended to ruin Russia economically, but rather to register its disapproval of Russian actions in Ukraine. Furthermore, German sanctions are not about Russia's internal policies, but only its actions abroad.

Some large German companies, especially in dual-use-technology sectors, have been hurt by sanctions. These companies, such as Siemens, are important and do interact with the German government, but the extent of corporate influence on government policy is unclear. The main lobbying organisation is the German Committee on Eastern European Economic Relations, which is affiliated with the main German industrial lobby, the Federation of German Industries (BDI). This committee is traditionally Russia-friendly and active in supporting German–Russian economic relations, but it modified its Russophile economic position after the Ukraine crisis, and accepted the *Primat der Politik*. Furthermore, as the rule of law in Russia is increasingly disregarded, German companies have less of a stake in investing there and less of a stake in defending Russia.

The Germans had hoped that the Minsk agreement would be implemented and lead to the resolution of the Ukraine crisis, but those hopes have been dashed. Real peace is unlikely and the Germans are pessimistic, particularly since the Ukrainians themselves did not fulfil all of the agreement's requirements. The Germans believe that they had offered Russia a way out of the conflict, but the Russians demurred. They further believe that Russia wants control over the Donbas as leverage over Ukraine and wants to force Ukraine into Russia's orbit, or, at the very least, out of the Western orbit. Russia's optimal goal is to reduce Ukraine to the status of a client state. Therefore, Russia would vigorously oppose not only Ukrainian membership in NATO, but also its membership in the EU. Ukrainian accession to the EU would require a dramatically different EU–Russian relationship. Russia views itself as a great power with control over its own space, which precludes control by others. Ukraine is within the Russian 'space' (as Moscow sees it), and so Russia, if strong enough, will not allow the emergence of an EU–Ukrainian economic space outside of Russian control.

Energy

Germany seems willing to accept a certain level of dependence on Russia for energy. There is major support within business circles, in particular for Nord Stream, despite the opposition to it by Poland and the Baltic states. Nord Stream will allow Russia to circumvent eastern EU countries and put direct pressure on Germany, but energy is a field where there have been very strong Russo-German ties since the 1970s. Influential German political–economic networks support this relationship, particularly since it is an area where cooperation is possible, as opposed to the greater conflict over purely political matters such as Ukraine. The Germans are confident that Russia will not cut off the flow of energy.

Human rights and the rule of law

The Russian regime's disregard for human rights and the rule of law within Russia are important to the Germans, but not central in determining German policy. While human rights and law shape the German view of Russia, these considerations are subordinated to political and economic factors that affect German interests. There are some parties within Germany, such as the Greens, that wish to increase the importance for German policy of rights and law within Russia, but for now the German focus is on Russia's foreign policy. However, as discussed, the *Atlantiker* view Russia's policy as a function of its domestic regime type.

German officials and the limits of antagonism

Senior German government officials view Putin as a rational and strategically predictable, albeit tactically unpredictable, actor. Putin wants Russia to be secure, powerful, respected and glorious. What he desires for Russia is therefore in no sense aberrant or unique in the history of international politics. Putin is neither self-destructive nor irrational, and will not precipitate a risky, highly dangerous military confrontation. His nuclear rhetoric is perceived by German officials as just that – rhetoric – and it does not concern them. However, while strategically rational, restrained and predictable, Putin's tactics are unpredictable; it is difficult to determine how and where he will use Russia's power to gain an incremental advantage and improved position. Would Russia's strategic caution, combined with tactical flexibility, change if Putin were replaced? The German officials interviewed for this article expressed concern that the likely alternatives to Putin would in fact be less restrained, less strategically predictable and more dangerous.

Is Russia under Putin a revisionist power? Yes, but in a limited sense. In contrast to its acquiescence and passivity in the 1990s, Russia wants to be a geopolitically important power, rather than subservient to the West. It intends to remain an independent, militarily important power. However, German officials do not believe Russia is revolutionary or maximally revisionist; it is not seeking to build a new USSR. Nor is it interested in conquering or seizing land or nations. Its actions in Ukraine are a special case for spiritual and historical reasons, and should not be interpreted as a general Russian desire to expand.

Nonetheless, Germany's hopes for Russia have been disappointed. After the Cold War, German officials cautiously hoped that Russia might develop into a 'normal' European country, governed by a fairly liberal political culture with the rule of law, and that Russia's foreign policy would reflect such a beneficent development. Until recently, the Germans were unsure about Russia's trajectory. However, German officials have now arrived at a conclusion: Russia is an 'antagonistic' power. It will not develop into a liberal polity for the foreseeable future. Its foreign policy, while neither irrational nor revolutionary, is, and will continue to be, opportunistic, calculating and transactional. Dreams of a pan-European political and security order, from the Atlantic to the Urals, are gone.

This is not to say that the German government expects major conflict with Russia, or dismisses mutually beneficial cooperation at either the EU or bilateral level. German officials have accepted that they must manage an antagonistic Russia on a case-by-case basis. In some cases, cooperation will be possible. In others, Russia must be checked, deterred, responded to or penalised, to change its calculations and influence its actions. German policymakers seek to pragmatically manage Germany's interactions with an opportunistic Russia. As an element of this pragmatism, though, Germany does not and will not seek to ruin Russia. A reasonably stable, well-off Russia is beneficial for Germany and Europe. A Russia in the throes of economic collapse or political chaos would eventually endanger German security. Germany therefore wants Russia, under Putin and in the future, to maintain itself as a relatively healthy and robust nation.

Therefore – and Americans in particular should clearly understand this – German officials will vigorously oppose sanctions which would ruin Russia. The view among German officials is that sanctions must be calibrated to signal EU or Western objections to specific Russian actions, in order to shift Russian calculations as to the costs and benefits of those actions. Sanctions must not be imposed if their purpose is to collapse the Russian economy, ruin Russia or destabilise its political structure. The German officials interviewed were clear that Germany will not accept or abide by extra-territorial American sanctions that seek to compel Germany or the EU to ruin Russia.

German officials and the limits of realpolitik

How do German officials view Russia within the broader geopolitical environment? They believe that Russia (unjustifiably, according to the Germans) fears NATO, but has no fear of the EU. So a putative expansion of the EU, according to these officials, is unlikely to provoke an extreme Russian response, particularly if the details of the expansion are discussed with Russia. NATO expansion eastward, on the other hand, would lead to greater fear in Russia. But German officials do not consider that NATO's past expansion to the east was an error. NATO expanded because Eastern European countries wanted to join the Alliance, and Russia wanted too much control over the terms, pace and scope of the Alliance's expansion. Russia should not have been granted a veto over whether the sovereign states of Europe could join the Alliance or not. On the other hand, although sovereign states, as a matter of principle, have the right to join the Alliance without subjecting their choice to a Russian veto, NATO itself should consider whether the prospective member enhances the Alliance's security or not. In other words, the Germans do not consider that all applicants should be accepted. If accepting a prospective member would diminish the security of the current members, then the applicant should be rejected. But Russia does not and should not have a veto over the actions of sovereign Eastern European states.

For similar reasons, and unsurprisingly given Germany's history, its officials adamantly reject suggestions that 'buffer zones' or 'spheres of influence' are acceptable responses to the dynamic of Russian fear and Europe's need for security.[11] The Germans view the Eastern European nations between their country and Russia as sovereign states with legitimate borders, aspirations and autonomy. They cannot be assigned to a Russian 'sphere' or demoted to a mere cordon sanitaire or buffer status. The Germans interviewed were strongly opposed to such a pure assertion of power and realpolitik, divorced from liberal-democratic beliefs that value the independence, rights and welfare of the Eastern Europeans.

Nonetheless, and perhaps incoherently, German officials assert that in Ukraine a political, negotiated solution is necessary. A long-term resolution cannot be imposed militarily by either side. Arming Ukrainian government forces with more advanced weaponry will only decrease the chances of arriving at a political solution, and German officials consider that such military support would be counterproductive, as Russia would match such an escalation.

Does the rise of China suggest that Russia has broader geopolitical options than either an accommodation with the West or isolation? Will a German and Western resigned acceptance of 'antagonism' with Russia push it into China's arms? German officials are sceptical that Russia will embrace a true partnership with China. Russia has been using its relationship with China as leverage against excessive Western pressure, but the Germans believe that Moscow, in the long term, sees China as too big and too powerful, and as threatening to subordinate Russia. Thus, Russia cannot play the 'China card' past a certain point – especially economically.

*   *   *

Compared with the immediate post-Cold War period, Germany's geopolitical position has deteriorated. While the United Kingdom might remain a significant power that contributes to the broader security of Europe, its departure from the EU has limited the prospects that Germany can reliably turn to the British to manage looming dangers and threats. Across the Atlantic, America is divided from within and increasingly preoccupied with the rise of a powerful, autocratic China. As America calibrates its political, military and economic strategy in response, there will be little surplus power left over to shape European affairs. America and Europe still have certain common interests and will undoubtedly work together at times, politically and economically. But with every passing year, the hard reality is that the Europeans are increasingly on their own. To the south of Europe, ecological decay, population growth, sclerotic regimes and religious extremism portend continual war and the movement of peoples, with combustible results.

A strong partnership with an assimilated, liberal, economically dynamic and normalised Russia would have profoundly strengthened the capacity of the Germans, and other Europeans, to successfully weather the coming storms. But that was not to be. Russia has not normalised and the Germans have given up hope that it will do so. A close partnership with Russia is not possible. However, Germany will carefully manage Russian antagonism so that it does not escalate, spin out of control or render all productive coopera-tion impossible. The Germans will carefully and pragmatically respond to Russian provocations while looking to simultaneously work with them in areas of mutual interest. Given the nature of the Russian regime, Germany's response is historically informed, rational and mature. Other nations might take it as a model to follow.

Acknowledgements

The author thanks his German interview subjects, as well as the PSC-CUNY Development Fund of the City University of New York, whose grant financed this research.

Notes

1   On success or failure in assimilating defeated powers, see Charles Doran, *The Politics of Assimilation: Hegemony and Its Aftermath* (Baltimore, MD: Johns Hopkins University Press, 1971); Henry Kissinger, *A World Restored: Metternich, Castlereagh and the Problems of Peace, 1812–22* (London: Weidenfeld and Nicolson, 1957); and Ludwig Dehio, *The Precarious Balance: Four Centuries of the European Power Struggle* (New York: Alfred Knopf, 1962).

2   See Klaus Hildebrand, 'Opportunities and Limits of German Foreign Policy in the Bismarckian Era, 1871–1890: A System of Stopgap?', in Gregor Schollgen (ed.), *Escape into War? The Foreign Policy of Imperial Germany* (Oxford: Berg Publishers, 1990); and W.N. Medlicott, *Bismarck and Modern Germany* (London: English Universities Press, 1965).

3   See David Calleo, *The German Problem Reconsidered: Germany and World Order, 1870 to the Present* (Cambridge: Cambridge University Press, 1978); and Fritz Fischer, *From Kaiserreich to Third Reich: Elements of Continuity in German History* (London: Unwin Hyman, 1986).

4   See Andreas Hillgruber, *Germany and the Two World Wars* (Cambridge, MA: Harvard University Press, 1981).

5   The Duke of Wellington, who was uncannily accurate in guessing the terrain on 'the other side of the hill' in the Peninsular War, is the source of the quotation. See Basil Liddell-Hart, *The Other Side of the Hill: Germany's Generals, Their Rise and Fall, with Their Own Account of Military Events, 1939–1945* (London: Cassell, 1973).

6   In 2018, the author interviewed Dr Hannes Adomeit, a professor at the American Institute for Contemporary German Studies at Johns Hopkins University, a Bosch Public Policy Fellow at the Transatlantic Academy and a Non-Resident Fellow at the Institut für Sicherheitspolitik an der Universität Kiel; Dr Susan Stewart of the Stiftung Wissenschaft und Politik; Sarah Pagung of the Deutsche Gesellschaft für Auswärtige Politik; and German government officials who requested anonymity.

7   When this author pointed out to German officials that Germany's geopolitical position was deteriorating in the east (Russian hostility), south (war in the Middle East) and west (Brexit and American unreliability), the response was something akin to shock. The Germans, for now, are unused to thinking in broad strategic terms.

8   Translated literally, *Russlandversteher* means 'those who understand Russia'. In this context, it denotes sympathy for the Russian position.

9   Lionel Barber, Neil Buckley and Catherine Belton, 'Laying Down the Law: Medvedev Vows War on Russia's "Legal Nihilism"', *Financial Times*, 24 December 2008, https://www.ft.com/content/e46ea1d8-c6c8-11dd-97a5-000077b07658.

10   See, in particular, Stephen Szabo, *Germany, Russia, and the Rise of Geo-economics* (London: Bloomsbury Academic, 2015).

11   Germany's experience with the 1939 Molotov–Ribbentrop pact is the most infamous historical episode informing this view.

Reforming Ukraine's Security Sector

Nicolò Fasola and Alyssa J. Wood

Russia and the West have conflicting interests in Ukraine's 'shared neigh-bourhood', and have adopted opposing strategies with respect to Ukraine.[1] While Ukraine has been an intense focus for NATO, revelations that US president Donald Trump withheld about $400 million in congressionally authorised security assistance for Ukraine and a head-of-state meeting at the White House to induce the Ukrainian government to advance his domestic political interests, prompting his impeachment, have distracted the Alliance from the ground-level exigencies of Ukrainian security.[2] One of these is the reform of its defence system.[3]

Ukraine inherited from the Soviet Union a sclerotic domestic political framework characterised by institutional inertia and ineffective leadership, commonly manifested in vicious circles of corruption.[4] After independ-ence in 1991, the government failed to seize the initiative in implementing reforms, especially in the security sector. Mismanagement, underfunding, outdated equipment and an ossified strategic culture left Ukraine unpre-pared to face Russian aggression in Crimea, Donetsk and Luhansk in 2014. Yet that crisis did present a new opportunity – arguably an imperative – to reform a system otherwise highly resistant to change. Since then, Ukraine

Nicolò Fasola is a doctoral researcher at the University of Birmingham. **Alyssa J. Wood** is a major in the United States Army. The views expressed herein are the personal views of the authors and do not necessarily reflect the official position of the US Department of Defense, the US Department of the Army, the North Atlantic Treaty Organization or its member governments.

Survival | vol. 63 no. 2 | April–May 2021 | pp. 41–54   https://doi.org/10.1080/00396338.2021.1905990

has undertaken an unprecedented effort to reform, making meaningful progress towards a healthier national system – which includes better prepared and more vigorous armed forces. The way ahead, however, is still long and arduous.

Foundations of Ukraine's security-sector reform

Ukraine's present security strategy is based on four core documents. The first is the National Security Strategy, which provides guidance for the re-establishment and maintenance of the country's security, broadly conceived.[5] Not surprisingly, the first such strategy following the Russian aggression – published in March 2015 – is rhetorically anchored in the traumatic events of the previous year. It clearly distinguishes pre- and post-crisis Ukraine, down to the level of sociopolitical cognition. The document frames the 2014 crisis as the result of Moscow's deliberately malign behaviour and rejects Moscow's view of history. In line with the spirit of that year's Maidan – that is, Dignity – Revolution, the National Security Strategy emphasises Kyiv's willingness to align itself with the Euro-Atlantic civilisational model. The new National Security Strategy, published in September 2020, introduces no substantial changes.[6] Thus, Russia is understood to have provoked Ukraine into rejecting its 'big brother'. Yet there are limits to the achievable degree of separation between the two countries, as their historical, cultural, economic and strategic ties are deeply rooted. This makes Kyiv's renewed orientation even more significant from a political perspective.[7]

Far from being mere rhetoric, the positioning of Ukraine within the European space mirrors and legitimises the overarching goal of securing a 'European future' for the country alongside that of restoring Ukraine's territorial integrity within 'internationally recognised borders'. Most perceived threats are linked directly or indirectly to Russia. But, to its credit, Ukraine also turns a critical eye on itself, pointing to its dysfunctional governance and poor political choices as additional threats to national security. While this disposition implicitly blames the pre-Maidan (that is, pro-Russian) leadership for today's situation, it also provides a basis for tackling domestic distortions that have been ignored for too long. In particular, the National Security Strategy identifies endemic corruption in public administration, the inefficiency of the security system, economic backwardness and environmental threats as key concerns.

Ukraine's Military Doctrine – published in September 2015 – echoes the language and tone of the political document. The doctrine describes the security environment in and around Ukraine, acknowledging internationally identified global trends, and clearly casts Russia as its greatest external threat. It also boldly highlights the challenges and risks to military security that are exacerbated by internal economic and sociopolitical factors, such as the low efficiency of the state-management system and its intelligence and counter-intelligence bodies. Military policy objectives focus on repulsing Russia's armed aggression and conforming the Ukrainian armed forces to the security and defence architectures of NATO and the European Union. Having set ambitious goals, the National Security Strategy and Military Doctrine call for a clear delineation of duties, responsibilities and operational authorities.

In May 2016, taking into account the unfolding military crisis in the east, Petro Poroshenko, then Ukraine's president, approved the Strategic Defense Bulletin.[8] This document's purpose is to serve as a road map for implementing best practices and efficiently managing the resources and external assistance for the defence sector, in order to attain Euro-Atlantic military standards. The bulletin – and now also the Ukrainian constitution – state that security-sector reform should aim to develop 'capabilities of the Ministry of Defense of Ukraine, the Armed Forces of Ukraine and other components of the defence forces in line with Euro-Atlantic standards and NATO membership criteria in order to adequately respond to national security threats'.

For accomplishing this rather grand outcome, the bulletin prescribes a unified military command and the improvement of the armed forces' planning, resource-management, combat, logistics and medical-support capabilities as well as its professional standards. These aims are further delineated in a series of operational objectives centred on reshaping the organisational logic of security institutions and radically upgrading the efficiency and effectiveness of Ukraine's armed forces, again with Western military culture as the guiding light of reform.

The fourth programmatic guidance for Ukraine's security-sector reform consists of the State Program for the Development of the Armed Forces, which directs the implementation of the bulletin's operational objectives by setting funding and a performance schedule for the years 2017–20.[9] On paper at least, this programme is very ambitious. In four years, the reform effort is to be formally completed, bringing Ukraine in line with NATO standards. To sustain such an effort, however, the available funding would have had to increase fivefold over the course of the four years, from 7,173m hryvnias ($255m) in 2017 to 38,152m hryvnias ($1.36 billion) in 2020. Although reliable figures on the actual military budgets for those years have not been disclosed, it is highly unlikely that they reached that level.

The new Law on National Security, approved in June 2018, was an attempt to bring some order to conflicting signals and mandates.[10] Originating from an accommodation of NATO and EU advice to Ukraine's political constraints, the new law attempts to simplify and update the country's legislation regarding national security, democratic control of the security sector and defence planning. Widely focused, the law does not provide very specific regulations but rather a normative framework setting general principles and interests (resonating with the ones already presented in the National Security Strategy), to be fleshed out with more specific laws that will define roles, responsibilities, means and procedures.[11]

The new law represents a clear step forward from the messy earlier regulations, but it also fails to fully address some issues, which could impair its effectiveness. Firstly, while the law states that the armed forces will finally become subject to civilian control from 1 January 2019, nothing is said about how this transition is to be effectuated. A civilian minister of defence does not per se guarantee compliance with democratic standards and good governance, especially if he is a retired military officer.[12] Minimising the nefarious influence of some individuals, groups and practices within the system is also necessary for the successful enforcement of civilian control. Before rushing through such a transformation, Kyiv and its partners have to make sure that the durable changes in political culture required to support it are well under way.

In addition, the new law provides inadequate guidance about the re-organisation of the roles and responsibilities of the Security Service –

which has plenary responsibility for homeland security – as well as the boundaries of state secrecy and the transparency of defence procurement. The over-classification of even the most basic information has produced a considerable lack of transparency and therefore reduced public accountability, which has enabled those with vested interests in the status quo to protect institutional power and resist reform. Complementary laws are needed but will inevitably come slowly.

Finally, the new law reiterates the National Security Strategy's requirement that no less than 5% of GDP should be spent on the security sector, with at least 3% on defence proper, without addressing the substance or quality of security expenditures.[13]

Allied support

While Ukraine itself must bear the primary burden of reform, external assistance enhances and bolsters the reform process.[14] NATO has played a major role. Cooperation between the Alliance and Ukraine started after the dissolution of the Soviet Union.[15] Kyiv joined the North Atlantic Cooperation Council in 1991 and three years later became an active member of the Partnership for Peace programme, which remains the largest framework for NATO's cooperative security efforts. On 9 July 1997, Ukraine and NATO signed the 'Charter on a Distinctive Partnership', establishing the NATO–Ukraine Commission and forming the basis for a privileged partnership.[16] The completion of a draft common action plan in November 2002 further consolidated the relationship.[17]

NATO–Ukraine cooperation has developed along political and military tracks. A number of committees, working groups and staffs composed of personnel from both sides meet regularly to discuss, plan and assess common activities. With the NATO–Ukraine Commission's guidance, they have shaped and strengthened the cooperation in order to improve the efficiency and effectiveness of Ukraine's military. The final goal is to reach full inter-operability with NATO.[18]

The Comprehensive Assistance Package, approved during NATO's Warsaw Summit in 2016, functions as the Alliance's keystone Ukraine document, outlining multiple lines of practical support. Here, NATO identifies and synchronises Ukraine's essential security- and defence-sector reforms as outlined by its strategic documents, with an eye to enabling Ukraine to become more resilient and better able to provide for its own security.[19] The document contains 40 tailored support measures, or work strands, which can be grouped into broader advisory efforts and vehicles. These include trust funds, which are voluntary financial or other resource contributions offered and managed by interested allies to advance security and defence projects.[20] Since 2014, ten trust funds, providing more than €40m, have assisted Ukraine in areas such as explosive-ordnance disposal; countering improvised explosive devices; command, control, communications and computers; medical rehabilitation; cyber defence; logistics and standardisation; military career transition; and destruction of small arms and light weapons.

At the behest of Stepan Poltorak when he was the Ukrainian minister of defence, the Defense Reform Advisory Board was established to provide 'high-level expertise and recommendations to senior Ukrainian political leaders regarding institutional reforms to Ukraine's armed forces'.[21] Six NATO allies – Canada, Germany, Lithuania, Poland, the United Kingdom and the United States – were asked to participate. This board, along with NATO itself and the Multinational Joint Commission, advise and assist within the scope outlined in the Strategic Defense Bulletin. Working in association with NATO but not under its direct supervision, the commission is a voluntary association of NATO allies and partners – comprising Canada, Denmark, Lithuania, Poland, Sweden, the UK and the US – that liaises with Ukraine's security and defence forces working to improve coordination, planning and implementation of security-cooperation activities. Each member participates in accordance with its nationally defined guidelines for providing advisory, consultative, military technical, training and other assistance to Ukraine's security forces. The commission coordinates with its members' national governments, the Defense Reform Advisory Board and NATO representatives.

On the basis of Kyiv's strong commitment to reforming the defence sector, Ukraine's requests for Enhanced Opportunities Partner status and even a Membership Action Plan have intensified in recent years. Both programmes offer chances to reinforce ties with NATO, focusing respectively on Ukraine's participation in allied operations and the delivery of tailored advice in support of reform. A Membership Action Plan is a formal prerequisite for NATO membership, while Enhanced Opportunities status is not; neither programme, however, prejudges any Alliance decision on NATO membership. Ukraine has cast itself as a unique case of reformist success devoted to NATO's cause – a portrayal which, though substantively debatable, has become increasingly popular with the domestic political audience. NATO is supportive of Ukraine's Euro-Atlantic ambitions and has in fact recently conferred Enhanced Opportunities Partner status on Ukraine.[22] This is not a profound change, as NATO's special partnership with Ukraine has long de facto included enhanced opportunities, but formalisation of its status does reflect increased political support. At the same time, although NATO's 'open door policy' remains the official stance, the Alliance cautiously manages Ukraine's expectations regarding membership. The Western commitment to supporting Ukraine's struggle for independence and non-interference from Russia is solid, but official NATO statements avoid open declarations that Ukraine will join the Alliance in the foreseeable future to minimise the risk of open political conflict with Moscow.[23] Accordingly, NATO will likely continue to foster its special relationship with Ukraine through security-sector assistance while keeping the country in the 'partner zone'.

A critical assessment

While Ukraine has managed to implement some meaningful reforms, their pace and impact have not been dramatic. The process remains equally susceptible to positive developments and serious regressions. Kyiv's strategic repositioning in favour of a 'European future' underpins the choices made in the context of security-sector reform, and strenuous efforts have been undertaken to align the country's planning and legislation with Euro-Atlantic standards. But important elements of reform are still lacking in content and coherence.

Ukraine's programmatic documents, though logical enough, fail to provide specific guidance for the armed forces on how they should function within the new and prevailing Euro-Atlantic political framework.

In particular, Ukraine has developed no consolidated concept of how its military will end the conflict in the Donbas, support the nation's desire for European integration or face future conflicts.

Furthermore, the National Security Strategy and the Strategic Defense Bulletin set ambitions that exceed Ukraine's reach. While enterprising pro-nouncements may keep partners engaged and materially supportive, they can also stretch the country's actual capabilities too much, distracting from goals that are less glamorous but equally relevant to the overall success of reforms. The new Law on National Security has the potential to reorient Kyiv's perspective on security-sector reform, but Ukrainian leaders should bear in mind that law and policy are not synonymous. A neat, workable legislative framework is a necessary but not sufficient condition for effective strate-gic decision-making. The new law will be of limited utility until more exacting complementary legislation fills nor-mative gaps. Only then will decisive movement towards NATO or EU membership be realistic – and even then it will depend on NATO and EU strategic choices that are largely beyond Ukraine's control.

The forces managed to hold their positions

Notwithstanding programmatic and political shortfalls, the actual per-formance of Ukraine's armed forces in conditions of war has been, on balance, positive and certainly improved since 2014. The armed forces are still unable to repel Russia and its proxy forces but have managed to hold their positions, reacting effectively to the attacks along the eastern line of contact while keeping their casualties relatively low. Unfortunately, this is not enough. Under Ukraine's strategic planning, the ultimate objective is to regain seized territory, and that cannot be achieved unless pro-Russian forces are forced to retreat. To accomplish this, Ukrainian forces would require a much more proactive military posture and higher force effec-tiveness, and would probably have to engage in something approaching full-scale war against Russia. On its own, Ukraine would not be able to meet these demands today or in the near future.

While the hybrid aspects of the Ukraine crisis have received a great deal of attention from both analysts and policymakers, a more conventional style of war is a salient possibility and poses significant risks. The conflict in the Donbas is still low intensity, but it is developing conventional aspects. Reportedly, Russian regular forces are at the head of two joint corps – clearly larger and more organised units of manpower and military assets than a mere group of insurgents could likely muster.[24] Two years ago, Ukrainian sources counted more than 700 Russian and proxy tanks on contested soil, and direct bombing via drones is becoming increasingly frequent. In addition, Russia's order of battle in the Western Military District clearly poses a conventional threat to Ukraine, which therefore needs to be ready to face multiple short-notice, mechanised attacks along different operational axes.[25]

Kyiv has recognised these realities and implemented an important strategic shift in its management of the eastern conflict. In particular, on the basis of a Ukrainian parliament decision, the *Anti-terrorist Operation* has been replaced by the *Joint Forces Operation*. This reflects a change of the understanding of the crisis in the east of the country.[26] As the name suggests, the former was linked to the original understanding of the crisis as necessitating a counter-guerrilla, counter-hybrid-warfare operation aimed at neutralising insurgents – by definition a domestic task, led by the Security Service. The transition to the latter operation, an integral part of security-sector reform, signals a new approach to the crisis. Russia is formally defined as an aggressor and the Donbas conflict is treated as an invasion that calls for a truly military response.[27] The General Staff of Ukraine's armed forces heads the operation. There remain problems of coherence, however. In line with Ukraine's strategic objectives, the operation aims at liberating the 'temporarily occupied territories', but apparently without any 'intensification of combat actions'. How this would be possible is unclear.

In general, security-force assistance is a cost-saving strategy that bolsters a partner's military effectiveness in order to defend one's own limited interests without the need of directly deploying one's own military assets.[28] But potential liabilities come with it. In particular, the patron and its partner may not share strategic goals. And if the patron does not have the means to impose strict conditionality on the use of its resources and to glean complete information about what the partner is doing on the ground, security-force assistance is less likely to have a positive impact on the assistance provider's strategic position.

NATO allies have helped Kyiv in a number of ways, most notably with funding and technical military assistance. But the West is not inclined to risk European security for the sake of Ukraine's sovereignty, and its external support has stopped well short of raising military tensions with Moscow. Western restraint is thus inconsistent with Ukraine's aspiration to regain territory as well as its vision of a 'European future' with full Alliance benefits. Conversely, while NATO allies' mentorship and support allows Ukraine to resist Russian depredations more effectively than it could if left solely to its own devices, the implicit political conditionality of Ukraine's advancement within Europe – namely, peace with Russia – constrains Kyiv's sovereign ambitions. The bottom line for the West is that as long as active military conflict with Russia plagues Ukraine's easternmost regions, Ukraine will not be accorded membership in NATO or the EU.[29] Yet no political settlement of the conflict is in sight due to Kyiv's coolness towards negotiations with Moscow, which it sees as inherently untrustworthy and a threat to Ukraine.

NATO itself is partly responsible. It has delivered assistance without taking the pre-existing institutional and ideational conditions of Ukraine's military landscape into sufficient account. The transmission of pre-packaged defence-planning models, managerial processes and technical, financial and legislative procedures has proceeded at a volume and pace that surpasses the ability of Ukraine to absorb it. Many senior Ukrainian military officers are still imbued with a rigid Soviet mentality, and have been able to internalise Western practices at best selectively.[30] Their inclination is to centralise all decision-making authority at the top of the military establishment, giving almost no latitude to subordinates to decide or act when circumstances change the course of an established plan. This clashes with effective reform, which requires decentralising decision-making to the appropriate levels and allowing subordinates room for manoeuvre within the strategic framework. Hence the lethargic institutional change.[31] The problem is likely to continue in the medium to long term. Its resolution will require NATO to shift the focus of its aid from hardware and capabilities to doctrine and standards.

In addition, effective civilian control of the armed forces and reasonably robust transparency and anti-corruption norms are critical to the success of Ukraine's security-sector reform. Both aims are difficult to achieve due to systemic resistance.[32] Tycoons and politicians who built their careers around illegal activities and state corruption strongly resist developments that may undermine their influence, depriving the armed forces of resources key to successful reform. Ukrainian political practices and traditions have afforded such actors the opportunity to retain their privileges, though political decentralisation reforms – motivated in part by Ukraine's political tilt towards Europe – may be slowly addressing this democratic deficit.[33]

*   *   *

The crisis of 2014 created an opportunity to end institutional inertia in the Ukrainian security sector. However, even that event's magnitude has not been enough to break all the chains constraining Ukraine's transition. Strategic aims are somewhat over-ambitious, and concepts and means are not completely fit for purpose. In trying to address these limitations, Kyiv and its partners need to extend their attention beyond tangible resources, quantitative parameters and a contingent checklist of short-term goals. They should concentrate more sharply on overcoming normative and ideational resistances to security-sector reform – in particular, the Soviet political–military mindset – in favour of Western thinking.

Acknowledgements

The authors would like to thank Derek Averre, Iryna Donets and Ben A. Paine for their useful comments on earlier drafts of this paper.

Notes

1   See, for example, Derek Averre and Kataryna Wolczuk (eds), *The Ukraine Conflict: Security, Identity and Politics in the Wider Europe* (Abingdon: Routledge, 2018); Lawrence Freedman, 'Ukraine and the Art of Limited War', *Survival*, vol. 56, no. 6, December 2014–January 2015, pp. 7–38; Pernille Rieker and Kristian L. Gjerde, 'The EU, Russia and the

Potential for Dialogue: Different Readings of the Crisis in Ukraine', *European Security*, vol. 25, no. 3, May 2016, pp. 304–25; Luigi Scazzieri, 'Europe, Russia and the Ukraine Crisis: The Dynamics of Coercion', *Journal of Strategic Studies*, vol. 40, no. 3, January 2017, pp. 392–416; and James Sperling and Mark Webber, 'NATO and the Ukraine Crisis: Collective Securitisation', *European Journal of International Security*, vol. 2, no. 1, December 2016, pp. 19–46.

2   See Dana H. Allin, 'Impeachment, Trump and US Foreign Policy', *Survival*, vol. 62, no. 1, February–March 2020, pp. 221–32; and Liana Semchuk, 'In Ukraine, Donald Trump Impeachment Controversy Is an Unwanted Distraction for Volodymyr Zelenskiy', *Conversation*, 27 September 2019, https://theconversation. com/in-ukraine-donald-trump-impeachment-controversy-is-an-unwanted-distraction-for-volodymyr-zelenskiy-124308.

3   One notable exception is Deborah Sanders, '"The War We Want; The War We Get": Ukraine's Military Reform and the Conflict in the East', *Journal of Slavic Military Studies*, vol. 30, no. 1, January 2017, pp. 30–49. Early policy-oriented analyses include Olga Oliker et al., *Security Sector Reform in Ukraine* (Santa Monica, CA: RAND Corporation, 2016); and Andrzej Wilk, *The Best Army Ukraine Has Ever Had: Changes in Ukraine's Armed Forces Since the Russian Aggression* (Warsaw: Centre for Eastern Studies, 2017).

4   For an analysis of recent developments, see Taras Kuzio, 'Ukraine's Other War: The Rule of Law and Siloviky After the Euromaidan Revolution', *Journal of Slavic Military Studies*, vol. 29, no. 4, December 2017, pp. 681–706; and Yuriy Matsiyevsky, 'Revolution Without Regime Change: The Evidence from the Post-Euromaidan Ukraine', *Communist and Post-Communist Studies*, vol. 51, no. 4, November 2018, pp. 349–59.

5   The text of the 2015 National Security Strategy is available, in Ukrainian, at https://zakon.rada.gov.ua/laws/show/en/287/2015/ed20150526#Text.

6   The text of the 2020 National Security Strategy is available, in Ukrainian, at https://www.president.gov.ua/documents/3922020-35037.

7   For an overview of Ukraine's changing orientation in foreign and security policy, see Elena Kropatcheva, 'Ukraine's Foreign Policy Choices After the 2010 Presidential Election', *Journal of Communist Studies and Transition Politics*, vol. 27, no. 3, September 2011, pp. 520–40; Taras Kuzio, 'The Domestic Sources of Ukrainian Security Policy', *Journal of Strategic Studies*, vol. 21, no. 4, 1998, pp. 18–49; Taras Kuzio, 'Ukrainian Foreign and Security Policy Since the Orange Revolution', *International Spectator*, vol. 41, no. 4, 2006, pp. 25–42; and Karina Shyrokykh, 'The Evolution of the Foreign Policy of Ukraine: External Actors and Domestic Factors', *Europe–Asia Studies*, vol. 70, no. 5, June 2018, pp. 832–50.

8   The text of the Strategic Defense Bulletin is available, in Ukrainian, at https://www.president.gov.ua/documents/2402016-20137.

9   Public official information on the State Program for Development of

the Armed Forces is available at http://www.mil.gov.ua/content/oboron_plans/2017-07-31_National-program-2020_en.pdf.

10 See 'Ukraine's New Law on National Security: Key Facts to Know', Ukraine Crisis Media Center Press Release, 22 June 2018, https://uacrisis.org/en/67656-ukraine-s-new-law-national-security-key-facts.

11 See Ukrainian Helsinki Human Rights Union, 'Law of Ukraine on National Security', 23 July 2018, https://helsinki.org.ua/en/articles/law-of-ukraine-on-national-security/.

12 In October 2018, Stepan Poltorak, then minister of defence, resigned from military service, effectively transitioning from military to civilian in January 2019. The current minister of defence is Andriy Taran, a retired lieutenant-general.

13 For an overview of Ukraine's economic resources, manpower and military hardware, see, for example, International Institute for Strategic Studies (IISS), *The Military Balance 2020* (Abingdon: Routledge, 2020), pp. 211–15.

14 For an early technical account on international support to Ukraine's security-sector reform, see Måns Hanssen, 'International Support to Security Sector Reform in Ukraine: A Mapping of SSR Projects', Folke Bernadotte Academy, 2016, https://fba.se/contentassets/9f9daa3815ac4adaa8 8fd578469fc053/international-support-to-security-sector-reform-in-ukraine--a-mapping-o....pdf.

15 On the origins of NATO–Ukraine cooperation, see Taras Kuzio, 'Ukraine and NATO: The Evolving Strategic Partnership', *Journal of Strategic Studies*, vol. 21, no. 2, 1998, pp. 1–30.

16 NATO, 'Charter on a Distinctive Partnership Between the North Atlantic Treaty Organization and Ukraine', 9 July 1997, https://www.nato.int/cps/en/natohq/official_texts_25457.htm?.

17 NATO, 'NATO–Ukraine Action Plan', 22 November 2002, https://www.nato.int/cps/en/natohq/official_texts_19547.htm?.

18 See NATO, 'Backgrounder: Interoperability for Joint Operations', 2006, https://www.nato.int/nato_static_fl2014/assets/pdf/pdf_publications/20120116_interoperability-en.pdf.

19 NATO, 'Comprehensive Assistance Package for Ukraine', 2016, https://www.nato.int/nato_static_fl2014/assets/pdf/pdf_2016_09/20160920_160920-compreh-ass-package-ukraine-en.pdf.

20 For an overview, see NATO, 'Trust Funds: Supporting Demilitarization and Defence Transformation Projects', 21 June 2016, https://www.nato.int/cps/en/natohq/topics_50082.htm?selectedLocale=en; and NATO, 'NATO–Ukraine Trust Funds', 28 March 2018, https://www.nato.int/cps/en/natolive/topics_153288.htm.

21 Stephen Fuhr, 'Canada's Support to Ukraine in Crisis and Armed Conflict: Report of the Standing Committee on National Defence', 2017, p. 15, https://www.ourcommons.ca/Content/Committee/421/NDDN/Reports/RP9313861/nddnrp08/nddnrp08-e.pdf.

22 NATO, 'NATO Recognises Ukraine as Enhanced Opportunities Partner', 12 June 2020, https://www.nato.int/cps/en/natohq/news_176327.htm.

[23] See Roman Sohn and Ariana Gic, 'Are the EU and NATO Serious About Bringing Peace to Ukraine? You Wouldn't Know It from Their Language', Atlantic Council, 19 July 2018, https://www.atlantic-council.org/blogs/ukrainealert/are-the-eu-and-nato-serious-about-bringing-peace-to-ukraine-you-wouldn-t-know-it-from-their-language/.

[24] Recent reports estimate 28,000 Russian military personnel in Crimea and 3,000 in the east of Ukraine. See IISS, *The Military Balance 2020*, p. 215.

[25] See Catherine Harris and Frederik W. Kagan, *Russia's Military Posture: Ground Forces Order of Battle* (Washington DC: Institute for the Study of War, 2018), http://www.understandingwar.org/report/russias-military-posture.

[26] See 'Old War, New Rules: What Comes Next as ATO Ends and a New Operation Starts in Donbas?', Ukraine Crisis Media Center Press Release, 4 May 2018, https://uacrisis.org/en/66558-joint-forces-operation.

[27] See Adam Coffey, 'Ukraine Declares "Anti-terrorist Operation in the Donbas" Officially Over: What Does that Mean?', RUSI Commentary, 6 May 2018, https://rusi.org/commentary/ukraine-declares-anti-terrorist-operation-donbas-officially-over-what-does-mean.

[28] See Stephen Biddle, Julia Macdonald and Ryan Baker, 'Small Footprint, Small Payoff: The Military Effectiveness of Security Force Assistance', *Journal of Strategic Studies*, vol. 41, nos 1–2, 2018, pp. 89–142.

[29] See Deborah Sanders and Christopher Tuck, 'The Ukraine Conflict and the Problems of War Termination', *Journal of Slavic Military Studies*, vol. 33, no. 1, January 2020, pp. 22–43; and Thomas-Durell Young, 'The Failure of Defence Planning in European Post-Communist Defence Institutions: Ascertaining Causation and Determining Solutions', *Journal of Strategic Studies*, vol. 41, no. 7, 2018, pp. 1,031–57.

[30] See Emily O. Goldman, 'Cultural Foundations of Military Diffusion', *Review of International Studies*, vol. 32, no. 1, January 2006, pp. 69–91.

[31] See Thomas-Durell Young, 'The Challenge of Reforming European Communist Legacy "Logistics"', *Journal of Slavic Military Studies*, vol. 29, no. 3, 2016, pp. 352–70; and Young, 'The Failure of Defence Planning in European Post-Communist Defence Institutions'.

[32] See Andrew Higgins, 'In Ukraine, Corruption Is Now Undermining the Military', *New York Times*, 19 February 2018, https://www.nytimes.com/2018/02/19/world/europe/ukraine-corruption-military.html.

[33] See Valentyna Romanova and Andreas Umland, 'Decentralising Ukraine: Geopolitical Implications', *Survival*, vol. 61, no. 5, October–November 2019, pp. 99–112.

Forum: The UN at 75

Editor's Note

Since it was established in 1945, the United Nations has been the world's most potent instrument of internationalism, and a beacon of hope for global governance. While the UN has proven valuable as a forum for its members to air grievances and seek solutions to common problems, the UN Security Council – its primary body for dealing with matters of peace and security – has also been a frustrated and frustrating institution, often falling short in addressing a range of challenges, from conflict resolution to peacekeeping to global health. In recent years, for example, the Security Council has been unable to make an effective impact on the Syrian civil war, and it has faltered in dealing with the COVID-19 pandemic. To a significant degree, the council's dysfunction is traceable to the realpolitik that prevailed at its inception: each of its five permanent members (P5) – China, France, the Soviet Union, the United Kingdom and the United States – insisted on retaining an effective veto over Security Council action. The veto has long been a vexing issue, but as great-power competition has intensified and the relative power of the P5 and other major states has shifted, the issue has become more acute and underpins burgeoning calls for Security Council reform. Three of the four articles presented here explore various challenges of reform. The fourth looks at the impediments COVID-19 has raised to peacekeeping – a key element of the Security Council's mandate – and examines how increased reliance on intelligence could ameliorate them. Earlier versions of

 https://doi.org/10.1080/00396338.2021.1906024

these articles were presented at the 2020 Global Order Colloquium at Perry World House, the University of Pennsylvania's global-affairs hub, with support from the Carnegie Corporation of New York. The statements made and views expressed are solely the responsibility of the authors.

Resolving the Dilemma of UNSC Reform

Kishore Mahbubani

United Nations Security Council (UNSC) reform has proven as difficult as it is necessary. Contrary to conventional wisdom, however, the problem is not the permanent-five members' (P5's) veto power. While the veto does seem unjust and undemocratic, it is essential for keeping great powers supportive of the UN. Perhaps the only reason the United States has not left the UN is that the veto is a powerful weapon that it would hate to lose. The real flaw in the P5 is rather its composition. To remain credible, effective and legitimate, the P5, which dominate and run the council, should constitute the great powers of today. Instead, the body includes two members, the United Kingdom and France, that are no longer ranking great powers. London and Paris implicitly recognise this reality, as they have not used their vetoes since 1989. Furthermore, the Security Council excludes one obvious contemporary great power, India. Martin Wolf, the influential *Financial Times* columnist, observed in 2009 that 'within a decade a world in which the UK is on the United Nations Security Council and India is not will seem beyond laughable'.[1] Also conspicuously left out are Brazil and Nigeria, the most populous states in Latin America and Africa, respectively.

Kishore Mahbubani is a Distinguished Fellow at the Asia Research Institute, National University of Singapore.
An earlier version of this article was presented at the 2020 Global Order Colloquium at Perry World House, the University of Pennsylvania's global-affairs hub, and made possible in part by a grant from the Carnegie Corporation of New York.

Survival | vol. 63 no. 2 | April–May 2021 | pp. 57–62   https://doi.org/10.1080/00396338.2021.1905983

Political stasis

The UN General Assembly has discussed reform continuously for almost three decades, since Boutros Boutros-Ghali, then secretary-general, first raised it in 1992, and made no progress. There are several obstacles to UNSC reform. Firstly, and most importantly, the most powerful member of the P5, the United States, opposes it. If there was any doubt about this, WikiLeaks removed it. In a leaked December 2007 cable, Zalmay Khalilzad, the US ambassador to the UN from 2007 to 2009, said: 'we believe expansion of the Council, along the lines of the models currently discussed, will dilute U.S. influence in the body ... Addition of new permanent members with veto rights would increase the risk to U.S. interests from Council expansion exponentially.'[2] Secondly, the other P5 members – China, France, Russia and the UK – have secretly blocked expansion of the permanent members' bloc while publicly pretending to support it. Thirdly, the permanent membership of the most qualified candidates – Brazil, India and Nigeria – has faced opposition from wary neighbours such as Argentina, Pakistan and South Africa, respectively. Fourthly, there is no consensus among regional groups. For example, the African Group cannot decide whether to support Egypt, Nigeria or South Africa for permanent membership.

This stasis favours the current P5, which want to preserve their privileges for as long as possible. To break the gridlock, I have proposed a novel 7-7-7 formula that would take on board the interests of all 193 UN member states. In brief, there would be seven permanent UNSC members: the European Union, Brazil, China, India, Russia, the United States and Nigeria or South Africa (this last member to be determined by the African Group). To accommodate the interests of the middle powers such as Argentina, Pakistan and South Africa (or Nigeria), a rotating group of seven out of a designated 28 semi-permanent members would serve once every four terms. The semi-permanent members would be selected on the basis of population size and GDP. Thus, they would represent the middle powers of the world. Instead of having to campaign for seats, they would return automatically. The final seven seats would be non-permanent and distributed among the smaller states.[3]

Generating political momentum

Although it is possible to find a formula that is both realistic and fair, such as the 7-7-7 framework, a formula alone is not sufficient. Political momentum behind its adoption is also required, and at present it seems almost impossible to generate. Such momentum could arise, however, if each of two critical parties made a strategic decision that UNSC reform was in its fundamental national interest and took certain critical steps towards that objective.

The most powerful force blocking UNSC reform is the United States. It believes, as noted above, that UNSC expansion is bad for America's national interests. This belief is reinforced by the ingrained US assessment that American interests are best served by weak multilateral institutions. But this calculation is correct only if it is assumed that the United States will remain the world's most powerful state indefinitely. This is not a sound assumption. It is likely that within a decade or two, the United States will become the number-two economic power, with China overtaking it. The interests of a second-ranking power are very different from those of a first-ranking one. Former US president Bill Clinton observed that the United States 'should be trying to create a world with rules and partnerships and habits of behavior that we would like to live in when we're no longer the military, political, economic superpower in the world'.[4] Those would be arrangements that limit and circumscribe the power of that country. In this light, the United States' liberal establishment – especially the media, universities and think tanks – would do well to start educating the US public that America's long-term interests are best served by stronger multilateral institutions. If this happens, UN reform can happen.

India is the other key player in UNSC reform. A major geopolitical contest has arisen between the United States and China. It will dominate global geopolitics in the next decade or more. To balance China, the United States is increasingly courting India. If the United States wants India to become an effective ally against China, it should support, not block, India's entry into the UNSC. And the most effective measure the US could take to win over India would be to announce that it will support India's admission as a permanent member immediately, even if India is the only new member admitted.[5]

To win permanent-member status, India itself would also have to become more ruthless and cunning. Although UN member states have occasionally banded together to defy UNSC resolutions – as the Organization of African Unity did with respect to UN sanctions against Libya in 1998 – they generally are not powerful enough by themselves to do so on a regular basis. The only plausible exception is India. It appears to be the only non-P5 country that can persuade the P5 to stop blocking UNSC reforms. A unilateral announcement by India that it would no longer comply with UNSC decisions could rattle the P5. If, in turn, other member states were inspired to declare openly that the composition of the P5 was illegitimate, and consequently that the decisions of the P5 were invalid, the P5 might be compelled to change course.

Such conduct on India's part might appear irresponsible. However, India would not be the first great power to refuse to abide by a compulsory UNSC decision. The United States has set a precedent. When the UNSC endorsed the Joint Comprehensive Plan of Action, the nuclear deal negotiated between the P5+1 (including Germany) and Iran, it made it compulsory for all UN member states to abide by the terms of the deal. Therefore, when the Trump administration withdrew from it, it was violating international law. In theory, the Security Council should have sanctioned the United States, but it did not even attempt to do so. Less provocatively, India could also promote the 7-7-7 formula to bring in Pakistan as a semi-permanent member, thereby showcasing its statesmanship and removing another obstacle to UNSC reform.

*   *   *

It may take a major diplomatic crisis to generate UNSC reforms, and India could trigger it. Many Indian officials would be reluctant to take such a bold step. But the United States could take advantage of the crisis to advance a new Security Council that would be more effective, credible and legitimate than the current one, and one that would serve America's national interest when it becomes the world's second-ranking power.

Notes

1   Martin Wolf, 'What India Must Do if It Is To Be an Affluent Country', *Financial Times*, 7 July 2009, https://www.ft.com/content/dc1a9462-6b1c-11de-861d-00144feabdc0.

2   Quoted in Vijay Sharma, 'Wikileaks Exposes US' Double-game on UN Security Council Expansion', Global Policy Forum, 25 July 2011, https://archive.globalpolicy.org/security-council/security-council-reform/membership-including-expansion-and-representation/50519-wikileaks-exposes-us-double-game-on-un-security-council-expansion.html.

3   See Kishore Mahbubani, *The Great Convergence: Asia, the West, and the Logic of One World* (New York: PublicAffairs, 2013).

4   *Ibid.*, p. 8.

5   See Kishore Mahbubani, *Has China Won? The Chinese Challenge to American Primacy* (New York: PublicAffairs, 2020).

The Intricacies of UN Security Council Reform

Martin Binder and Monika Heupel

United Nations member states widely agree that reforms to the UN Security Council are necessary to bolster the body's legitimacy. Over the years, myriad reform proposals have arisen. Scholars speak of a norm of Security Council reform, as it has become dubious for member states to deny its necessity.[1] Yet Security Council reform is hard to achieve, and states that have invested the most in the reform debate are increasingly frustrated by the lack of progress.

What reforms are needed?

Legitimacy is crucial for any institution to survive and thrive. While scholars have traditionally argued that strong performance is the best way for international organisations to establish legitimacy, recent scholarship on the UN Security Council suggests that the fairness of the body's procedures is equally crucial.[2] Three aspects of reform appear most important in this regard.

The first is representation. The council's five permanent members (P5) do not equitably reflect the world's population, nor does the P5's composition correspond to current realities of global power distribution. The UK's and

Martin Binder is an associate professor of international relations at the University of Reading. **Monika Heupel** is a professor of political science at the University of Bamberg. An earlier version of this article was presented at the 2020 Global Order Colloquium at Perry World House, the University of Pennsylvania's global-affairs hub, and made possible in part by a grant from the Carnegie Corporation of New York.

Survival | vol. 63 no. 2 | April–May 2021 | pp. 63–68   https://doi.org/10.1080/00396338.2021.1905984

France's permanent seats are remnants of the past, while the African continent, though the centre of much of the council's work, has no permanent seat. The composition of the council's ten rotating elected members is more balanced, especially since the reforms of the mid-1960s, but Western states remain over-represented in the body.

The second aspect is participation. The P5 exercise significant influence on the council's agenda-setting and policy formulation. Changes in the council's working methods now provide for better access for troop-contributing countries, as well as for civil-society actors, by way of informal 'Arria formula' meetings. But this has not fundamentally changed council practices, and in fact has created incentives for the P5 to employ insular, informal debates among themselves. The COVID-19 pandemic has also reduced Security Council access for non-governmental organisations and for delegations with limited technological capacities even further.

Thirdly, there is decision-making. The council's decision-making rules accord vast powers to the P5. The veto allows each permanent member to block any decision that goes against its interests, or to credibly threaten to do so (via the so-called 'hidden' veto), preventing the council from taking action. The council's sustained inability to authorise even a limited intervention in the war in Syria, with Russia and China vetoing multiple draft resolutions, shows the dire consequences of a decision-making structure that accords individual members that may not always subscribe to the values enshrined in the UN Charter the power to prevent the council from responding to mass atrocities.

What reforms are possible?

Unsurprisingly, status quo powers and reformists differ greatly on the urgency and direction of reform. China, Russia and the US disapprove of charter amendments that would give permanent seats on the Security Council to additional member states or curtail the P5's vetoes, and are reluctant to agree to far-reaching reforms to the council's working methods. In contrast, reform-minded blocs, most notably Brazil, Germany, India and Japan – known as the G4 – and the African Group demand substantial reforms ranging from the expansion of the permanent membership to the extension of the veto power to additional council members, which is not acceptable to China, Russia or the US. These blocs are hardly unified themselves, however. One reformist faction, the Uniting for Consensus group, is opposed to adding new permanent members to the council.

Given the wide gulf between the main camps, the only way forward would be a grand bargain under which actors holding maximalist positions gave them up and agreed to a compromise. To win consent, the bargain would have to embody a 'reforms lite' approach. Such a bargain could be attractive to the P5 in that it would enable them to fend off demands for more meaningful reforms, and to reformists in that it would yield at least some of the changes they desire.

Expanding the number of permanent members and extending the veto right to new members is unacceptable to China, Russia and the US. But the Intergovernmental Negotiations process seems to have forged some common ground between status quo countries and reformers. They agree in principle that non-permanent council membership could be expanded to a number in the mid-20s, increasing the representation of developing countries.[3] The additional criterion of more equitable geographical representation also appears to be negotiable.

It is hard to see how the P5 could agree to formal rules providing for more meaningful participation for non-permanent members, non-members and civil-society actors in the council's work. However, UN members have expressed their general willingness to guarantee 'full participation' of all UN members in the activities of the council, to 'improve the participation in and access to the work of the Security Council' for all states in the General Assembly and to commit to 'informal interactive dialogues and Arria-formula meetings'.[4] These admittedly generic concessions could provide space to explore more substantive enhancements of council participation.

Given that the abolition of the veto remains anathema to the P5, the only veto-related reform proposal with even a limited chance of success is that the P5 voluntarily renounce their veto rights with respect to resolutions on action to halt genocide, crimes against humanity or widespread war crimes.[5]

At present, the chances for even these 'reforms lite' are slim, as neither the status quo powers nor the reformists have sufficient incentives to compromise, although France and the United Kingdom support the G4 proposal, and with it an expansion of the permanent membership of the council. The permanent members retain considerable leverage, as there are no institutional alternatives to the Security Council.[6] Thus, even in the absence of meaningful reforms, reformists have little choice but to remain committed to the council, assuming they prefer a world with a body through which great powers can coordinate, however imperfect, to a world without one. Further, the reformists are divided and unlikely to agree on a common set of demands. Some may see advantages in merely agitating for reform. For example, simply pushing for permanent seats on the council with the prospect of gaining veto power after a transitional period allows the G4 to signal their great-power status.

*   *   *

Notwithstanding ongoing reform gridlock and the council's dramatic policy failures, there are many areas in which the body makes important contributions to maintaining and restoring international peace and security. In the past 20 years, the council has authorised a large number of peacekeeping operations and sanctions regimes; pressured states to step up their efforts to tackle cross-cutting security threats such as terrorism and proliferation; and provided governments with a channel of communication and a forum for managing their mutual relationships. These alone are important functions, especially in the context of the intensifying rivalry between the US and China.

Furthermore, the persistence of the reform debate shows that states care about the Security Council, wish to make it more effective and legitimate, and do not question its overarching value. But the fact remains that meaningful procedural reform is still needed to ensure the council's long-term relevance in world affairs. With this reality in mind, reformists would do well to pave over their differences and collectively push for those limited reforms that are feasible, rather than insisting on maximal demands. Permanent members, for their part, should bear in mind that ultimately the council is useful to them only if UN member states believe in its legitimacy and are willing to heed its decisions.

Notes

1   See Kai Schaefer, 'Reforming the
    United Nations Security Council:
    Feasibility or Utopia?', *International
    Negotiation*, vol. 22, no. 1, February
    2017, pp. 62–91.

2   See Martin Binder and Monika
    Heupel, 'The Legitimacy of the UN
    Security Council: Evidence from
    Recent General Assembly Debates',
    International Studies Quarterly, vol.
    59, no. 2, May 2014, pp. 238–50;
    Martin Binder and Monika Heupel,
    'Rising Powers, UN Security Council
    Reform, and the Failure of Rhetorical
    Coercion', *Global Policy*, vol. 11,
    Supplement 3, October 2020, pp.
    93–103; and Lisa Maria Dellmuth,
    Jan Aarte Scholte and Jonas Tallberg,
    'Institutional Sources of Legitimacy for
    International Organisations: Beyond
    Procedure Versus Performance',
    Review of International Studies, vol. 45,
    no. 4, March 2019, pp. 1–20.

3   See Co-Chairs IGN GA73, 'Revised
    Elements of Commonality and Issues
    for Future Consideration: On the
    Question of Equitable Representation
    on and Increase in the Membership
    of the Security Council and Related
    Matters', United Nations, 7 June
    2019, pp. 2, 4, https://www.un.org/
    pga/73/wp-content/uploads/
    sites/53/2019/06/06.07.19-Revised-
    Elements-of-Commonality-paper.pdf.

4   *Ibid.*, pp. 3, 5.

5   See 'Code of Conduct Regarding
    Security Council Action against
    Genocide, Crimes against Humanity
    or War Crimes', A/70/621–S/2015/978,
    14 December 2015, pp. 3–4, https://
    undocs.org/pdf?symbol=en/A/70/621.
    Among the P5, France and the United
    Kingdom support the regulation of
    the veto in the council.

6   See Phillip Y. Lipscy, *Renegotiating
    the World Order: Institutional Change
    in International Relations* (Cambridge:
    Cambridge University Press, 2017).

What's the UN Security Council For?

Sergio Aguirre and William Wagner

The United Nations Security Council's (UNSC) inaugural responsibility was to maintain international peace and security – nothing less than preventing the Third World War. As the UN turned 75 last year, that worst case had not come to pass. But for the UNSC to stay relevant in helping to protect future generations, its members will have to renew its agenda to keep pace with new threats. This may seem like a mammoth task as the UNSC's five permanent, veto-wielding members – the P5 – remain sharply divided. But the UNSC has reinvented itself before, and can do so again.

The Security Council starts with a few distinct advantages. Governments still appeal to it in times of crisis because it has unmatched international legitimacy and tools, including coercive powers, that exceed those of any other multilateral body. It can authorise the use of force. It can set up sanctions regimes to deter and punish bad behaviour. It can galvanise a sprawling UN system to deploy mediators, ceasefire monitors and assistance experts to places where most other governments would hesitate to tread. So it is worth investing in the UNSC's revitalisation. This requires addressing twenty-first-century threats to international peace and security that are not currently on the UNSC agenda.

Sergio Aguirre is a co-founder and a managing partner of WestExec Advisors. **William Wagner** was a senior policy adviser to the US Mission to the United Nations. An earlier version of this article was presented at the 2020 Global Order Colloquium at Perry World House, the University of Pennsylvania's global-affairs hub, and made possible in part by a grant from the Carnegie Corporation of New York.

Survival | vol. 63 no. 2 | April–May 2021 | pp. 69–76   https://doi.org/10.1080/00396338.2021.1905982

The UNSC has long had a tendency to tackle the issues of its non-members. The lion's share of the council's agenda is still taken up by crises in Africa, while entire regions of the world, such as Asia and Latin America, are largely overlooked. The P5 also block serious consideration of most issues pertaining to themselves, including emerging transnational threats. Among the most pressing, yet still largely unaddressed, issues are cyber and emerging technology, climate and the environment, and global health – all deeply connected to international peace and security, and therefore within the UNSC's remit. To be worthy of its name, the Security Council will need to engage with these new threats more deliberately and resolutely.

Cyber threats

Despite widespread recognition of the gravity of cyber threats, the UNSC has been almost completely silent on the matter. Estonia, which joined the council as a non-permanent member for the 2020–21 term, pledged to put the matter on the council's radar, but these efforts are still at an embryonic stage. Since 2016, the council has periodically held informal meetings to discuss cyber threats, but these have been unfocused, with little discussion of how the council could apply its concrete tools.[1] To date, the council has never held a formal meeting dedicated to cyber security, though Estonia, the United Kingdom and the United States did call out Russia's cyber attacks on Georgia at the end of an unrelated closed-door meeting on Syria in March 2020.

UNSC members need a plan to move from scattershot rhetorical engagement on cyber to establishing and endorsing frameworks to prevent escalation and discussing cyber crises in a timely fashion. The 2015 Group of Governmental Experts' conclusions could be the basis for workable rules of the road in the cyber domain. And there should be consequences for state-sponsored and non-state-actor attacks. For example, few would oppose a UNSC resolution protecting hospitals from cyber attacks during peacetime, especially amid the COVID-19 pandemic. Such a resolution could commission independent investigations and reports, establish a sanctions committee and panel of experts, or set forth more granular standards for what capabilities states need to hold malicious actors accountable and to share and report information about attacks. The UNSC could tackle other emerging technology-related issues as well, including disinformation and surveillance.

The council's engagement in counter-terrorism demonstrates how the body could coalesce around a new threat like cyber and set useful norms for all UN member states to follow. After the 9/11 attacks, the council quickly adopted UNSC Resolution 1373, which made it an obligation for states to outlaw terrorism and created a structure whereby the UN could track implementation. Beyond that, the resolution established a new process for debating counter-terrorism standards that has remained intact and productive, spawning landmark resolutions such as Resolution 2178 in 2014, which outlined how states should deal with foreign terrorist fighters. The UN has also built up and maintained a strong institutional capacity to report on threats posed by al-Qaeda and the Islamic State.

There are numerous existing processes promoting clearer rules for cyber, some of which are productive and could feed into a renewed cyber initiative at the Security Council. Their aim is to develop a broad policy community, which the UN has thus far failed to do. The Paris Call for Trust and Security in Cyberspace, driven by France, is the most ambitious such initiative. Prominent international lawyers kicked off the Oxford Process earlier this year to advance discussion on the applicability of international law to cyber attacks on health-care facilities. This was especially urgent, as hackers were impeding the efforts of hospitals, pharmaceutical companies and university researchers to cope with the pandemic. But there is a limit to what institutions of international civil society, or intergovernmental bodies like the Group of Governmental Experts and Open-Ended Working Group, can actually do. While they can promulgate basic, lowest-common-denominator norms, they cannot do much to compel state compliance. The UNSC has the authority to do so.

Climate change

It is no longer controversial that droughts and famines caused by climate change contribute to conflict. If the Paris agreement and the UN Climate Change Conference processes are meant to produce broad cooperation by all member states, the UNSC is the body that has to step in when the world's poorest countries end up suffering from climate-related stresses. The

Security Council's tools range from shining a spotlight on bad behaviour to equipping UN mediators and peacekeeping missions to deal with the political and security fallout from climate-driven crises. But here again, the council has done almost nothing to reckon with the nexus between climate change and insecurity.

While Estonia made cyber security the centrepiece of its campaign for non-permanent UNSC membership, Germany decided to emphasise climate during its 2019–20 term.[2] Discussion of the latter issue is more advanced. Germany has sponsored formal UNSC meetings on the connection between climate and security. A growing number of resolutions about conflicts in Africa contain references to climate.[3] As part of its February 2021 UNSC presidency, the UK also held a high-level open debate on climate and security, during which US Special Presidential Envoy for Climate John Kerry made clear that 'the climate crisis is indisputably a Security Council issue'.[4] Ireland and Niger now also chair an expert working group on climate for UNSC members. But these efforts have yet to generate a tangible outcome.

The council needs a landmark resolution on climate and security, just as it has belatedly recognised other key factors that affect the maintenance of international peace and security. For example, in 2000, the council adopted Resolution 1325, which calls on member states to 'ensure increased representation of women at all decision-making levels' in the institutions and mechanisms to prevent, manage and resolve conflict, among other measures.[5] This resolution spawned an agenda focused on women, peace and security that has influenced the UN's work in conflicts around the world. Twenty years later, council members routinely press the UN about including women in peace talks. The UN has commissioned reports showing the positive impact of women's inclusion on peace talks; governments publish action plans on women, peace and security; and a robust coalition of civil-society groups holds the UN and its members accountable.

A similar model could help the council find its voice on issues of climate. The UNSC lacks the capacity to act as the world's climate police. But as new dimensions of the challenge are recognised, the UNSC can ensure that the UN system and governments around the world acknowledge the threat and take steps to mitigate it.

Global health

The UNSC can also be used as a bully pulpit to mobilise resources in response to a global health emergency. But the council's anaemic response to the COVID-19 pandemic shows how far the body has to go. In March 2020, UN Secretary-General António Guterres called for an immediate global cease-fire to allow for all parties to focus on fighting COVID and delivering aid to populations in need. It took the council more than three months to adopt a brief resolution supporting his call. In February 2021, the UNSC, at the UK's urging, adopted Resolution 2565, which calls for ceasefires in conflict zones to allow for the delivery of COVID vaccines. However, the UNSC has yet to take any other tangible steps to address COVID or prepare for future pandemics.

Some would argue that discussions about COVID and responding to global health emergencies generally belong with the World Health Organization (WHO) and its decision-making body of member states, the World Health Assembly, in Geneva. But the secretary-general's own plea for a global COVID ceasefire demonstrates the nexus between pandemics and the council's peace and security remit. Moreover, the Security Council could move quickly to compel the UN system and member states to act while also pushing member states to marshal resources to combat these threats – functions that the WHO struggles to perform.

Contrast the UNSC's response to COVID with its 2014 response to the Ebola virus in West Africa. In Resolution 2177, the UNSC unabashedly declared that Ebola was a threat to international peace and security, and it pushed member states to adopt best practices to contain the pandemic. Perhaps more importantly, the resolution galvanised the UN to accelerate its response to Ebola, including through the creation of a special system-wide coordinator, and cast the UNSC as a forum to press member states to deliver assistance.[6]

While council reports and sanctions are not ideal for global health responses, a set of pre-approved procedures for responding to pandemics, including the prompt sharing of information and guidelines for how the UN system can deliver aid quickly to those most in need, would be useful. As the WHO begins its own effort to assess the adequacy of its response to COVID-19, member states could also consider whether there could be a more formal mechanism for the WHO to refer health emergencies to the UNSC, along the lines of the International Atomic Energy Agency's referral of nuclear-related matters of concern to the UNSC for follow-up action.

Taking action

At the moment, putting these contemporary threats on the council's agenda may seem like an impossible task. The P5 is beset by deepening divisions, and the council obviously would be stymied if a P5 member used its veto. To the extent that new thematic issues are explored in the Security Council, this is typically done in one-off meetings with little substance that are quickly forgotten. Every UNSC member has a tendency to pick a topic to explore when it holds the rotating presidency, but the discussions quickly dissipate as the presidency changes.

Focusing the council's agenda calls for a long-term strategy; it will not work as a one-off vanity project. This process would start by assembling the right coalition of member states to bring an issue forward. To ensure continuity and legitimacy, a P5 champion – ideally more than one – and a broad range of representatives from the UN's geographical blocs would be needed. They must explain the issue and identify what practical steps the UNSC can take to address it. To convince member states to back new initiatives, diplomats at UN headquarters, generalists by training, would do well to bring leading experts to New York to brief the issues.

Having laid a foundation for advocacy, there is an established progression for how to elevate an issue on the council's agenda. First comes a high-level side event. Next, an informal 'Arria-formula' meeting – such as those Estonia and Indonesia employed to try to get cyber on the agenda in 2020 – is convened. No UNSC member can block the agenda for this kind of meeting, unlike one for a formal UNSC meeting. When planned carefully, an Arria meeting can illuminate what sources of opposition need to be overcome and how to frame an issue for the UNSC's formal consideration. Then comes a formal meeting, ideally paired with the adoption of a presidential statement laying out overarching principles to guide what the UNSC wants member states to do. Finally, members build on the presidential statement to develop a resolution that uses UNSC tools and authorities to tangible effect.

This progression may sound easy enough to advance, but there are myriad ways it can be frustrated. UNSC members looking for quick wins sometimes prefer to skip systematic steps and rush towards half-baked resolutions that do little more than restate basic principles. The time involved in following each step may also exceed what members are willing to invest. To succeed, therefore, the strategy has to extend beyond diplomacy in New York. Governments serious about bringing new issues to the Security Council need to marshal support from their foreign ministers and even heads of state to push recalcitrant UNSC members to buy in. Ministerial summits and the like may be necessary to shape the content of any prospective UNSC resolution they seek to have adopted.

Finally, while diplomats see the UN's meetings as inherently important, most discussions attract scant media attention. Proponents of bold UNSC action may need to mobilise international attention by recruiting powerful public voices (for instance, Nadia Murad on the Islamic State's human trafficking), and to encourage officials of UNSC member states to venture beyond New York to understand challenges first-hand – whether to the Sahel to witness climate risk or to the operations centre of a technology company to appreciate the scale of twenty-first-century cyber threats.

*   *   *

The UNSC has a unique standing among the world's multilateral institutions, but this position of privilege is not guaranteed. Its continuing relevance hinges on effectively confronting new and future threats to international peace and security. At bottom, that requires member states committed to revitalising the Security Council's agenda.

Notes

[1] See 'In Hindsight: The Security Council and Cyber Threats', *Security Council Report*, January 2020 Monthly Forecast, https://www.securitycouncil-report.org/monthly-forecast/2020-01/ the-security-council-and-cyber-threats.php.

[2] Federal Foreign Office of Germany, 'Germany Is Putting the Impact of Climate Change on the Agenda of

the UN Security Council', 22 January 2019, https://www.auswaertiges-amt.de/en/aussenpolitik/internationale-organisationen/vereintenationen/climate-change-security-council/2179806.

3   See United Nations Foundation, 'Climate Change at the UN Security Council: Seeking Peace in a Warming World', 29 June 2020, https://unfoundation.org/blog/post/climate-change-a-un-security-council-seeking-peace-warming-world/#:~:text=We%20Do%20It-,Climate%20Change%20at%20the%20UN%20Security%20Council,Peace%20in%20a%20Warming%20World&text=The%20impacts%20of%20climate%20change,multipliers%2C%E2%80%9D%20intensifying%20preexisting%20orisks.

4   US Department of State, 'Secretary Kerry Participates in the UN Security Council Open Debate on Climate and Security', 23 February 2021, https://www.state.gov/secretary-kerry-participates-in-the-un-security-council-open-debate-on-climate-and-security/.

5   United Nations Security Council, Resolution 1325, 31 October 2000, http://unscr.com/en/resolutions/doc/1325.

6   See United Nations Security Council, Resolution 2177, 18 September 2014, http://unscr.com/en/resolutions/doc/2177.

UN Peacekeeping After the Pandemic: An Increased Role for Intelligence

Allison Carnegie and Austin Carson

United Nations peacekeepers have a tough job, and the coronavirus is making it much tougher. Effective peacekeeping requires detailed information about rebel movements, troop levels and other ground-level conditions. However, the coronavirus has reduced peacekeepers' abilities to obtain this information by diminishing their physical presence in conflict areas.

Worries abound that peacekeepers will either contract the virus if sent into hot spots, or spread the virus to a country that has not had a severe outbreak. As a result, traditional suppliers of peacekeepers, such as Bangladesh, Ethiopia, India, Pakistan and Rwanda, have expressed reluctance to contribute them, and potential host countries have been hesitant to accept them.[1] Troop rotations thus have been put on hold.[2] Those states that have deployed troops have minimised their interactions with local populations.[3] The UN has suspended training for local partners if physical contact or close proximity is involved, and reduced military patrolling.[4] This reduction in peacekeepers' physical presence has undoubtedly impaired the situational awareness and tactical knowledge that peacekeepers depend on. They are compelled to figure out how to do more with less.

One partial solution may be to increase peacekeepers' access to information derived from intelligence sources. While no technical intelligence platform can fully substitute for local knowledge gained on the ground,

Allison Carnegie is an associate professor of political science at Columbia University. **Austin Carson** is an assistant professor of political science at the University of Chicago. An earlier version of this article was presented at the 2020 Global Order Colloquium at Perry World House, the University of Pennsylvania's global-affairs hub, and made possible in part by a grant from the Carnegie Corporation of New York.

Survival | vol. 63 no. 2 | April–May 2021 | pp. 77–83   https://doi.org/10.1080/00396338.2021.1905985

expanding and enhancing available intelligence will greatly assist the UN as it seeks to advance its traditional peacekeeping goals, providing new streams of information as UN peacekeepers' traditional means of gathering it are inhibited. But ramping up intelligence does have costs. These include leaks and a loss of transparency, which the UN has been keen to avoid. Its concerns could be mitigated through better protections for confidential information. While such an approach may challenge established UN practices, the world is changing, and the UN may need to change with it.

The qualified utility of intelligence

Peacekeepers are called upon to interpose themselves between hostile parties, monitor peace processes, implement peace agreements and pre-empt violence.[5] All of these activities require detailed knowledge of conditions on the ground, both to enable them to effectively keep the peace and to ensure their safety. Peacekeepers may need to navigate difficult terrain, monitor disease outbreaks, locate refugees, detect security threats or learn about military activities.

The necessary information can be gleaned on site, but it can also be obtained via intelligence systems. Satellites and uninhabited aerial vehicles, thermal sensors and signals intercepts can relay detailed information to peacekeepers to supplement existing knowledge or to direct their movements. Open-source information can also help, though it is rarely as detailed and probative as professionally generated intelligence.

Such intelligence typically comes from outside actors or is gathered by the UN itself. Many large member states invest significant resources in developing sophisticated intelligence bureaucracies and collect peacekeeping-related information either on a dedicated basis or as a by-product of other collection activities.[6] They then choose whether to share this information with the UN. These states have also equipped the UN with technology to allow it to obtain some of this information itself.

At the same time, intelligence is often highly sensitive, making governments hesitant to share it and leading them to restrict how much intelligence the UN itself can collect. In particular, in providing intelligence to the UN, member states risk exposing the sources and methods they used to collect it.[7] Such exposure can endanger their national-security interests, as intelligence targets may learn to avoid detection once they understand how they are monitored. Moreover, other states may mimic their advanced methods of intelligence collection, eroding their advantage. While states could omit sensitive details in providing intelligence to the UN, such information would be considered less credible.

The UN's direct collection of intelligence is one alternative. But member states may oppose it owing to sovereignty concerns. They may also fear that the UN could uncover information that they wish to keep secret, such as detailed security arrangements or personal data. The pandemic may exacerbate these sensitivities, as states may wish to hide outbreaks in their countries to avoid trade and travel restrictions that negatively impact their economies.[8]

Protecting confidential information

To mitigate such factors, the UN could implement strong confidentiality measures to reassure intelligence providers that their information will be kept secure. The UN already has some experience with this, as it has collected intelligence sporadically for some time.[9] For example, the Security Council allowed the UN to use drones for intelligence collection during its mission in the Democratic Republic of the Congo. Joint mission-analysis centres have been adopted and used as mission-specific locations for states to share peacekeeping-related intelligence. Member states have also robustly shared intelligence for the UN peacekeeping mission in Haiti. For the most part, however, these intelligence-sharing efforts remain ad hoc.

Today, peacekeeping missions are able to both collect their own intelligence and receive it from member states, sometimes even from other international organisations.[10] The Department of Peace Operations' intelligence framework, developed in 2017 and revised in 2019 in response to members' concerns, highlights and recognises the need to keep this information secure. The framework states that 'missions will put in place procedural, technological and physical security tools … to ensure secure information management and communications'. Such tools might include protection measures for computers and servers, encryption, access control, training for personnel and other tools. It further calls for information to be shared on a need-to-know basis and for labels based on levels of classification.[11]

Implementation of this framework has faced difficulties, however. UN headquarters has long had a reputation for leaking information, based in considerable part on a particularly egregious instance that occurred during the peacekeeping mission in Somalia, when the US found unprotected classified documents in a deserted UN office. The leak led to the cancellation of planned intelligence-sharing initiatives and has contributed to a lack of trust in the UN's existing confidentiality systems. On account of a 'general lack of trust', peacekeeping missions now use two official databases with different levels of access, along with their own unofficial systems and personalised platforms.[12]

Perceptions of corruption and bias have also impeded the expanded use of intelligence in UN peacekeeping efforts.[13] Previous instances of wrongdoing, neglect and corruption, including alleged sexual misconduct during peacekeeping missions and peacekeepers abandoning their stations, have left states wary of giving the UN too much power and fed worries about intelligence-gathering by the organisation. Indeed, rather than turning towards secrecy, the UN has made transparency and accountability critical goals.[14] States worry that the UN will use intelligence to favour particular members, and that secrecy may obscure who is calling the shots.

As a result of these concerns, the UN's capacity for intelligence integration is relatively weak, and defining what peacekeeping intelligence means in practice has been left unclear.

Moving forward

Leaks, corruption and biases cannot be completely eliminated. But because of the pandemic, the benefits of adopting new technologies that allow the UN to access or collect intelligence now arguably exceed the costs. International organisations other than the UN Department of Peace Operations – including the International Atomic Energy Agency, the World Trade Organization and the Organisation for the Prohibition of

Chemical Weapons – have dealt effectively with similar obstacles to intelligence collection and have successfully implemented strong confidentiality systems.[15] These include stand-alone computers, document-classification systems and penalties for leaks, among other measures. The UN could draw from these models.

The UN has already started to improve its confidentiality system in specific missions. For the UN Multidimensional Integrated Stabilization Mission in Mali, for instance, it has introduced the All Source Information Fusion Unit intelligence structure. But stronger measures are possible. In particular, the UN should work towards integrating its multiple peace-keeping databases to allow personnel to access information that has been gathered by other units and prevent unnecessary delays in securing useful information. Confidentiality classifications and clearance levels could then be standardised rather than determined by who trusts whom on an ad hoc basis. For such reforms to be practically feasible, the UN would need to build a track record of securely handling information to gain the trust of its members. The organisation might, for example, visibly redact sensitive information from published documents, and ensure that its information-gathering and -sharing processes are transparent. The UN could also recruit technocratic experts to help incorporate and enforce systemic measures and protocols that guarantee information security.

* * *

A dearth of detailed information is only one of several challenges that the current pandemic has posed to UN peacekeeping. Indeed, peacekeeping was already on the decline prior to the coronavirus outbreak, with reduced funding and no new missions authorised since 2014. As governments slash budgets and prioritise public health, peacekeeping is unlikely to regain substantial momentum in the medium term. Yet the demand for peacekeepers is likely to rise due to pandemic-induced instability in fragile states. Greater reliance on intelligence cannot completely close the gap, but it could help UN peacekeepers to continue to work effectively at relatively low cost.

Notes

1   See Cedric de Coning, 'Examining the Longer-term Effects of COVID-19 on UN Peacekeeping Operations', *IPI Global Observatory*, 13 May 2020, https://theglobalobservatory.org/2020/05/examining-longer-term-effects-covid-19-un-peacekeeping-operations/.

2   See Richard Gowan and Louise Riis Andersen, 'Peacekeeping in the Shadow of Covid-19 Era', reliefweb, 12 June 2020, https://reliefweb.int/report/world/peacekeeping-shadow-covid-19-era.

3   See 'Community Outreach and COVID-19', UN Peacekeeping, 22 May 2020, https://peacekeeping.un.org/sites/default/files/20200522_peacekeeping_community_outreach_and_covid.pdf.

4   See Namie De Razza, 'UN Peacekeeping and the Protection of Civilians in the COVID-19 Era', *IPI Global Observatory*, 22 May 2020, https://theglobalobservatory.org/2020/05/un-peacekeeping-protection-of-civilians-in-covid-19-era/.

5   See Virginia Page Fortna, *Does Peacekeeping Work? Shaping Belligerents' Choices after Civil War* (Princeton, NJ: Princeton University Press, 2008).

6   See David Carment and Martin Rudner (eds), *Peacekeeping Intelligence: New Players, Extended Boundaries* (Abingdon and New York: Routledge, 2006).

7   See Allison Carnegie and Austin Carson, *Secrets in Global Governance: Disclosure Dilemmas and the Challenge of International Cooperation* (Cambridge: Cambridge University Press, 2020).

8   See Catherine Z. Worsnop, 'Concealing Disease: Trade and Travel Barriers and the Timeliness of Outbreak Reporting', *International Studies Perspectives*, vol. 20, no. 4, November 2019, pp. 344–72.

9   See A. Walter Dorn, 'United Nations Peacekeeping Intelligence', in Loch Johnson (ed.), *The Oxford Handbook of National Security Intelligence* (Oxford: Oxford University Press, 2010), pp. 275–95.

10 See UN Security Council, Resolution 2547, 27 February 2019, https://www.securitycouncilreport.org/atf/cf/%7B65BFCF9B-6D27-4E9C-8CD3-CF6E4FF96FF9%7D/s_res_2457.pdf.

11 See UN Department of Peace Operations, 'Policy: Peacekeeping Intelligence', 2 May 2017 (reviewed 2 May 2019), https://www.confluxcenter.org/wp-content/uploads/2018/11/2017.07-Peacekeeping-Intelligence-Policy.pdf.

12 Sarah-Myriam Martin Brûlé, 'Finding the UN Way on Peacekeeping-Intelligence', International Peace Institute, 20 April 2020, https://www.ipinst.org/wp-content/uploads/2020/04/2004-Finding-the-UN-Way.pdf.

13 See, for example, Rick Gladstone, 'Armies Used by U.N. Fail Watchdog Group's Test', *New York Times*, 3 April 2016, https://www.nytimes.com/2016/04/04/world/armies-used-by-un-fail-watchdog-groups-test.html.

14 See UN Peacekeeping, 'Standards of Conduct', https://peacekeeping.un.org/en/standards-of-conduct.

15 See Carnegie and Carson, *Secrets in Global Governance*.

Noteworthy

Coup in Myanmar

'I urge people not to accept this, to respond and wholeheartedly to protest against the coup by the military.'
From a statement attributed to Aung San Suu Kyi after she and other civilian leaders were detained as part of a military takeover of Myanmar's government on 1 February 2021.[1]

'The abject failure of the security council, thanks to the likes of China and Russia, to hold Myanmar's military leaders accountable for their crimes helps them feel they can engage in horrific abuses and pay little or no cost.'
Louis Charbonneau, UN director at Human Rights Watch, criticises the UN Security Council for failing to condemn the coup.[2]

'Our country was a bird that was just learning to fly. Now the army broke our wings.'
Burmese student activist Si Thu Tun.[3]

'Protesters are now inciting the people, especially emotional teenagers and youths, to a confrontation path where they will suffer the loss of life.'
Myanmar's State Administration Council issues a warning on 21 February to protesters demonstrating against the coup in a broadcast on state-run MRTV.[4]

'I knelt down … begging them not to shoot and torture the children, but to shoot me and kill me instead.'
Sister Ann Rose Nu Tawng, a Catholic nun, explains why she placed herself between armed police officers and protesters in the city of Myitkyina on 8 March 2021.[5]

A damning acquittal

'You were just 58 steps away.'
Democratic House impeachment manager Representative Eric Swalwell tells members of the US Senate during the second impeachment trial of former president Donald Trump how close they came to confronting violent rioters in the US Capitol on 6 January 2021.[6]

'I have listened to the arguments presented by both sides and considered the facts. The facts are clear.

The President promoted unfounded conspiracy theories to cast doubt on the integrity of a free and fair election because he did not like the results. As Congress met to certify the election results, the President directed his supporters to go to the Capitol to disrupt the lawful proceedings required by the Constitution. When the crowd became violent, the President used his office to first inflame the situation instead of immediately calling for an end to the assault.

As I said on January 6th, the President bears responsibility for these tragic events. The evidence is compelling that President Trump is guilty of inciting an insurrection against a

     DOI 10.1080/00396338.2021.1905986

coequal branch of government and that the charge rises to the level of high Crimes and Misdemeanors. Therefore, I have voted to convict.

I do not make this decision lightly, but I believe it is necessary.

By what he did and by what he did not do, President Trump violated his oath of office to preserve, protect, and defend the Constitution of the United States.

My hope is that with today's vote America can begin to move forward and focus on the critical issues facing our country today.'

Republican Senator Richard Burr comments on his vote to convict Trump on 13 February 2021.[7]

'I voted to convict President Trump because he is guilty.'

Republican Senator Bill Cassidy.[8]

'It is a sad commentary on our times that one political party in America is given a free pass to denigrate the rule of law, defame law enforcement, cheer mobs, excuse rioters, and transform justice into a tool of political vengeance, and persecute, blacklist, cancel and suppress all people and viewpoints with whom or which they disagree. I always have, and always will, be a champion for the unwavering rule of law, the heroes of law enforcement, and the right of Americans to peacefully and honorably debate the issues of the day without malice and without hate.'

Former US president Donald Trump comments on his acquittal by the US Senate on 13 February 2021 on the charge of inciting the riot at the US Capitol on 6 January 2021.[9]

'There's no question, none, that President Trump is practically, and morally, responsible for provoking the events of the day … The people who stormed this building believed they were acting on the wishes and instructions of their president, and having that belief was a foreseeable consequence of the growing crescendo of false statements, conspiracy theories and reckless hyperbole, which the defeated president kept shouting into the largest megaphone on planet Earth.'

Senate Republican minority leader Mitch McConnell, who voted to acquit Trump, gives a speech following the vote.[10]

Australia vs Facebook

'In response to Australia's proposed new Media Bargaining law, Facebook will restrict publishers and people in Australia from sharing or viewing Australian and international news content.

The proposed law fundamentally misunderstands the relationship between our platform and publishers who use it to share news content. It has left us facing a stark choice: attempt to comply with a law that ignores the realities of this relationship, or stop allowing news content on our services in Australia. With a heavy heart, we are choosing the latter.'

In a statement released on 17 February 2021, Facebook explains its decision to block the sharing of news and the accessing of public information by Australian users on its platform.[11]

'Facebook's actions to unfriend Australia today, cutting off essential information services on health and emergency services, were as arrogant as they were disappointing. I am in regular contact with the leaders of other nations on these issues.

These actions will only confirm the concerns that an increasing number of countries are expressing about the behaviour of BigTech companies who think they are bigger than governments and that the rules should not apply to them. They may be changing the world, but that doesn't mean they run it.

We will not be intimidated by BigTech seeking to pressure our Parliament as it votes on our important News Media Bargaining Code. Just as we weren't intimidated when Amazon threatened to leave the country and when Australia drew other nations together to combat the publishing of terrorist content on social media platforms.

I encourage Facebook to constructively work with the Australian Government, as Google recently demonstrated in good faith.'
Australian Prime Minister Scott Morrison uses his Facebook account to comment on the company's decision.[12]

'The timing could not be worse. Three days before our Covid-19 vaccine rollout, Australians using Facebook as their primary source of news can no longer get access to credible information about vaccination from news organisations and some government and public health organisation pages.'
Julie Leask, professor at the University of Sydney's school of nursing.[13]

'Nobody benefits from this decision as Facebook will now be a platform for misinformation to rapidly spread without balance.'
Australia's Nine media group supports the government's position.[14]

'They are behaving more like North Korea than an American company.'
Mark McGowan, premier of Western Australia.[15]

'Facebook has re-friended Australia.'
Australian Treasurer Josh Frydenberg announces the end of Facebook's news ban after discussions with the company.[16]

Sources

1 Rebecca Ratcliffe, 'Fears Army Will Tighten Grip in Myanmar After Aung San Suu Kyi Detained', *Guardian*, 1 February 2021, https://www.theguardian.com/world/2021/feb/01/further-army-clampdown-feared-in-myanmar-after-aung-san-suu-kyi-detained.
2 Rebecca Ratcliffe and Julian Borger, 'Myanmar Coup: Civil Disobedience Campaign Begins amid Calls for Aung San Suu Kyi's Release', *Guardian*, 2 February 2021, https://www.theguardian.com/global-development/2021/feb/02/myanmar-coup-military-tightens-grip-amid-calls-for-suu-kyi-to-be-freed.
3 Ratcliffe, 'Fears Army Will Tighten Grip in Myanmar After Aung San Suu Kyi Detained'.
4 Helen Regan, 'Huge Demonstrations Across Myanmar Despite Military's Warning that Protesters Could Suffer "Loss of Life"', CNN, 23 February 2021, https://edition.cnn.com/2021/02/21/asia/myanmar-general-strike-military-warning-intl-hnk/index.html.
5 '"Shoot Me Instead": Myanmar Nun's Plea to Spare Protesters', *Guardian*, 9 March 2021, https://www.theguardian.com/world/2021/mar/09/shoot-me-instead-myanmar-nuns-plea-to-spare-protesters.
6 Luke Broadwater and Emily Cochrane, '"We Have to Relive It": Images Revive Painful Memories in Senate', *New York Times*, 10 February 2021, https://www.nytimes.com/2021/02/10/us/politics/impeachment-violence-senate.html?action=click&module=Spotlight&pgtype=Homepage.
7 'Senator Burr Statement on Vote to Convict Former President Trump on Article of Impeachment', press release, 13 February 2021, https://www.burr.senate.gov/press/releases/senator-burr-statement-on-vote-to-convict-former-president-trump-on-article-of-impeachment.
8 Luke Broadwater, 'Here Are the Seven Republicans Who Voted to Convict Trump',

New York Times, 13 February 2021, https://www.nytimes.com/2021/02/13/us/politics/republicans-vote-to-impeach.html?action=click&module=Spotlight&pgtype=Homepage.
9 Lisa Kashinsky, 'Full Text of Trump's Statement on Impeachment Acquittal', *Boston Herald*, 13 February 2021, https://www.bostonherald.com/2021/02/13/full-text-of-trumps-statement-on-impeachment-acquittal/.
10 'Mitch McConnell Speech Transcript After Vote to Acquit Trump in 2nd Impeachment Trial', Rev, 13 February 2021, https://www.rev.com/blog/transcripts/mitch-mcconnell-speech-transcript-after-vote-to-acquit-trump-in-2nd-impeachment-trial.
11 William Easton, 'Changes to Sharing and Viewing News on Facebook in Australia', Facebook, 17 February 2021, https://about.fb.com/news/2021/02/changes-to-sharing-and-viewing-news-on-facebook-in-australia/.
12 Scott Morrison, Facebook post, 18 February 2021, https://www.facebook.com/scottmorrison4cook/posts/3992877800756593.
13 Jamie Smyth, Hannah Murphy and Alex Barker, 'Facebook Ban on News in Australia Provokes Fierce Backlash', *Financial Times*, 18 February 2021, https://www.ft.com/content/cac1ff54-b976-4ae4-b810-46c29ab26096.
14 *Ibid.*
15 Jamie Smyth, 'Facebook "Behaving Like North Korea" as Australia Wakes Up to News Ban', *Financial Times*, 19 February 2021, https://www.ft.com/content/9e519b57-4e48-4221-9622-facd83cd0e42.
16 'Facebook Reverses Ban on News Pages in Australia', BBC News, 23 February 2021, https://www.bbc.co.uk/news/world-australia-56165015.

The Sino-American World Conflict

Peter Rudolf

In Beijing a new consensus has emerged: that, in the words of Yonsei University professor Xiangfeng Yang, 'a shift in the tectonic plates of China's relations with the United States is afoot, or indeed already complete'.[1] Chinese officials had noted the Trump administration's stated determination to undertake a 'fundamental restructuring' of the relationship with China and to adopt a 'whole-of government approach' to managing US–Chinese competition.[2] President Joe Biden's China policy may be less confrontational and more nuanced than his predecessor's, but Secretary of State Antony Blinken has stated that although 'extreme competition', a phrase used by Biden,[3] does not exclude engagement with China, any such engagement will need to take place 'from a position of strength'.[4] Meanwhile, the dominant view in China seems to be that its strategic rivalry with the US will be intense and long-lasting.[5] It is widely expected that the United States, as the world's most powerful country, will use its resources to preserve its status and privileges, and to prevent China from rising further.[6] The coronavirus pandemic has only worsened the deterioration of US–China relations.[7]

The danger for international politics is that the intensifying strategic rivalry between the two states threatens to harden into what might be called a 'structural world conflict', with the attendant economic and military risks.[8] In this sense, talk of a 'new cold war' is not entirely misplaced,

Peter Rudolf is a Senior Fellow at Stiftung Wissenschaft und Politik (SWP), the German Institute for International and Security Affairs, Berlin.

Survival | vol. 63 no. 2 | April–May 2021 | pp. 87–114   https://doi.org/10.1080/00396338.2021.1905980

despite the problems and limitations of the analogy. In the United States, China's rise is widely seen as a threat to America's pre-eminent international position. The expectation among elites and the public alike is that China will threaten traditional US predominance not only in the Western Pacific and East Asia, but also globally.[9] Perceptions of China's 'unstoppable' economic and military rise, and of a relative decline in US power, may be based on questionable assumptions and projections.[10] However, China can arguably be described as an 'emerging potential superpower', a status with implications both for the United States and its allies, and for the international order more generally.[11]

Debating the Thucydides Trap

History shows that integrating a rising power into the international system is not an easy task.[12] Power-transition theory holds that even states without an aggressive, revisionist or risk-prone foreign policy tend to come into conflict with other powers as they attempt to secure raw materials, markets and military bases.[13] Thus, power shifts pose a considerable risk to the stability of the international system. This is sometimes known as 'Thucydides Trap', following Thucydides' interpretation of the Peloponnesian War as an inevitable result of the rising power of Athens, which forced a fearful Sparta to go to war.[14] The idea has been widely debated in both the United States and China.

Discussion about the Thucydides Trap in both countries testifies to an awareness of the risks associated with China's rise. Top Chinese officials, including President Xi Jinping himself, have repeatedly declared their intention to avoid the trap.[15] Sensitivity to the risks resulting from China's rise has been reflected in talk of seeking a 'new type of great power relationship' between the United States and China.[16]

The power-transition theories underpinning this discussion are not without their problems, however. Above all, it is important to note that such theories, by acting as frames that influence perceptions, are political constructs.[17] Frames contextualise facts and structure the flow of events. They serve to define problems and to diagnose their causes. They provide criteria for assessing developments, offer solutions and set the boundaries of debate. In this way, they contribute to the construction of political reality.[18]

Within the power-transition frame, conflicts that might otherwise be seen as regional or local in character gain such salience that they add up to a global hegemonic rivalry. To the extent that Chinese policies nourish and strengthen this perception in the United States, this might lead to a kind of self-fulfilling prophecy. At the very least, this frame can have a conflict-hardening effect resulting from the built-in expectation that a rising power will inevitably question the existing international order.[19] From this perspective, China is by definition a revisionist power.

If one takes official documents and statements as a yardstick, the prevailing perception in the United States is that China is thoroughly revisionist. Any hope that China's integration into international institutions and the global economy would make it a reliable partner has given way to the view that China – as well as Russia – is aiming to shape 'a world antithetical to U.S. values and interests'.[20] The 2017 US National Security Strategy states that both powers 'are contesting [the United States'] geopolitical advantages and trying to change the international order in their favor'.[21] According to the Pentagon, China 'seeks Indo-Pacific regional hegemony in the near-term and, ultimately global preeminence in the long-term'.[22] As then-secretary of state Mike Pompeo put it in 2019, 'China wants to be the dominant economic and military power of the world, spreading its authoritarian vision for society and its corrupt practices worldwide'.[23] As these statements indicate, the Trump administration based its China policy on worst-case assumptions about the long-term intentions of China's leadership.[24]

The Trump White House saw the relationship with China through the lens of a zero-sum logic, resolutely propagating the narrative of great-power competition and thereby shaping the China debate in the unique way that only authoritative speakers such as presidents and members of their administrations can do.[25] Narratives present an interpretation of the past ('the cooperative China policy has failed'), they interpret the current situation ('China is disputing US supremacy') and they offer strategic instruction for future action ('offensively compete using every available resource').[26]

While the revisionist label may serve a range of domestic and foreign-policy purposes in the United States, it does not necessarily provide an accurate picture of Chinese behaviour.[27] Indeed, China is not fundamentally questioning the existing international order. This order consists of many principles, norms and functional regimes. China supports some of them and rejects others.[28] The term 'revisionist stakeholder' is a more precise way of describing the Chinese position: China operates within the framework of existing international organisations, especially the United Nations system, and insists on a traditional understanding of state sovereignty. However, it rejects US and Western dominance in international institutions and is dissatisfied with its own status. From the Chinese perspective, this status no longer corresponds to the country's increased power and the relative decline of the United States.[29]

Within Chinese discourse, the US narrative of great-power competition has been criticised as reflecting a Cold War, zero-sum mentality.[30] The Chinese government denies striving for hegemony or establishing spheres of influence. Beijing insists it will not follow the path taken by other rising powers.[31] President Xi's vision is for a rejuvenated China to become an economic, technological and cultural world power that exerts greater influence over the rules of international politics.[32] In this way, he has linked the Communist Party's claim to legitimacy with China's emergence as a leading world power.[33]

A new cold war?

A Cold War analogy is often used to interpret current conflicts in US–China relations, if only to highlight the differences between the Sino-American and the US–Soviet conflicts.[34] Indeed, some elements of American–Chinese relations lend themselves well to a comparison with the East–West conflict, such as the presence of an emerging bipolarity and ideological antagonism; a security dilemma and arms competition; and global power rivalry.[35] Like any analogy, however, Cold War comparisons are problematic and of limited use.

Status competition

The US–Chinese conflict encompasses regional and global competition for status in an international system characterised by an emerging bipolarity, even though there is no parity of power between America and China.[36] This is comparable to the Cold War era, during which the international order was generally regarded as bipolar even though power resources were by no means equally distributed between the United States and the Soviet Union. Because the gap between these two states and the remaining powers was considerable, they were both regarded as superpowers.

In contrast to the Cold War, however, the relationship between the United States and China is not a confrontation between two mutually exclusive, opposing blocs, but a competition for influence within a globalised international system in which the two powers are highly intertwined economically.[37] In 2018, China was America's number-one trading partner – the third-largest export market for American products and the main source of the country's imports. For China, the United States tops the list of buyers of Chinese products.[38] There is also a high degree of industrial interdependence between the two economies, which has developed since the early 1990s as a result of an almost revolutionary change in the organisation of industrial production.[39] Today, components manufactured in China are used in many US products. Mutual dependencies have also arisen because China had long held the largest share of US treasury bonds until Japan overtook it in July 2019.[40]

China's actual and projected increase in power has aroused anxiety in the United States that it might lose its status as the predominant international superpower. States (or more precisely, the officials representing them) may aspire to high status as an end in itself: a high status creates the satisfying feeling of superiority over other people or states, while the prospect of losing one's status can threaten one's identity. But status is also associated with material gains. In the long run, China threatens not only the status of the United States as the lone superpower, but also its privileges and economic advantages.[41] If China were to become the world's predominant political, economic and technological power, it could, as the US fears, widely set rules and standards, and establish a kind of illiberal sphere of influence. If this were to happen, American security and prosperity would no longer be as secure as before.[42] The fear is that the US dollar would no longer dominate as the international reserve currency, and that the US would no longer attract the financial inflows that help secure American prosperity. Under these conditions, the United States would see its freedom of action curtailed.[43]

Ideological differences

It may be that, were China a liberal democracy, its rise would appear less threatening to the US. Since it is not a liberal democracy, the competition between China and the US contains an element of ideological antagonism. Unlike in the case of the East–West confrontation, however, this is not the core feature of the US–Chinese rivalry. During the Cold War, Soviet ideology completely ruled out any permanent coexistence with the capitalist system led by the United States, and the supposedly inevitable victory of communism worldwide was seen as guaranteeing the security of the Soviet Union. This element is missing in the Sino-American conflict. China's stance is better described as 'nationalist' rather than 'internationalist'.[44]

It is true that the human-rights situation in China has long been a source of friction in Sino-American relations, but as long as China's rise was not perceived as a global challenge, and as long as there was hope that China would liberalise, the country was not seen in the United States as an ideological antagonist. From the Chinese perspective, the ideological dimension has always been more pronounced, since Western ideas of liberal democracy and freedom of expression threaten the ideological dominance of the Communist Party.[45]

Recent debates in the United States, however, suggest that Americans have begun to perceive the ideological conflict between the American and Chinese systems as being of a similar dimension to that between Western democracy and Soviet communism. It has been argued that China's economically successful 'authoritarian capitalism' could find international resonance at a time when confidence in the systemic superiority of 'democratic capitalism' is weakening. In this scenario, competition for geopolitical power is mixed with a struggle for ideological superiority.[46]

China has even been portrayed as an existential threat both to the United States and to the world order.[47] The Trump administration, for example, characterised the conflict with China as an ideological clash between 'civilizations'.[48] China was accused of trying to 'reorder the world' by constructing 'a worldwide socialist order with Beijing at the center'.[49] This view plays down the fact that China lacks a 'coherent ideology with international appeal', as Cornell professor Jessica Chen Weiss has argued,[50] and that

Chinese policies are not aimed at establishing clientelist relationships with countries that share its own ideological orientation, as the Soviet Union once did.[51] The Chinese leadership under Xi may promote a development model that implicitly calls into question liberal democracy as a political ideal, and China's model of governance may be attractive for authoritarian states.[52] However, China's economic success is based on specific preconditions, including a large domestic market, an abundance of labour, the government's willingness to experiment and a spirit of pragmatic improvisation. Yes, China supports many authoritarian regimes, exports surveillance technology and exerts pressure on critical voices abroad. But this does not add up to a struggle against democracy or a strategy to undermine democratic systems.[53] Nevertheless, it is likely that a narrative of systemic conflict between 'digital authoritarianism' and 'liberal democracy' will become predominant in the US discourse, since it might help to mobilise long-term domestic political support for a costly competitive policy towards China.[54]

Security dilemma

Although the ideological element in the Sino-American rivalry is not its dominant feature, an increasing emphasis on the ideological differences between the two sides can be expected to influence their threat perceptions, thus reinforcing the security dilemma between them.[55] In an anarchic international system, no state can be certain that it will not be attacked, dominated or even extinguished. Measures to strengthen one's own security, however, whether through arms, territorial expansion or alliances, can reduce the security of other states, and thus lead to a competition for weaponry and power.[56] In its classical form, a security dilemma arises when offensive military doctrines and capabilities pose a threat to a state's territorial integrity, either in the form of an invasion or a nuclear first strike. In the context of the US–China rivalry, the United States has not accepted mutual nuclear vulnerability as the basis of its strategic relationship.[57] This could, it is feared, be understood as a lack of American resolve to defend its allies and interests in Asia. Moreover, Beijing would probably not be convinced by any US statements that it does not have plans to eliminate China's nuclear capability in the case of an escalating crisis.[58] Similarly, China does not trust American assurances that the development of missile-defence systems is not directed against China's strategic nuclear potential.[59]

China has rejected the first use of nuclear weapons in its declaratory nuclear doctrine; it relies on a minimum-deterrence strategy and thus on the ability to retaliate.[60] Beijing fears that Washington's development of reconnaissance, surveillance and conventional prompt global-strike capabilities, as well as missile-defence systems, could jeopardise China's second-strike capability. China maintains a relatively small nuclear arsenal of an estimated 290 warheads.[61] However, there are plans to expand this arsenal by acquiring a greater number of missiles with multiple warheads. The United States is faced with the question of whether to accept its nuclear vulnerability in relation to China, which may result from the deployment of mobile intercontinental and sea-based ballistic missiles, or to pursue a damage-limitation strategy that at least opens up the possibility of limiting its own losses should deterrence fail. In accordance with the traditional logic of American deterrence policy, the US would need options for pre-emptively eliminating the enemy's nuclear arsenal.[62]

According to fears voiced in the US debate, a secure Chinese second-strike capability could lead to a greater Chinese willingness to take risks in crises. In the debate on nuclear strategy, this is referred to as the 'stability–instability paradox'.[63] This means that stability at the strategic level could tempt one side to use limited force in the expectation that the other will shy away from a massive nuclear strike, as this would lead to mutual destruction. According to this scenario, a secure Chinese second-strike capability threatens to raise doubts among America's Asian allies about the credibility of extended deterrence. If the United States follows the traditional line of its operational deterrence strategy by pursuing pre-emptive damage-limiting 'counterforce' options as a prerequisite for credible extended deterrence, the result will probably be an intensified arms competition.[64] The US nuclear posture, which is geared to limiting damage in the event of war, must be perceived as threatening by China – irrespective of the defensive motives of the American side.

In Sino-American relations a security dilemma is also present in the Taiwan question. This unresolved conflict over the sovereignty of Taiwan carries the risk of war.[65] The Chinese leadership expressly reserves the right to use military force to prevent Taiwan's complete independence, as President Xi reiterated in January 2019.[66] Once it had normalised relations with the People's Republic of China in 1978, the United States ended official diplomatic ties with Taiwan and terminated the defence treaty between them. However, the Taiwan Relations Act of 1979 states that it is US policy to regard any attempt to decide Taiwan's future other than by peaceful means as a threat to peace and security in the Western Pacific. Consequently, the US policy is one of 'strategic ambiguity'; although Washington has promised to respond to any threat to Taiwan, it is not formally committed to doing so. For China, the goal of preventing Taiwan's lasting independence from mainland China is a defensive one. Beijing wants to militarily deter Taiwan from changing the status quo and declaring independence. However, Chinese military options might be perceived in an offensive sense, as enabling Beijing to compel reunification. The United States sees its security assurance to Taiwan, and the weapons systems it supplies to prevent an invasion by the People's Republic, as defensively motivated. Nevertheless, Washington's arming of Taiwan and maintaining of its own ability to intervene in a crisis might be perceived by Beijing as a protective umbrella enabling Taiwan to declare independence.[67]

The US policy is one of 'strategic ambiguity'

China sees the development of its own anti-access/area-denial capabilities in the South and East China seas as necessary to safeguard its core interests, which include preventing Taiwan from declaring independence. China may see this development as defensively motivated, but it is perceived in the United States as aimed at developing offensive capabilities which could make US power projection in the region more difficult and risky.[68]

Breaking out of a security dilemma is rarely easy. In order to assure an opponent of one's own defensive intentions, steps are needed that may be considered too risky – certainly if the opponent's present or future intentions are perceived as offensive.[69] Security dilemmas between states can be mitigated by mutual transparency, confidence-building measures and arms control.[70] However, in the case of Sino-American relations, each side continues to insist that its intentions are purely defensive. Officially, China sees itself as a power that is retaking its position as a respected nation after a century of humiliation. Chinese history is interpreted as demonstrating that the country is peacefully minded, non-aggressive and non-expansive, whose rise has been hindered by the United States.[71] The US sees itself as a liberal democracy that does not pose a threat to other states and whose superior military strength serves the interests of all well-meaning people by guaranteeing international stability.[72] The danger is that each side's tendency to see itself as defensive and peaceful while attributing offensive and aggressive intentions to the other side will trigger a conflict spiral.[73]

Dissecting the strategic rivalry

The US–Chinese relationship is perhaps best interpreted as a complex 'strategic rivalry'. Both countries are not only competitors for power and influence, but also potential military opponents.[74] Their intensifying strategic rivalry, rooted in incompatible goals and mutual threat perceptions, has a regional dimension, a global dimension and a technological dimension.

The regional dimension

China has been expanding its military options to counter US intervention capabilities on its periphery and to project its own military power into the East Asian region and beyond. In conjunction with increased economic influence, this might enable China to 'decouple' the United States from Asia and thereby to gain supremacy in the region.[75] The US–China conflict is especially pronounced in the Western Pacific.[76] In 'maritime Asia', the relationship is antagonistic, imbued with military threat perceptions.[77] In the United States, it is widely believed that China intends to establish an exclusive 'maritime sphere of influence' in the South China Sea.[78]

In Chinese discourse, the prevailing self-perception seems to be that China does not intend to exclude non-regional actors from the region as is often assumed in the United States. Chinese behaviour in the South China Sea, however, can be taken as an indication that China is moving towards a policy of exclusion. Beijing has resolutely asserted legally questionable territorial claims and established military outposts on artificial islands.[79] In the

South China Sea, China's claims to some islands, rocks, reefs and low-tide elevations clash with those of four other littoral states (Brunei, Malaysia, the Philippines and Vietnam). In addition, China's sovereignty claims within what it calls the 'nine-dash line' (an area encompassing most of the South China Sea) conflict with the exclusive economic zones of these states and Indonesia. Moreover, China's interpretation of the United Nations Convention on the Law of the Sea (an interpretation that is shared by some other governments) is that states have the right to regulate and prohibit the military activities of other states in their exclusive economic zones, which extend up to 200 nautical miles from the coast. The United States firmly rejects this interpretation.[80]

The South China Sea is where the two sides' incompatible interpretations of the law of the sea are most apparent.[81] The US claims to be upholding the freedom of the seas, while the Chinese have been asserting a claim to a sphere of influence. The conflict is heightened by the mutual perception that in a crisis the other side could block important maritime lines of communication. If China were to block them, the economic costs would probably be bearable if shipping traffic to Australia, Japan and South Korea could be diverted, for example via the Sunda or Lombok straits. However, a large proportion of the goods shipped across the South China Sea come from China or go there. It is therefore in China's interest to ensure maritime transport remains unhindered in the region. The Chinese fear that the US military could block the Strait of Malacca in the event of a crisis, thus severely affecting China's energy supply.[82]

The geopolitical conflict over the South China Sea also has a nuclear dimension.[83] China seems to be fortifying the South China Sea as a protected bastion for ballistic-missile submarines as part of a survivable second-strike capability. According to information from the United States, at least four ballistic-missile submarines are already in service, and construction of a follow-on class, with a more advanced design, is expected to begin in the early 2020s.[84] China still has no sea-based ballistic missiles in service that could reach the continental United States from the South China Sea. The new missile (JL-3) in development for the planned next generation of submarines will have a significantly greater range than the current design, but even this may not be enough.[85] Due to the limited range of the sea-based nuclear missiles currently in service, in the event of a serious international crisis, China may try to relocate ballistic-missile submarines to the deeper and thus safer waters of the Pacific, through the bottlenecks of the 'first island chain' (which extends from the Kuril Islands via the principal Japanese islands and Taiwan to Borneo). Securing the South China Sea against US anti-submarine forces is already an enormous challenge, a consideration that is relevant to China's expansion of its artificial islands.[86]

While the East–West conflict was stabilised to a significant degree by the establishment of clear spheres of influence in Europe, the geostrategic situation in East Asia is less stable. There is no clear demarcation between spheres of influence in Asia, and there are no acknowledged buffer zones. China's efforts to establish a kind of security zone within the first island chain are regarded as highly provocative in the United States as the region's leading sea power.[87]

A worsening crisis between the United States and China poses a considerable risk of military instability in Asia. US military planners assume that China will pursue offensive pre-emptive options in a crisis. Certainly, there are significant incentives for pre-emptive action against US armed forces in the region – for example, in the form of massive missile salvoes. Since the termination of the Intermediate-range Nuclear Forces Treaty, Washington has been free to deploy medium-range systems in Asia. These could be based on the island of Guam, or – should America's allies agree – in the north of Japan, the southern Philippines or the northern part of Australia. With conventionally equipped medium-range systems, the US military could destroy Chinese forces in the South and East China seas without sending naval units into these risk zones. This would also obviate the need to initially eliminate missile systems on the Chinese mainland that would endanger US surface ships. Such an attack could inadvertently neutralise Chinese nuclear forces or their command-and-control facilities since, according to available information, China's conventional and nuclear forces seem to be entangled. It cannot be ruled out that, in the event of a serious confrontation, China will be tempted to use nuclear weapons before they are put out of action.[88]

The global dimension

The Trump administration believed that any gains in influence by China would come at the expense of the United States. In particular, China's Belt and Road Initiative (BRI) was viewed with suspicion. The BRI and the Asian Infrastructure Investment Bank (AIIB) have allowed China to open new markets as outlets for its industrial overcapacities; to build road and rail networks to reduce its dependence on vulnerable sea lanes; and to widen its economic leverage and shore up its position in the global power competition.[89]

The Trump administration pushed the idea of a 'Free and Open Indo-Pacific' as a kind of counter-narrative to the BRI. The idea has been rightly characterised as a 'strategic narrative' that promotes American interests.[90] Like all narratives, it is intended to reduce complexity and mobilise domestic and international support. At the international level, the narrative contrasts a rules-based international order with an order shaped by China; at the national level, it signals the antithesis of democracy and autocracy; and at the thematic level, it highlights the difference between a defensive policy aimed at maintaining the status quo and an expansive, revisionist one.

The United States is trying to dissuade other countries from further developing economic ties with China. Washington has warned Israel against participating in infrastructure projects with China. Particularly worrisome is the prospect that the state-owned Shanghai International Port Group will operate the port of Haifa.[91] Similarly, during his visit to Panama in 2018, Pompeo warned the country's president against expanding economic relations with China. Washington is apparently concerned that Panama could become a 'bridgehead' for China's growing economic influence in the western hemisphere. China, whose ships are heavily reliant on the Panama Canal, is already involved in several infrastructure projects in Panama.[92]

Africa is regarded as the new front in the Sino-American struggle for influence. The Trump administration believed that Beijing was trying to make African countries submissive to Chinese interests through loans, bribery and dubious agreements. Introducing the United States' 'new Africa strategy' in December 2018, then-national security advisor John Bolton warned against China's 'predatory' practices in Africa.[93] Shortly before leaving office, UN ambassador Nikki Haley tried to prevent a Chinese diplomat from being appointed UN Special Ambassador for the Great Lakes region in Africa. There may have been some concern that a Chinese ambassador could use this role to expand China's influence in the region. There is also more general concern about China's growing clout within the UN; China has been seeking to place its own diplomats in UN leadership positions. In addition, Beijing has considerably expanded its participation in UN peace missions, both financially and in terms of personnel. These developments have prompted the United States to scrutinise Chinese influence in the UN and other international organisations.[94]

Washington also sees the Arctic as an arena for great-power rivalry. China has displayed a growing interest in the region, releasing its own Arctic policy in January 2018. Not only does the Northern Sea Route shorten the distance between China and Europe considerably, but China is also interested in exploiting Arctic energy resources.[95]

The United States views China's presence in the Arctic as a potential security threat. In its 2019 report on Chinese military power, the US Department of Defense warned against China's growing presence in the region, including the possibility that China could deploy submarines there.[96] The Pentagon's report on its Arctic strategy published in June 2019 describes the region as a 'potential vector for an attack on the U.S. homeland'.[97] The deployment of ballistic-missile submarines in the Arctic would have two advantages for China. Firstly, if Chinese strategic submarines were able to operate under the ice, this would probably reduce their vulnerability to American anti-submarine warfare. Secondly, the flight times to targets in the continental United States are considerably shorter from the Arctic than from the Western Pacific. However, these scenarios are not likely to occur in the short term, in part because Chinese submarines would likely require a developed infrastructure in Arctic Russia.[98] Nevertheless, US military planners appear to be incorporating Arctic scenarios into their worst-case assumptions. Although China's White Paper on Arctic policy does not explicitly mention military aspects, the strategic importance of the Arctic is an important topic in Chinese military discourse.[99]

The technological dimension

The Sino-American conflict has a pronounced technological dimension as each side struggles for technological supremacy in the digital age. America wants to maintain its technological superiority over China, which is favourably positioned to benefit from the 'fourth industrial revolution', in which artificial intelligence plays an important role.[100] Competition for technological leadership is so pronounced because the introduction of new technologies creates economic growth and secures competitive advantages with military implications.[101] Many Americans now view China as a serious threat to the industrial foundations of the United States, and therefore as a threat to national security.[102] For the Chinese leadership, which believes that the technological superiority of the West has secured its global dominance, catching up and even surpassing the West in the field of advanced technology is a key priority.[103] It aims to do so through industrial-policy initiatives within the Made in China 2025 framework, technology transfer and industrial espionage.

The technological component of the US–China rivalry differs considerably from the United States' arms race with the Soviet Union. During the Cold War, the United States faced a technologically backward opponent, and was therefore able to shift military competition to areas where the Soviet Union was weak. With China, the United States faces an opponent against whom this option does not exist, since China has caught up technologically and is even leading in some areas, such as quantum computing and robotics. Maintaining or restoring technological leadership is thus of eminent military importance for the United States.[104]

The Trump administration undertook several initiatives aimed at impeding China's technological progress and protecting the United States' technological base. The Committee on Foreign Investment in the United States began to examine Chinese investments in the United States more closely, and even to restrict them. The Foreign Investment Risk Review Modernization Act of 2018 extended the scope of the review to include 'critical technology'.[105] The Export Control Reform Act, which came into force in August 2018, authorises export restrictions on 'emerging and foundational' technologies that are considered essential for US national security but are not subject to existing controls. Among the technologies that the Bureau of Industry and Security within the US Department of Commerce (which is responsible for administering and enforcing the restrictions) has in mind are those that are central to Made in China 2025, including biotech, artificial intelligence and quantum computing.[106] There are also efforts under way to reduce the transfer of knowledge to China by Chinese students and scientists resident in the United States.

By decoupling the two economies as much as possible, the White House hoped to reduce US economic, technological and security vulnerabilities created by the countries' interdependence. (The pandemic appears only to have hastened these efforts.) Perhaps the most high-profile initiative was the Trump administration's campaign against Huawei, one of China's most important technology groups. For the 'China hawks' within the administration – particularly Peter Navarro, a presidential advisor on trade issues and director of the Office of Trade and Manufacturing Policy – the fight against Huawei was an important stage in the competition for future technological supremacy and control of information systems employing 5G networks.[107] Washington has especially sought to restrict Huawei's access to cutting-edge semiconductors, thereby focusing on an area where Chinese firms are heavily dependent on foreign suppliers.[108]

The campaign against Huawei reflects the abandonment of the positive-sum logic in economic relations. This logic, which was based on absolute gains, was linked to the expectation that economic interdependence would promote political cooperation. Now that China is seen as a global strategic rival, economic logic has given way to a security-policy logic, the dominant concern of which is the relative distribution of gains and the negative consequences of economic interdependence for preserving the technological basis of military superiority.[109]

The defensive and offensive measures adopted by the US will likely lead China to seek to reduce its own dependence on the United States and any other countries that might partner with the US in denying China access to advanced technology. As James Crabtree has written, Donald Trump's 'erratic and aggressive policies have succeeded in convincing Chinese elites that the U.S. is now irrevocably set on blocking China's technological rise'.[110]

Beijing's response, combined with US actions, could lead to the emergence of a new 'geoeconomic world order', in which the question of the relative distribution of gains, and concerns about the security consequences of economic interdependence, play a far more important role in determining government policy than in recent decades.[111] It is possible that as the economic interdependence between the United States and China dissolves, the world will experience de-globalisation and the emergence of economic blocs or closed economic spaces.[112]

The Sino-American world conflict could even trigger the emergence of two 'bounded orders', one led by the United States and the other by China.[113] This kind of bipolarisation would present dilemmas for American allies that favour a multipolar world order.[114]

*   *   *

Martin Wolf has suggested that the United States' strategic rivalry with China has the potential to develop into the 'organising principle of US economic, foreign and security policies'.[115] Certainly, there is ample reason to believe that Washington increasingly perceives all of its international relationships through a 'China prism', including its relationship with Europe.[116] The Biden administration can be expected to increase the pressure on US allies to take a stand in the intensifying Sino-American conflict and to join with the United States in balancing against China by restricting Chinese access to advanced technologies and screening Chinese foreign investments.[117]

From a European perspective, it is an open and vexing question whether Washington will rely on the power of persuasion or resort to economic pressure by means of its extraterritorial sanction levers to obtain European cooperation. US and European interests with regard to China are by no means identical, although European perceptions of China primarily as a source of economic opportunities have been giving way to a more nuanced view. A European Commission paper from March 2019 reflects this shift, referring to China as a 'cooperation partner', an 'economic competitor' and a 'systemic rival promoting alternative models of governance' depending on the policy field.[118] Even so, China's rise affects the United States and Europe to different degrees, so their threat perceptions will continue to diverge. There is neither a status conflict nor a global competition for influence between Europe and China. Moreover, no security dilemmas are shaping the relationship, meaning that security concerns do not overshadow all aspects of the relationship. The coronavirus pandemic has led to some discussion of how much dependence on China is tolerable, but only with respect to a diversification of supply chains and production sites, rather than in the sense of a broad decoupling.[119]

Given partly converging, partly diverging interests on each side of the Atlantic, as well as within the European Union, there is a widespread sense that transatlantic policy coordination on China will have to become an institutionalised feature in US–EU relations, whether in the guise of the US–European Dialogue on China initiated in 2020 by Josep Borrell, the EU high representative for foreign affairs and security policy, or in more functional formats occasionally suggested in the US debate and apparently taken up by the Biden administration in its evolving 'modular approach' to restricting Chinese access to advanced technology.[120] Certainly, European allies are faced with the question of how far and under which conditions they will support the United States in its strategic rivalry with China.

Acknowledgements

This article is adapted from a research paper published by Stiftung Wissenschaft und Politik (SWP), the German Institute for International and Security Affairs.

Notes

1   Xiangfeng Yang, 'The Great Chinese Surprise: The Rupture with the United States Is Real and Is Happening', *International Affairs*, vol. 96, no. 2, 2020, p. 420.

2   See remarks by Vice President Pence at the Frederic V. Malek Public Service Leadership Lecture, Washington DC, 24 October 2019, https://www.wilsoncenter.org/event/video-vice-president-pence-delivers-inaugural-frederic-v-malek-public-service-leadership; and White House, 'United States Strategic Approach to the People's Republic of China', 20 May 2020, p. 16, https://www.whitehouse.gov/wp-content/uploads/2020/05/U.S.-Strategic-Approach-to-The-Peoples-Republic-of-China-Report-5.20.20.pdf.

3   Quoted in Cassidy McDonald, 'Biden Says There Will Be "Extreme Competition" with China, but Won't Take Trump Approach', CNBC, 7 February 2021, https://www.cnbc.com/2021/02/07/biden-will-compete-with-china-but-wont-take-trump-approach.html.

4   US Department of State, 'Secretary Antony J. Blinken with Wolf Blitzer of CNN's The Situation Room', 8 February 2021, https://www.state.gov/secretary-antony-j-blinken-with-wolf-blitzer-of-cnns-the-situation-room/.

5   See Minghao Zhao, 'Is a New Cold War Inevitable? Chinese Perspectives on US–China Strategic Competition', *Chinese Journal of International Politics*, vol. 12, no. 3, 2019, pp. 371–94.

6   See Andrew J. Nathan and Andrew Scobell, 'How China Sees America: The Sum of Beijing's Fears', *Foreign Affairs*, vol. 91, no. 5, 2012, pp. 32–47; and Suisheng Zhao, 'A New Model of Big Power Relations? China–US Strategic Rivalry and Balance of Power in the Asia-Pacific', *Journal of Contemporary China*, vol. 24, no. 93, 2015, pp. 377–97.

7   See, for example, Richard Haass, 'The Pandemic Will Accelerate History Rather than Reshape It: Not Every Crisis Is a Turning Point', *Foreign Affairs*, 7 April 2020. On the more structural factors driving the competition, see Evan S. Medeiros, 'The Changing Fundamentals of US–China Relations', *Washington Quarterly*, vol. 42, no. 3, 2019, pp. 93–119.

8   On 'structural world conflicts', see Werner Link, *Der Ost-West-Konflikt. Die Organisation der internationalen Beziehungen im 20. Jahrhundert* (Stuttgart:
W. Kohlhammer, 1988), pp. 35–53.

9   See Kim Parker, Rich Morin and Juliana Menasce Horowitz, 'America in 2050', Pew Research Center, 21 March 2019.

10 See Michael Beckley, 'Stop Obsessing About China: Why Beijing Will Not Imperil U.S. Hegemony', *Foreign Affairs*, 21 September 2018; and Michael Beckley, *Unrivaled: Why America Will Remain the World's Sole Superpower* (Ithaca, NY: Cornell University Press, 2018).

11 See Stephen G. Brooks and William C. Wohlforth, 'The Rise and Fall of the Great Powers in the Twenty-first Century: China's Rise and the Fate of America's Global Position', *International Security*, vol. 40, no. 3, Winter 2015/16, pp. 7–53.

12 See, for example, Yuen Foong Khong, 'Primacy or World Order? The United States and China's Rise – A Review Essay', *International Security*, vol. 38, no. 3, Winter 2013/14, pp. 153–75; and John J. Mearsheimer, 'Can China Rise Peacefully?', *National Interest*, 25 October 2014.

13 See Randall L. Schweller, 'Managing the Rise of Great Powers: History and Theory', in Alastair Iain Johnston and Robert S. Ross (eds), *Engaging China: The Management of an Emerging Power* (London and New York: Routledge, 1999), pp. 1–31.

14 Political scientist Graham Allison has helped to popularise this term and the associated power-transition theories in a wealth of publications since 2012, such as Graham Allison, 'The Thucydides Trap: Are the U.S. and China Headed for War?', *Atlantic*, 24 September 2015.

15 See Rosemary Foot, 'Constraints on Conflict in the Asia-Pacific: Balancing "the War Ledger"', *Political Science*, vol. 66, no. 2, 2014, pp. 129–31.

16 See Jinghan Zeng, 'Constructing a "New Type of Great Power Relations": The State of Debate in China (1998–2014)', *British Journal of Politics and International Relations*, vol. 18, no. 2, 2016, pp. 422–42.

17 See Steve Chan, *The Power-transition Discourse and China's Rise* (Oxford: Oxford Research Encyclopedia of Politics, May 2017), p. 17; and Steve Chan, 'More than One Trap: Problematic Interpretations and Overlooked Lessons from Thucydides', *Journal of Chinese Political Science*, vol. 24, no. 1, 2019, pp. 1–24.

18 On the role of framing, see Robert M. Entman, *Projections of Power: Framing News, Public Opinion, and U.S. Foreign Policy* (Chicago, IL: University of Chicago Press, 2004), pp. 5–6.

19 For a critical view, see Richard Ned Lebow and Benjamin Valentino, 'Lost in Transition: A Critical Analysis of Power Transition Theory', *International Relations*, vol. 23, no. 3, 2009, pp. 389–410.

20 White House, 'National Security Strategy of the United States of America', December 2017, p. 25, https://trumpwhitehouse.archives.gov/wp-content/uploads/2017/12/NSS-Final-12-18-2017-0905.pdf.

21 *Ibid.*, p. 27.

22 US Department of Defense, 'Indo-Pacific Strategy Report: Preparedness, Partnerships, and Promoting a Networked Region', 1 June 2019, p. 8, https://media.defense.gov/2019/Jul/01/2002152311/-1/-1/1/ DEPARTMENT-OF-DEFENSE-INDO-PACIFIC-STRATEGY-REPORT-2019.PDF.

23 As quoted in Edward Wong and Catie Edmonson, 'Trump Administration Plans to Sell More than $2 Billion of Arms to Taiwan', *New York Times*, 6 June 2019.

24 On the scholarly debate as to whether states can safely assess the intentions of other powers, see Sebastian Rosato, 'The Inscrutable Intentions of Great Powers', *International Security*, vol. 39, no. 3, Winter 2014/15, pp. 48–88.

25 On the different logics, see Thomas J. Christensen, 'Fostering Stability or Creating a Monster? The Rise of China and U.S. Policy Toward Asia', *International Security*, vol. 31, no. 1, 2006, pp. 81–126.

26 For a general discussion on the role of narratives, see Ronald R. Krebs, *Narrative and the Making of US National Security* (Cambridge: Cambridge University Press, 2015), p. 3.

27 See Steve Chan, Weixing Hu and Kai He, 'Discerning States' Revisionist and Status-quo Orientations: Comparing China and the US', *European Journal of International Relations*, vol. 25, no. 2, 2019, pp. 613–40.

28 See Alastair Iain Johnston, 'China in a World of Orders: Rethinking Compliance and Challenges in Beijing's International Relations', *International Security*, vol. 44, no. 2, 2019, pp. 9–60.

29 See Suisheng Zhao, 'A Revisionist Stakeholder: China and the Post-World War II World Order', *Journal of Contemporary China*, vol. 27, no. 113, 2018, pp. 643–58.

30 See Michael D. Swaine, 'Chinese

Views on the U.S. National Security and National Defense Strategies', Carnegie Endowment for International Peace, China Leadership Monitor, 1 May 2018.

31 See, for example, Ministry of National Defense of the People's Republic of China, 'Speech at the 18th Shangri-La Dialogue by Gen. Wei Fenghe, State Councilor and Minister of National Defense, PRC', 2 June 2019, http://eng. mod.gov.cn/leadership/2019-06/02/ content_4842884.htm.

32 See Chu Shulong and Zhou Lanjun, 'The Growing U.S.–China Competition Under the Trump Administration', in National Committee on American Foreign Policy, U.S.–China Relations: Manageable Differences or Major Crisis? (New York: NCAFP, 2018), pp. 10–18.

33 See Elizabeth C. Economy, The Third Revolution: Xi Jinping and the New Chinese State (Oxford and New York: Oxford University Press, 2018), p. 190.

34 See, for example, Charles Edel and Hal Brands, 'The Real Origins of the U.S.–China Cold War', Foreign Policy, 2 June 2019; and David L. Roll, 'The Key to Avoiding a New Cold War with China', Washington Post, 10 July 2019.

35 For interpretations of the East–West conflict, see Ernst-Otto Czempiel, Weltpolitik im Umbruch. Das internationale System nach dem Ende des Ost-West-Konflikts (Munich: C.H. Beck, 1991), pp. 20–6.

36 See Øystein Tunsjø, The Return of Bipolarity in World Politics: China, the United States, and Geostructural Realism (New York: Columbia University Press, 2018); and Richard Maher, 'Bipolarity and the Future of U.S.–China Relations', Political Science Quarterly, vol. 133, no. 3, 2018, pp. 497–525.

37 See 'Policy Roundtable: Are the United States and China in a New Cold War?', Texas National Security Review, 15 May 2018.

38 See Andres B. Schwarzenberg, U.S.–China Trade and Economic Relations: Overview (Washington DC: Congressional Research Service, 7 August 2019).

39 See Barry C. Lynn, 'War, Trade and Utopia', National Interest, no. 82, Winter 2005/06, pp. 31–8.

40 See Andres B. Schwarzenberg, U.S.–China Investment Ties: Overview and Issues for Congress (Washington DC: Congressional Research Service, 28 August 2019).

41 See William C. Wohlforth, 'Unipolarity, Status Competition, and Great Power War', World Politics, vol. 61, no. 1, 2009, pp. 28–57; Tudor A. Onea, 'Between Dominance and Decline: Status Anxiety and Great Power Rivalry', Review of International Studies, vol. 40, no. 1, 2014, pp. 125–52; Timothy R. Heath, 'The Competition for Status Could Increase the Risk of a Military Clash in Asia', RAND Blog, 2 February 2018, https://www.rand. org/blog/2018/02/the-competition-for-status-could-increase-the-risk.html; Michael Mastanduno, 'System Maker and Privilege Taker: U.S. Power and the International Political Economy', World Politics, vol. 61, no. 1, 2009, pp. 121–54; Daniel W. Drezner, 'Military Primacy Doesn't Pay (Nearly as Much as You Think)', International Security, vol. 38, no. 1, 2013, pp. 52–79; and Doug Stokes and Kit Waterman, 'Security Leverage, Structural Power

and US Strategy in East Asia', *International Affairs*, vol. 93, no. 5, 2017, pp. 1,039–60.

42 See Ely Ratner, 'There Is No Grand Bargain with China', *Foreign Affairs*, 27 November 2018.

43 See Ashley J. Tellis, *Balancing Without Containment: An American Strategy for Managing China* (Washington DC: Carnegie Endowment for International Peace, 2014), pp. 14, 18–19.

44 See Odd Arne Westad, 'The Sources of Chinese Conduct: Are Washington and Beijing Fighting a New Cold War?', *Foreign Affairs*, 12 August 2019.

45 See Elsa Kania, 'The "Regime Security Dilemma" in US–China Relations', *Strategist*, 21 March 2019.

46 For this view, see Tarun Chhabra, 'The China Challenge, Democracy, and U.S. Grand Strategy', Brookings Institution, Policy Brief, 15 February 2019.

47 See David Brooks, 'How China Brings Us Together: An Existential Threat for the 21st Century', *New York Times*, 14 February 2019.

48 Kiron Skinner, during her tenure as the director of policy planning at the US State Department, said that the US is engaged in a 'fight with a really different civilization and a different ideology, and the United States hasn't had that before … It's the first time that we'll have a great power competitor that is not Caucasian.' Quoted in Abraham M. Denmark, 'Problematic Thinking on China from the State Department's Head of Policy Planning', *War on the Rocks*, 7 May 2019.

49 Christopher A. Ford, Assistant Secretary of State for International Security and Nonproliferation, 'Technology and Power in China's Geopolitical Ambitions', testimony before the U.S.–China Economic and Security Review Commission, Washington DC, 20 June 2019, https://www.state.gov/technology-and-power-in-chinas-geopolitical-ambitions/; and Policy Planning Staff, Office of the Secretary of State, 'The Elements of the China Challenge', November 2020, p. 45.

50 Jessica Chen Weiss, 'No, China and the U.S. Aren't Locked in an Ideological Battle. Not Even Close', *Washington Post*, 4 May 2019.

51 See Kevin Rudd, 'How to Avoid an Avoidable War: Ten Questions About the New U.S. China Strategy', *Foreign Affairs*, 22 October 2018.

52 See Andreas Møller Mulvad, 'Xiism as a Hegemonic Project in the Making: Sino-Communist Ideology and the Political Economy of China's Rise', *Review of International Studies*, vol. 45, no. 3, 2019, pp. 449–70; and Economy, *The Third Revolution*, p. 221.

53 See Jessica Chen Weiss, 'A World Safe for Autocracy? China's Rise and the Future of Global Politics', *Foreign Affairs*, vol. 98, no. 4, 2019, pp. 92–102; and Emily S. Chen, *Is China Challenging the Global State of Democracy?* (Honolulu, HI: Pacific Forum, June 2019).

54 See Nicholas Wright, 'How Artificial Intelligence Will Reshape the Global Order: The Coming Competition Between Digital Authoritarianism and Liberal Democracy', *Foreign Affairs*, 10 July 2018. On the ideological dimension of great-power conflicts, see Hal Brands, 'Democracy vs Authoritarianism: How Ideology

Shapes Great-power Conflict', *Survival*, vol. 60, no. 5, October–November 2018, pp. 61–114. For a view critical of accentuating the ideological dimension, see Elbridge Colby and Robert D. Kaplan, 'The Ideology Delusion: America's Competition with China Is Not About Doctrine', *Foreign Affairs*, 4 September 2020.

55   On the general role of 'ideological difference' in threat perceptions, see Mark L. Haas, *The Ideological Origins of Great Power Politics, 1789–1989* (Ithaca, NY: Cornell University Press, 2005).

56   See John H. Herz, 'Idealist Internationalism and the Security Dilemma', *World Politics*, vol. 2, no. 2, 1950, pp. 157–80; and Robert Jervis, 'Cooperation Under the Security Dilemma', *World Politics*, vol. 30, no. 2, 1978, pp. 67–214. For a further elaborated view, see Ken Booth and Nicholas J. Wheeler, *The Security Dilemma: Fear, Cooperation and Trust in World Politics* (Basingstoke: Palgrave Macmillan, 2008), pp. 4–7.

57   See Adam Mount, *The Case Against New Nuclear Weapons* (Washington DC: Center for American Progress, May 2017), p. 41.

58   See Brad Roberts, *The Case for U.S. Nuclear Weapons in the 21st Century* (Stanford, CA: Stanford University Press, 2016), p. 173.

59   See Susan Turner Haynes, 'China's Nuclear Threat Perceptions', *Strategic Studies Quarterly*, vol. 10, no. 2, 2016, pp. 25–62.

60   For more detail, see Eric Heginbotham et al., *China's Evolving Nuclear Deterrent: Major Drivers and Issues for the United States* (Santa Monica, CA: RAND Corporation, 2017); David C.

Logan, 'Hard Constraints on a Chinese Nuclear Breakout', *Nonproliferation Review*, vol. 24, nos 1–2, 2017, pp. 13–30; and M. Taylor Fravel, *Active Defense: China's Military Strategy Since 1949* (Princeton, NJ: Princeton University Press, 2019), pp. 236–69.

61   See Hans M. Kristensen and Matt Korda, 'Chinese Nuclear Forces, 2019', *Bulletin of the Atomic Scientists*, vol. 5, no. 4, 2019, pp. 171–8.

62   See Peter Rudolf, *US Nuclear Deterrence Policy and Its Problems* (Berlin: Stiftung Wissenschaft und Politik, November 2018), p. 14.

63   See Bryan R. Early and Victor Asal, 'Nuclear Weapons, Existential Threats, and the Stability–Instability Paradox', *Nonproliferation Review*, vol. 25, no. 3, 2018, pp. 223–47.

64   See Austin Long, 'U.S. Strategic Nuclear Targeting Policy: Necessity and Damage Limitation', in International Security Studies Forum, 'Policy Roundtable 1–4 on U.S. Nuclear Policy', 22 December 2016, https://networks.h-net.org/node/28443/discussions/157862/issf-policy-roundtable-9-4-us-nuclear-policy#_Toc470037165; Charles L. Glaser and Steve Fetter, 'Should the United States Reject MAD? Damage Limitation and U.S. Nuclear Strategy Toward China', *International Security*, vol. 41, no. 1, 2016, pp. 49–98; and Fiona S. Cunningham and M. Taylor Fravel, 'Assuring Assured Retaliation: China's Nuclear Posture and U.S.–China Strategic Stability', *International Security*, vol. 40, no. 2, 2015, pp. 7–50.

65   See Scott L. Kastner, 'Is the Taiwan Strait Still a Flash Point? Rethinking the Prospects for Armed Conflict

Between China and Taiwan', *International Security*, vol. 40, no. 3, Winter 2015/16, pp. 54–92.

66 See Chris Buckley and Chris Horton, 'Xi Jinping Warns Taiwan that Unification Is the Goal and Force Is an Option', *New York Times*, 1 January 2019.

67 See Thomas J. Christensen, 'The Contemporary Security Dilemma: Deterring a Taiwan Conflict', *Washington Quarterly*, vol. 25, no. 4, 2002, pp. 5–21.

68 See James Johnson, *The US–China Military and Defense Relationship During the Obama Presidency* (Basingstoke: Palgrave Macmillan, 2018), pp. 97–8. As Sulmaan Wasif Khan writes in his book *Haunted by Chaos*, even a 'defensive policy can look suspiciously aggressive' in an apparently threatening environment. Sulmaan Wasif Khan, *Haunted by Chaos: China's Grand Strategy from Mao Zedong to Xi Jinping* (Cambridge, MA: Harvard University Press, 2018), p. 218.

69 On this problem, see Evan Braden Montgomery, 'Breaking Out of the Security Dilemma: Realism, Reassurance, and the Problem of Uncertainty', *International Security*, vol. 31, no. 2, 2006, pp. 151–85.

70 See Adam P. Liff and G. John Ikenberry, 'Racing Toward Tragedy? China's Rise, Military Competition in the Asia Pacific, and the Security Dilemma', *International Security*, vol. 39, no. 2, 2014, pp. 88–90.

71 See Merriden Varrall, *Chinese Worldviews and China's Foreign Policy* (Sydney: Lowy Institute, November 2015); and Andrew Scobell, 'Learning to Rise Peacefully? China and the Security Dilemma', *Journal of Contemporary China*, vol. 21, no. 76, 2012, pp. 713–21.

72 See Christopher J. Fettweis, 'Unipolarity, Hegemony, and the New Peace', *Security Studies*, vol. 26, no. 3, 2017, pp. 443–5.

73 See Nicholas J. Wheeler, *Trusting Enemies: Interpersonal Relationships in International Conflict* (Oxford: Oxford University Press, 2018), pp. 92f., 273f. On the 'spiral model', see Robert Jervis, *Perception and Misperception in International Politics* (Princeton, NJ: Princeton University Press, 1976), pp. 62–7.

74 See Manjeet S. Pardesi, *Image Theory and the Initiation of Strategic Rivalries* (Oxford: Oxford Research Encyclopedia of Politics, March 2017). On the many aspects of rivalry, see Barbara Lippert and Volker Perthes (eds), *Strategic Rivalry Between the United States and China: Causes, Trajectories, and Implications for Europe* (Berlin: Stiftung Wissenschaft und Politik, April 2020).

75 See Ashley J. Tellis, 'Protecting American Primacy in the Indo-Pacific', testimony before the Senate Armed Services Committee, Washington DC, 25 April 2017, https://www.armed-services.senate.gov/imo/media/doc/Tellis_04-25-17.pdf.

76 For a more detailed discussion, see Michael Paul, *Kriegsgefahr im Pazifik? Die maritime Bedeutung der sino-amerikanischen Rivalität* (Baden-Baden: Nomos, 2017).

77 See Joel Wuthnow, 'Asian Security Without the United States? Examining China's Security Strategy in Maritime and Continental Asia', *Asian Security*, vol. 14, no. 3, 2018, pp. 230–45.

[78] Kurt M. Campbell and Ely Ratner, 'The China Reckoning: How Beijing Defied American Expectations', *Foreign Affairs*, 13 February 2018.

[79] See Steven F. Jackson, *China's Regional Relations in Comparative Perspective: From Harmonious Neighbors to Strategic Partners* (London: Routledge, 2018), pp. 146–52; and Denny Roy, 'Assertive China: Irredentism or Expansionism?', *Survival*, vol. 61, no. 1, 2019, pp. 51–74.

[80] See Michael McDevitt, 'Whither Sino-U.S. Relations: Maritime Disputes in the East and South China Seas?', in National Committee on American Foreign Policy, *U.S.–China Relations*, pp. 41–52; and Ronald O'Rourke, *U.S.–China Strategic Competition in South and East China Seas: Background and Issues for Congress* (Washington DC: Congressional Research Service, 23 August 2019).

[81] See Huiyun Feng and Kai He, 'The Bargaining Dilemma Between the United States and China in the South China Sea', in Huiyun Feng and Kai He (eds), *US–China Competition and the South China Sea Disputes* (London: Routledge, 2018), pp. 14–28.

[82] See James Laurenceson, 'Economics and Freedom of Navigation in East Asia', *Australian Journal of International Affairs*, vol. 71, no. 5, 2017, pp. 461–73; Bobby Andersen and Charles M. Perry, *Weighing the Consequences of China's Control over the South China Sea* (Cambridge, MA: Institute for Foreign Policy Analysis, November 2017), pp. 12–13; and Marc Lanteigne, 'China's Maritime Security and the "Malacca Dilemma"', *Asian Security*, vol. 4, no. 2, 2008, pp. 143–61. For further detail on the option of a naval blockade, see

Fiona S. Cunningham, 'The Maritime Rung of the Escalation Ladder: Naval Blockades in a US–China Conflict', *Security Studies*, vol. 29, no. 4, 2020, pp. 730–68.

[83] See Andrew Scobell, 'The South China Sea and U.S.-China Rivalry', *Political Science Quarterly*, vol. 133, no. 2, 2018, pp. 199–224.

[84] See US Department of Defense, 'Military and Security Developments Involving the People's Republic of China 2020: Annual Report to Congress', p. 45, https://media. defense.gov/2020/Sep/01/2002488689/-1/-1/1/2020-DOD-CHINA-MILITARY-POWER-REPORT-FINAL.PDF; Michael Paul, *Chinas nukleare Abschreckung. Ursachen, Mittel und Folgen der Stationierung chinesischer Nuklearwaffen auf Unterseebooten*, SWP-Studie 17/2018 (Berlin: Stiftung Wissenschaft und Politik, September 2018); and Tong Zhao, *Tides of Change: China's Nuclear Ballistic Missile Submarines and Strategic Stability* (Washington DC: Carnegie Endowment for International Peace, 2018).

[85] Recent estimates for the maximum range of the JL-3 missile vary between 9,000 and 10,000 km. See Kristensen and Korda, 'Chinese Nuclear Forces, 2019', pp. 175–6; and National Air and Space Intelligence Center, Defense Intelligence Ballistic Missile Analysis Committee, '2020 Ballistic and Cruise Missile Threat', p. 33, https://media.defense.gov/2021/Jan/11/2002563190/-1/-1/1/2020%20BALLISTIC%20AND%20CRUISE%20MISSILE%20THREAT_FINAL_2OCT_REDUCEDFILE.PDF.

86 See Tong Zhao, *The Impact of Chinese Supporting Capabilities* (Beijing: Carnegie–Tsinghua Center for Global Policy, 24 October 2018).

87 See Tunsjø, *The Return of Bipolarity in World Politics*, pp. 133–8.

88 See Nathan Levine, 'Why America Leaving the INF Treaty Is China's New Nightmare', *National Interest*, 22 October 2018; and Eric Sayers, 'The Intermediate-range Nuclear Forces Treaty and the Future of the Indo-Pacific Military Balance', *War on the Rocks*, 13 February 2018. On the risks of escalation, see James M. Acton, 'Escalation Through Entanglement: How the Vulnerability of Command-and-control Systems Raises the Risks of an Inadvertent Nuclear War', *International Security*, vol. 43, no. 1, 2018, pp. 56–99; and Caitlin Talmadge, 'Would China Go Nuclear? Assessing the Risk of Chinese Nuclear Escalation in a Conventional War with the United States', *International Security*, vol. 41, no. 4, 2017, pp. 50–92.

89 See Kevin G. Cai, 'The One Belt One Road and the Asian Infrastructure Investment Bank: Beijing's New Strategy of Geoeconomics and Geopolitics', *Journal of Contemporary China*, vol. 27, no. 114, 2018, pp. 831–47.

90 See Giulio Pugliese, 'The "Free and Open Indo-Pacific" as a Strategic Narrative', *China–US Focus*, 18 February 2019, https://www.chinausfocus.com/foreign-policy/the-free-and-open-indo-pacific-as-a-strategic-narrative; and Bruce Vaughn et al., *The Trump Administration's 'Free and Open Indo-Pacific': Issues for Congress* (Washington DC:

Congressional Research Service, 3 October 2018).

91 See William A. Galston, 'What's Beijing Doing in Haifa?', *Wall Street Journal*, 29 May 2019; and Amos Harel, 'With Its National Security at Stake, Israel Takes Sides in U.S.–China Trade War', *Haaretz*, 26 May 2019.

92 See Edward Wong, 'Mike Pompeo Warns Panama Against Doing Business with China', *New York Times*, 19 October 2018. For more detail on Chinese activities in Latin America, see Katherine Koleski and Alec Blivas, *China's Engagement with Latin America and the Caribbean* (Washington DC: U.S.–China Economic and Security Review Commission, 17 October 2018).

93 'Remarks by National Security Advisor Ambassador John R. Bolton on the Trump Administration's New Africa Strategy', Washington DC, 13 December 2018, https://www.whitehouse.gov/briefings-statements/remarks-national-security-advisor-ambassador-john-r-bolton-trump-administrations-new-africa-strategy/.

94 See Robbie Gramer and Colum Lynch, 'Haley Tried to Block Appointment of Chinese Diplomat to Key U.N. Post. He Got the Job Anyway', *Foreign Policy*, 14 February 2019.

95 See Steven Lee Myers and Somini Sengupta, 'Latest Arena for China's Growing Global Ambitions: The Arctic', *New York Times*, 27 May 2019.

96 US Department of Defense, 'Annual Report to Congress: Military and Security Developments Involving the People's Republic of China 2019', May 2019, p. 114, https://media.defense.gov/2019/May/02/2002127082/-

1/-1/1/2019_CHINA_MILITARY_ POWER_REPORT.pdf. See also US Department of the Navy, 'A Blue Arctic: A Strategic Blueprint for the Arctic', January 2021, https://media. defense.gov/2021/Jan/05/2002560338/- 1/-1/0/ARCTIC%20BLUEPRINT%20 2021%20FINAL.PDF/ARCTIC%20 BLUEPRINT%202021%20FINAL.PDF.

97 US Department of Defense, 'Report to Congress: Department of Defense Arctic Strategy', June 2019, p. 6, https://media.defense.gov/2019/ Jun/06/2002141657/-1/-1/1/2019-DOD- ARCTIC-STRATEGY.PDF.

98 See Lyle J. Goldstein, 'Chinese Nuclear Armed Submarines in Russian Arctic Ports? It Could Happen', *National Interest*, 6 June 2019.

99 See State Council of the People's Republic of China, 'Full Text: China's Arctic Policy', January 2018, http://english.www.gov.cn/ archive/white_paper/2018/01/26/ content_281476026660336.htm; and David Curtis Wright, *The Dragon and Great Power Rivalry at the Top of the World: China's Hawkish, Revisionist Voices with Mainstream Discourse on Arctic Affairs* (Calgary: Canadian Global Affairs Institute, September 2018).

100 See James A. Lewis, *Technological Competition and China* (Washington DC: Center for Strategic and International Studies, November 2018).

101 See Timothy R. Heath and William R. Thompson, 'Avoiding U.S.–China Competition Is Futile: Why the Best Option Is to Manage Strategic Rivalry', *Asia Policy*, vol. 13, no. 2, 2018, pp. 105–7.

102 See, for example, Peter Navarro, 'Our Economic Security at Risk', *New York Times*, 5 October 2018.

103 See Julian Baird Gewirtz, 'China's Long March to Technological Supremacy: The Roots of Xi Jinping's Ambition to "Catch up and Surpass"', *Foreign Affairs*, 27 August 2019.

104 See Robert O. Work and Greg Grant, *Beating the Americans at Their Own Game: An Offset Strategy with Chinese Characteristics* (Washington DC: Center for a New American Security, 2019), p. 16.

105 See James K. Jackson, *The Committee on Foreign Investment in the United States (CFIUS)* (Washington DC: Congressional Research Service, 6 August 2019), pp. 24–5.

106 For a more detailed discussion, see Peter Lichtenbaum, Victor Ban and Lisa Ann Johnson, 'Defining "Emerging Technologies": Industry Weighs in on Potential New Export Controls', *China Business Review*, 17 April 2019; and Kevin Wolf, 'Confronting Threats from China: Assessing Controls on Technology and Investment', testimony before the US Senate Committee on Banking, Housing, and Urban Affairs, 4 June 2019, https://www.banking. senate.gov/imo/media/doc/Wolf%20 Testimony%206-4-19.pdf.

107 See Richard Waters, Kathrin Hille and Louise Lucas, 'Trump Risks a Tech Cold War', *Financial Times*, 25 May 2019.

108 See Eurasia Group, 'The Geopolitics of Semiconductors', September 2020.

109 See Anthea Roberts, Henrique Choer Moraes and Victor Ferguson, 'Toward a Geoeconomic Order in International Trade and Investment', *Journal of International Economic Law*, vol. 22, no. 4, 2019, pp. 655–76.

110 James Crabtree, 'China's Radical New Vision of Globalization', *Noema*, 10 December 2020, https://www.noemamag.com/chinas-radical-new-vision-of-globalization/.

111 See Anthea Roberts, Henrique Choer Moraes and Victor Ferguson, 'The Geoeconomic World Order', Lawfare, 19 November 2018, https://www.lawfareblog.com/geoeconomic-world-order.

112 See David A. Lake, 'Economic Openness and Great Power Competition: Lessons for China and the United States', *Chinese Journal of International Politics*, vol. 11, no. 3, pp. 237–70.

113 See John J. Mearsheimer, 'Bound to Fail: The Rise and Fall of the Liberal International Order', *International Security*, vol. 43, no. 4, 2019, pp. 49–50.

114 For a Chinese perspective, see Yan Xuetong, 'The Age of Uneasy Peace: Chinese Power in a Divided World', *Foreign Affairs*, 11 December 2018; and Ngaire Woods, 'Can Multilateralism Survive the Sino-American Rivalry?', *Strategist*, 10 July 2019.

115 Martin Wolf, 'The Looming 100-year US–China Conflict', *Financial Times*, 4 June 2019.

116 See Noah Barkin, 'The U.S. Is Losing Europe in Its Battle with China', *Atlantic*, 4 June 2019.

117 On how leading actors in the Biden administration viewed relations with China before they entered the White House, see Kurt M. Campbell and Jake Sullivan, 'Competition Without Catastrophe: How America Can Both Challenge and Coexist with China', *Foreign Affairs*, September/October 2019; and Kurt M. Campbell and Rushi Doshi, 'How America Can Shore Up Asian Order: A Strategy for Restoring Balance and Legitimacy', *Foreign Affairs*, 12 January 2021.

118 European Commission, 'EU–China: A Strategic Outlook', 12 March 2019, p. 1, https://ec.europa.eu/info/sites/info/files/communication-eu-china-a-strategic-outlook.pdf.

119 See Andrew Small, 'The Meanings of Systemic Rivalry: Europe and China Beyond the Pandemic', European Council on Foreign Relations, Policy Brief, May 2020.

120 See Bob Davis, 'U.S. Eyes Tech Alliance Against China', *Wall Street Journal*, 1 March 2021.

Why Global Order Needs Disorder

Dominic Tierney

In 1991, US president George H.W. Bush said that the end of the Cold War would herald a 'new world order' based on international law and institutions. A generation later, in 2017, when Donald Trump's national-security team gave him a primer on the global liberal order, the president was reportedly so bored that the secretary of state called him a 'moron'.[1] Trump's lack of interest in the architecture of the international system symbolises the broader erosion of liberal order, marked by Brexit, Russian aggression in Ukraine and the emergence of populist regimes around the world. Why, after the Cold War ended, did the United States evolve from sentinel to subverter of the system?

The answer is something of a paradox: the global liberal order requires disorder. A grave menace like the Soviet Union is a clear and present danger to the liberal system, but it also prompts the United States to buttress the order by strengthening alliances and constructing institutions. By contrast, when there is no major peril, as there was not after the Cold War ended, the system may seem to be in optimal health and yet decay from within as Americans lose interest in global order and turn their attention to domestic issues. Therefore, the liberal order rests on an uneasy balance. Too much disorder and the system will weaken. Too much order and the system may also start to weaken. As a result, the liberal order is never as

Dominic Tierney is a professor of political science at Swarthmore College and a senior fellow at the Foreign Policy Research Institute. His most recent book is *The Right Way to Lose a War: America in an Age of Unwinnable Conflicts* (Little, Brown, 2015).

Survival | vol. 63 no. 2 | April–May 2021 | pp. 115–138   https://doi.org/10.1080/00396338.2021.1905981

weak or as strong as it looks. At the time of greatest peril, the order may be primed for renewal. At the apex of its triumph, the order can become a victim of its own success.

Understanding these vexing dynamics is vital because the liberal order is an engine of peace and prosperity. After the Second World War, there were no big global financial crises until the 1970s; major wars between countries largely disappeared (although civil wars remained prevalent); and the United States and its allies ultimately won the Cold War. By contrast, eras of US retreat from liberal order, such as the 1920s, encouraged beggar-thy-neighbour economics and the rise of hyper-nationalist states like Germany, Italy and Japan.

Today, Chinese economic growth is often viewed as a significant – and perhaps existential – challenge to the liberal model of global governance.[2] But the rise of Beijing may spur revitalisation. Order requires disorder, and the Chinese threat could inspire Americans to re-engage with alliances and global institutions.

Law and order

Global order refers to an international arrangement of norms, laws and institutions, or as Hedley Bull put it, 'a pattern of activity that sustains the elementary or primary goals of the society of states, or international society'.[3] The variety of possible global orders is almost limitless. They can be globally integrated or regionally varied, based on state sovereignty or a suzerainty model, more or less coercive, and driven by communist, fascist, monarchical or theocratic ideologies.[4] More specifically, a global liberal order is a set of rules and structures designed to promote democracy and human rights, encourage free trade and diminish war by fostering the pursuit of mutual gain and giving weaker countries a voice.[5]

The debate about whether the system the US has led since 1945 approximates a liberal order hinges on the metric employed. Compared to a pure model of liberal order, the US-led system comes up short. Washington has repeatedly engaged in illiberal behaviour, including covert and overt regime change, electoral meddling, partnerships with unsavoury dictatorships, and unilateral wars in Vietnam and Iraq.[6] Furthermore, for much of the post-war era, the US-led system was mainly a North Atlantic security community rather than a truly global structure.[7] However, compared to the systems that prevailed in previous eras of international relations, the US-led system can be meaningfully described as 'liberal' because of its distinctive architecture, including institution-building, democracy promotion and a reduction in barriers to trade.

According to liberal scholars, the order exists because it works. 'Above all, the case for optimism about liberalism rests on a simple truth', write G. John Ikenberry and Daniel Deudney. 'The solutions to today's problems are more liberal democracy and more liberal order.'[8] A rules-based system can best handle the challenges of modernity – from globalisation to public health – by facilitating international cooperation and the provision of public goods. From the liberal perspective, the spread of democracy, the construction of international institutions and the increase of trade are all mutually reinforcing in a virtuous cycle. Democracies trade more with one another, rarely fight among themselves and are more active in institutions; in turn, economic exchange and institutions promote the spread of representative government.[9] But the flip side is also true: if illiberal actors emerge, the order may become increasingly fragile in a vicious cycle.

Liberals are right that the liberal order works for most countries most of the time. The question is whether this is a sufficient motive for powerful actors to make costly sacrifices to protect the system. Why would strong countries tolerate weak countries making relative gains or faring better than the leviathan state, or accept free-riding by an ally who receives the benefits of a public good without helping to defray the costs?[10] In recent decades, the benefits of a liberal order have been consistently evident, but the United States' willingness to build the order has varied dramatically. The liberal order worked in 1918 when Woodrow Wilson outlined the Fourteen Points, as well as in 1945 when the United States helped found the United Nations, but it also worked in 1919 when the US Senate rejected membership of the League of Nations, in 1935 when the United States passed neutrality legislation to ensure its isolation from foreign wars, in 2003 when George W. Bush invaded Iraq, and in 2016 when Americans elected an avowed opponent of liberal order as president.

A second prominent explanation for liberal order is the need for a benevolent hegemon. Charles Kindleberger wrote in his book *The World in Depression, 1929–1939* that a single stabiliser was required to maintain open markets, offer counter-cyclical financing and be the lender of last resort.[11] A liberal economic system is much more likely when one state has a preponderance of power, as the United Kingdom did in the nineteenth century or the United States did after 1945.[12] In this view, the strength of the order is tied to the health of the hegemon: as it grows more powerful, so the order is reinforced; as the hegemon weakens, the order begins to crumble.[13] Anne-Marie Slaughter notes that 'the post-1945 world order that is now coming to an end required a hegemon, a nation among nations that was willing to absorb the costs of making the global machinery work, insisting that other nations meet the commitments they had agreed to'.[14]

Hegemonic-stability theorists are right to highlight the importance of US leadership for the health of the liberal order. Historically, the United States has been essential in creating institutions, anchoring alliances and providing public goods.[15] 'We are the giant of the economic world', said Harry Truman in 1947. 'The future pattern of economic relations depends upon us.'[16] Four decades later, Madeleine Albright as secretary of state described America as the 'indispensable nation'.[17]

But hegemonic-stability theory is less convincing in arguing that an uncontested hegemon is the key to liberal order. Why would an unrivalled great power sacrifice to provide public goods, willingly hand power over to weaker actors or otherwise do the hard yards of order-building? What would deter a colossus from unilaterally pursuing its interests, jealously guarding its sovereignty or coercing other actors by weaponising interdependence and taking advantage of its control of key nodes in the global supply chain?[18] Without any rival, why would the hegemon not simply become insular and focus on internal issues? At the domestic level, democracies create checks and balances precisely because unbridled power is prone to abuse. Similarly, at the international level, no hegemon in history has, at the zenith of its power, and without any competitor, acted with sustained restraint and benevolence.[19]

The liberal and hegemonic-stability explanations offer distinctive logics, but they both predicted that the end of the Cold War would encourage a renewed liberal order. Following the collapse of communism, the democratic community expanded at a rapid clip and faced few viable challengers. Meanwhile, the United States achieved almost unparalleled primacy. Contrary to expectations, however, the liberal order has confronted gathering crises, first gradually and then suddenly.

Threat matrix

The vital motor behind the liberal order is threat, or the existence of a peer competitor with the capability and desire to harm the US homeland. The nemesis can either be fighting America already (a hot war) or be engaged in sustained competition with a significant risk of conflict (a cold war). It is easy to miss the role of threat in bolstering the liberal order. One does not usually see a knife pointed at the heart as a source of wellness. In a similar vein, an existential peril is an obvious hazard to rules-based governance. The enemy may try to demolish the entire global structure, and the fierce contest could spur Washington to embrace illiberal or even barbarous measures, from assassination attempts to the carpet-bombing of enemy cities. Nevertheless, threat is a critical force behind liberal order-building. Constructing an edifice of alliances and institutions is a monumental task that requires a liberal state with the requisite power and motivation. In the modern era, only the United States has had the capacity to erect such an ambitious structure, and only threat provides America with sufficient incentive to act.[20]

At a basic level, sensitivity to threat is a core element of human psychology. All mammals have evolved sophisticated vigilance systems to detect danger, often subconsciously. People tend to be more responsive to human and purposeful threats than to environmental dangers (like climate change).[21] The gravest possible human threat is a hostile great power.

For the United States, the emergence of an aggressive peer competitor transforms how Americans think about liberal order in five ways. Firstly, the grand contest provides a powerful strategic rationale for order-building. In his book *Orders of Exclusion*, Kyle Lascurettes shows that, over the centuries, international orders were usually designed to block a dangerous rival.[22] In times of peril, the United States has sought to overcome challengers by constructing a liberal order of alliances and institutions. Shared danger is the most powerful glue for international alliances because the menace lessens concerns about free-riding and relative gains. Everyone is fighting for the same team and Washington will underwrite the security of weak states seen as vital for US interests.[23]

Secondly, an existential threat unleashes an idealistic streak in American foreign policy. The United States tends to cast major campaigns as righteous struggles between good and evil. The existence of a non-democratic 'other' means that Americans see fellow democracies as brothers-in-arms engaged in a common struggle, which suppresses concerns about free-riding. Furthermore, as the expenditure of American blood and treasure rises, the moral pay-off must also increase to justify the sacrifice. A return to the status quo ante is unacceptable, and America must craft a new world order.

External peril increases national unity

Thirdly, threat encourages order-building by shaping US domestic politics. External peril increases national unity and bipartisanship as the public 'rallies around the flag' and becomes more trusting of elites and the 'establishment', which provides the president with a wellspring of domestic support for ambitious international projects.

Fourthly, threat boosts the prestige and power of the federal government. Fareed Zakaria has argued that the key driver of an expansive foreign policy is not national power or overall resources, but state power, or the government's access to those resources.[24] In wartime, the US federal government is dramatically strengthened through new taxes and regulatory authority, giving Washington the capacity to build order by, for example, providing resources to international agencies.

Fifthly, threat has an especially strong effect on how American conservatives think about liberal order. Studies suggest that right-wing Americans are even more sensitive to threats than liberals.[25] Conservatives also tend to be more retributive and seek to exact vengeance on transgressors, whether they are criminals at home or despots abroad.[26] In the face of foreign peril, conservatives will do whatever it takes to win and punish the enemy, including building a liberal order.

In the absence of an existential threat, all five routes to order are partially or entirely closed off, the US commitment to order-building wanes and there is a temptation to tear down what was earlier constructed. There is no longer a strategic imperative to create alliances and institutions, and concerns about free-riding and relative gains resurface. The other disappears, and the differences between democracies seem more glaring. The idealistic wave that peaked during the campaign may crash as Americans believe the war's outcome fell short of the leadership's grand promises. Domestically, US society becomes less cohesive, partisanship may increase and there can be growing distrust of elites. There is also a decrease in the federal government's capacity and prestige as taxes and regulations are cut, and Washington may lack the means for expansive global projects.

Order needs disorder. In nature, the predator menaces the bird's nest, but it is also the reason the nest exists. In international politics, threat both imperils the system and is the catalyst for building the system.

To be clear, threats do not automatically strengthen the liberal order. The issue is whether the adversary's destructive acts are greater than America's constructive acts. The United States is not a nimble guardian that addresses any attack on the system with a calibrated and proportionate response. Instead, it is closer to George Kennan's image of 'one of those prehistoric monsters' that is slow to be provoked but, once aggravated, acts with 'blind determination'.[27] Washington may ignore small and moderate threats, and then react to grave danger with an extraordinary mobilisation and ambitious plans to re-invent the entire structure of international politics.

The liberal order is most likely to thrive with an enemy that is not too strong and not too weak. At one extreme, if the adversary is feeble, the United States may cease guarding the system altogether, causing it to disintegrate internally. The liberal order is also vulnerable when a relatively weak state manages to chip away at the structures of global governance in a covert manner, without reaching the threshold of peril that will galvanise Americans.

A sweet spot for order-building arises when a threat prompts creation without equivalent destruction. If the enemy looks dangerous because of an alien ideology but does not actually seek to tear down the order, the system may end up being bolstered. Truly grave perils can also lead to significant order-building. Although the adversary's acts may be highly destructive to global order, that effect is outweighed by US and allied resistance to it. Flagrant violations of human rights can produce greater global protection for human rights, and overt aggression may lead to a decline in inter-state war. The German decision to launch unrestricted submarine warfare in 1917 and the Japanese attack on Pearl Harbor in 1941 were extreme challenges to liberal principles, but they also produced a transformation in US order-building – a result opposite to that envisaged by German and Japanese war planners. Of course, there are limits to the stabilising impact of threat. If the enemy is too potent, it may succeed in toppling the order entirely.

Accordingly, there is a cycle of global order. When grave threats arise, Americans seek to build a liberal system. When the enemy is defeated, US enthusiasm for transforming the world dissolves and many people stop caring much about what lies beyond the water's edge. The success of the system leads Washington to retreat until a new hazard emerges, and then the cycle starts over again. George Shultz, secretary of state in the Reagan administration, once described foreign policy as tending the garden of international order, but Americans only cultivate the common when there is a peril looming and otherwise allow the weeds to grow back.[28]

In summary, liberals view destructive contests as challenges that the liberal order overcame, but those very contests are also the fuel that propels the order.[29] Scholars also tend to see America's hard-hitting or barbarous acts as deviations from the liberal model, but harsh measures are less a bug than a feature of the US-led liberal order. The system was built in the midst of a terrible contest and therefore accompanies tough wartime measures.

Ikenberry has defined liberal order as 'order that is open and at least loosely rules-based' such that 'it can be contrasted with order that is organized into rival blocs or exclusive regional spheres'.[30] This distinction between open and closed orders is not merely a useful definitional device; it lies at the heart of liberal order-building. The existence of an opposing closed bloc, and the contrast drawn by Americans between the free world and the unfree world, has driven the formation and unity of the US-led open bloc. The liberal needs the illiberal.

Hegemonic-stability theorists see a single uncontested state as the key for global order, but it is precisely contestation that impels a powerful actor to build the liberal order. Washington defends the order when it is threatened, not when it is unthreatened, as a brief survey of American history will reveal.

The cycle of global liberal order

During the decades before the First World War, America was largely secure from external threat. In 1895, the US secretary of state proclaimed that 'the United States is practically sovereign on this continent, and its fiat is law upon the subjects to which it confines its interposition'.[31] Washington did not seek to build a global liberal order, and instead tended to follow Thomas Jefferson's dictum: 'Peace, commerce, and honest friendship with all nations – entangling alliances with none.'[32] In his inaugural address in 1913, Woodrow Wilson did not even mention foreign policy, and the following year, the United States was largely irrelevant in the July Crisis that led to the outbreak of the war.[33]

In the early years of the Great War, with America on the sidelines, Wilson began to formulate his thinking about a post-war system. In January 1917, he contemplated US participation in a future 'concert of power', but it was a hazy concept and conditional on the belligerents agreeing to a 'peace without victory'.[34] The US entry into the war in April 1917 revolutionised how Americans thought about global order, as Wilson proposed a millennial vision of universal freedom. In January 1918, he outlined the Fourteen Points programme to transform international relations and end all war based on the principles of self-determination and disarmament, and a new collective-security organisation, the League of Nations. In July 1918, Wilson stated: 'What we seek is the reign of law, based upon the consent of the governed, and sustained by the organized opinion of mankind.'[35]

Americans did not suddenly realise that law and institutions would solve the problems of modernity. Neither did the United States achieve uncontested hegemony. Rather, the catalyst for US order-building was the threat posed by imperial Germany and Bolshevik Russia. Berlin was the mightiest industrial power in Europe, and in 1917 it declared unrestricted submarine warfare against all shipping around Britain, including US vessels, and incited Mexico to ally with Japan and Germany in an attack on the United States. If Germany won the war, it could become the European hegemon and oversee an empire stretching from the English Channel to Ukraine, cutting America off from European trade. Meanwhile, in late 1917, a second threat loomed as Bolshevik Russia preached global revolution.[36]

Threat thus provided a powerful strategic imperative for building a liberal order. Wilson believed that a new US-led system would consolidate the peace and prevent another conflagration. The League of Nations would sweep away the morass of balance-of-power politics and shadowy alliances that incubated German aggression. The Fourteen Points also countered the Bolshevik promise of self-determination with Wilson's own defence of the principle.[37] As long as the Great War was ongoing, questions about potential relative gains and free-riding in a new world order were put aside. German militarism was a stark other that underscored the shared values of democratic societies such as France, the United Kingdom and the United States.

The Great War also unleashed an idealistic strain in American politics that boosted ambitions for the post-war world. Ironically, right at the moment when the fate of the world hinged on blood and iron, the White House believed that power politics could be transcended. William McAdoo, the secretary of the treasury, saw the campaign as 'a kind of crusade; and, like all crusades, it sweeps along on a powerful stream of romanticism'.[38] As the scale of the US war effort increased, so the nobility of the post-war vision grew, and Wilson urged a 'peace worth the infinite sacrifices of these years of tragical suffering'.[39]

The war had a profound impact on American domestic politics, which fuelled the drive for order-building. *The Nation* described a 'rebirth of American patriotism'.[40] With extraordinary speed, the US press, elites and public abandoned the traditional commitment to unilateralism and supported the idea of leading a global liberal order, although few bothered to think through the details. During the war, Republicans and Democrats alike backed Wilson's vision of the League of Nations.[41] 'When Woodrow Wilson speaks to the American people, he speaks for them', wrote the *New York Times*. 'He has an instinctive understanding of their will.'[42]

The war effort dramatically expanded the federal government's capabilities and widened leaders' horizons. The top tax rate grew to 77% and Washington established a cornucopia of boards and institutions to unite US industries in the war effort, from steel to railroads. It was a natural step from creating domestic structures to win the war, to creating international ones to win the peace.

In 1918, at the eleventh hour of the eleventh day of the eleventh month, the war ended in triumph for the United States and its allies. The crusading wave crashed, and Americans turned inward and lost interest in order-building. Wilson's plans for US entry into the League of Nations were defeated in the Senate. In the 1920 election, Republican Warren Harding won 61% of the vote with a promise of 'normalcy'. In the 1920s and 1930s, Washington repeatedly hiked tariffs, triggering an international trade war. Americans also sought isolation from Old World intrigues, and by 1936, 95% of the public opposed getting involved in a future European conflict under any circumstances.[43]

Security killed the liberal order

Liberals readily admit that their arguments cannot explain why the United States failed to ratify the League of Nations.[44] Meanwhile, if uncontested power is the key to liberal order, the United States in the decade after the First World War might have seemed primed for global leadership. The war immensely strengthened US power, and during the 1920s the United States accounted for around 40% of world manufacturing output.[45] Despite these vast capabilities, however, Americans chose splendid isolation.

Security killed the liberal order. After 1918, the United States no longer faced a grave threat. Germany was stripped of a tenth of its territory as well as its colonies, and was restricted to a small army of 100,000 men. Meanwhile, the Bolsheviks failed to export the Russian revolution, and were crippled by civil war, famine and the loss of the Baltic states, Finland and Poland.

Without a clear and present foreign danger, Americans pivoted to domestic problems. The passionate idealism of the Great War produced a backlash against the entire enterprise. Despite the great victory in 1918, Americans quickly concluded that US entry into the war had been a terrible mistake. In 1919, *The Nation* described Wilson as 'the one-time idol of democracy' who now stands 'discredited and condemned'.[46]

In the 1940s, the cycle turned, and Americans engaged in the most sustained era of order-building in US history. Washington began planning for a post-war system in 1941, before America had entered the war, and even as the fascist states continued to score victories. In his memoir, Dean Acheson, Truman's secretary of state, described the task that Americans faced in the 1940s as being only slightly easier than the challenge laid down in Genesis. 'That was to create a world out of chaos; ours, to create half a world, a free half, out of the same material without blowing the whole to pieces in the process.'[47]

The new architecture of institutions and alliances included the Bretton Woods monetary system and the International Monetary Fund (1944); the International Bank for Reconstruction and Development (1944), which later became part of the World Bank Group; the United Nations (1945); the General Agreement on Tariffs and Trade (1947), which later became the World Trade Organization; the Marshall Plan (1948); and the North Atlantic Treaty Organization, America's first peacetime alliance (1949). The United States economically revived its former enemies, Germany and Japan, cut US tariffs and kept the dollar overvalued to help other states recover. America may be the first great power in history that sought to weaken its own dominant position.

It was not the sudden effectiveness of liberal order that enabled Washington to create a world out of chaos. After all, tariffs and isolationism had eroded American and global security for two decades. And uncontested American hegemony did not induce America to build the order. It was precisely the challenge to US security that drove Washington to act.[48]

US order-building was unparalleled because the threat was unrivalled. During the 1940s, three hostile peer competitors emerged – Nazi Germany, imperial Japan and the Soviet Union – armed with new technologies that could strike US territory. In 1940, Germany overran much of Western Europe, and Franklin Roosevelt outlined a nightmare vision of America in a fascist-dominated world: 'a people lodged in prison, handcuffed, hungry, and fed through the bars from day to day by the contemptuous, unpitying masters of other continents'.[49] The following year, Japan struck American territory at Pearl Harbor, and Germany declared war on the United States.

In the wake of the Second World War, the Soviet Union occupied much of Eastern Europe (in Winston Churchill's formulation, the 'iron curtain' fell from 'Stettin in the Baltic to Trieste in the Adriatic'), became a nuclear power and looked to expand its influence among the newly decolonising states of Africa and Asia.[50] In 1946, Kennan wrote the 'Long Telegram', which claimed that Moscow was 'committed fanatically to the belief that with US [sic] there can be no permanent *modus vivendi*'.[51]

The triple threat provided a profound strategic rationale for order-building. During the Second World War, America sought to prevent another conflagration by designing institutions to tackle the root causes of war, such as economic protectionism and hyper-nationalism.[52] The United Nations was forged in war: Roosevelt coined the term in 1942 to describe the military coalition arrayed against the fascist states, and envisaged the wartime alliance continuing to police the world after victory was achieved.

The Soviet Union was an ideal other

After 1945, order-building was primarily designed to contain the Soviet Union and win the Cold War. Extraordinary danger trumped concerns about free-riding and relative gains. To maintain alliance cohesion, Washington rewarded partners with access to US markets, and offered Europeans disproportionate representation in the UN Security Council and the IMF. The US public backed the Marshall Plan not as an act of charity but to stop the spread of communism.[53]

The Soviet Union was an almost ideal other: a strategic rival and the ideological and religious antithesis of the United States. The contrast between the 'free world' and the 'evil empire' effectively masked differences within the Western coalition. Many American conservatives were deeply sceptical about foreign aid, meddling institutions and ungrateful partners. But defeating the threat trumped these worries.

As they had during the Great War, US leaders portrayed the struggle in idealistic terms and argued for a transformation of global policies to justify the investment. Democratic senator Joseph Ball called the creation of the UN 'the greatest crusade since Jesus sent his twelve disciples out to preach the brotherhood of man'.[54] In 1955, president Dwight D. Eisenhower said, 'either man is the creature whom the Psalmist described as "a little lower than the angels" … or man is a soulless, animated machine to be enslaved, used and consumed by the state for its own glorification'.[55]

Threat gave rise to an era of bipartisanship and trust in elites that smoothed the path to order-building. Unity at home was the foundation for ambition abroad. In the Second World War, despite hundreds of thousands of casualties, large popular majorities backed the fight for unconditional surrender and the creation of the UN. During the 'Cold War consensus' of the 1940s and 1950s, Republicans and Democrats agreed to fight a global struggle against communism. Americans placed their faith in the foreign-policy establishment. In 1958, polls found that 73% of Americans said they trusted the government most or all the time.[56]

During the war, the size of the federal government increased tenfold and it naturally began to think bigger on the global stage. The top rate of income tax increased to 94%, and Washington regulated all aspects of economic life, including wages and prices. Government activism at home encouraged greater engagement abroad. In her book *A New Deal for the World*, Elizabeth Borgwardt observes: 'America's receptivity to multilateral institutions such as the United Nations was enhanced by more cosmopolitan sensibilities growing out of widespread wartime service and vastly increased mobility on the home front.'[57]

In 1945, there were signs that the wave of internationalism might crash as it did in 1918–19. In October 1945, just 7% of the public said that world peace was the biggest problem facing the country, and there was pressure to quickly demobilise and get the boys home.[58] Post-war America remained internationalist precisely because it was not post-war. A new, grave peril emerged – the Soviet Union – and the Second World War blurred into the Cold War.

In 1989, Brent Scowcroft, then George H.W. Bush's national security advisor, recalled to the president Acheson's lines about the book of Genesis, and urged the White House to 'pick up the task where they left off'.[59] The United States would complete the global liberal order by drawing the former communist world and the developing countries into a cohesive, rules-based system. When Iraq invaded Kuwait in 1990, Washington assembled a broad coalition, with UN support, to liberate Kuwait. The United States helped to oversee German unification, set Eastern Europe on the road to membership of NATO and the European Union, and integrate the North American economies through the North American Free Trade Agreement.

The system, however, began to corrode internally. In 1992, H. Ross Perot ran for president as an outsider candidate on a proto-Trump unilateralist platform and received 19% of the vote, despite quitting and re-entering the race. Bill Clinton showed where his priorities lay by bluntly stating that 'foreign policy is not what I came here to do'.[60] The Republican Party's 'Contract with America' had ten planks: nine were about domestic politics; the lone plank about foreign policy stressed that US troops should never be placed under UN command.[61] In the following years, the United States rejected an array of international treaties: the Law of the Sea Convention, the Comprehensive Test-Ban Treaty, the Kyoto Protocol, the Ottawa Convention on anti-personnel landmines and the International Criminal Court. After the 9/11 attacks, the 'war on terror' triggered a new era of US unilateralism, including the invasion of Iraq without UN Security Council approval.

Barack Obama lauded the US alliances and institutions of the post-war era, but he also dramatically expanded the use of drone strikes, criticised allied 'free-riding' during the 2011 intervention in Libya and proved unable to craft an effective coordinated response to the Syrian civil war.[62] During Obama's second term, order-building almost ground to a halt. As Mira Rapp-Hooper and Rebecca Lissner put it, 'in 2012, for the first time since World War II, the United States joined zero treaties, and then it did the same in 2013 and 2015'.[63]

In 2016, Americans elected a president who overtly opposed the liberal order. Trump claimed that allies took America for a ride, excoriated institutions like NATO and the EU and assailed NAFTA as 'the worst trade deal in ... the history of this country'.[64] He favoured a transactional, zero-sum approach that put 'America first' by encouraging the break-up of the EU, withdrawing from the Iran nuclear deal and the Paris climate accord, and praising despots. In 2016, according to Francis Fukuyama, America switched from 'the liberal internationalist camp, to the populist nationalist one'.[65]

Why did Scowcroft and Bush's vision not come to pass? Liberals have no obvious answer. The surge in democracy and trade after the Cold War ought to have produced a virtuous cycle. A declining hegemon was not to blame, as the United States enjoyed almost unprecedented economic and military primacy into the early 2000s and nevertheless chose military adventurism rather than order-building. Even in 2016, the year that Trump was elected, Washington spent three times as much on its military as its closest rival, Beijing.[66]

The core reason the liberal order eroded is the disappearance of the Soviet threat. Bush senior hoped that the end of the Cold War would liberate the United Nations to achieve its original mission, but the fall of communism may have actually doomed the global system. When the superpower antagonism ended, Soviet official Georgi Arbatov told a US audience, 'we are going to do a terrible thing to you. We are going to deprive you of an enemy.'[67] The post-Cold War period echoed, in some respects, the previous era of threatlessness – the 1920s – as Americans questioned the system that delivered victory, and retreated into unilateralism and protectionism. The Pax Americana had too much peace.

Americans viewed allies and institutions through the lens of safety. As Ikenberry and Deudney put it, 'the collapse of the Soviet Union, although a great milestone in the annals of the advance of liberal democracy, had the ironic effect of eliminating one of its main drivers of solidarity'.[68] There was no longer an imperative to pay for the system's upkeep, and worries about relative gains and free-riding re-emerged. Without an other to identify against, the divisions within the West loomed larger. NATO absorbed many of its former adversaries and became more diverse and fractious. 'As long as Soviet divisions could reach the Rhine in hours, we obviously had a blood brotherhood with our cousins overseas', wrote the Belgian prime minister in 2003. 'But now that the Cold War is over, we can express more freely our differences of opinion.'[69] America did not lavish money on Russia to aid its transition to democracy and capitalism in the same way that Washington had helped Germany and Japan decades earlier. Instead, the vogue was for shock therapy, and, as US diplomat Strobe Talbot commented, there was too much shock and not enough therapy.[70]

Without a compelling peril, the American public became more sceptical of order-building. Americans wanted to focus on domestic issues or carry out 'nation building at home', as Obama put it.[71] By the late 1990s, only 2–3% of the public said foreign policy was the greatest issue facing the country, and in 2016, 57% wanted the United States to 'mind its own business internationally'.[72] Free trade had always created winners and losers, but now the losers were more vocal because there was no security imperative for boosting economic ties with allies.

Domestic politics became increasingly partisan and Americans were much less trusting of the establishment. Americans elected 'outsider' presidents with little or no prior experience with foreign policy, such as Clinton, George W. Bush, Obama and, most emphatically, Trump. The elite architects of liberal order were no longer celebrated as 'wise men', but were instead derided as 'globalists', 'Davoisie' or 'the Blob'. In one 2019 poll, only 17% of Americans said they trusted the federal government to do the right thing.[73]

Threatlessness had a particularly strong effect on American conservatives. The political right's attachment to liberal order is conditioned on external peril. After the Cold War ended, the Republican Party evolved from supporting free trade to embracing Trump, the self-described 'Tariff Man', and in 2018, Republican voters were evenly split on whether the United States should leave NATO.[74]

If threat spurs US order-building, why did the 9/11 attacks trigger unilateralism and preventive war rather than stronger alliances and institutions? The answer is that the terrorists were too weak. The United States embraces order-building when there is an existential threat on a par with Nazi Germany or the Soviet Union. By contrast, al-Qaeda was a tiny band of fanatics who succeeded beyond their wildest dreams on 9/11.[75] During the 'war on terror', there was no pressing strategic need to construct global alliances, and no national mobilisation akin to the one that arose during the Second World War, which produced a spirit of shared sacrifice and trust in elites. Instead of aligning against a single fearsome focal point, the liberal order faced ambiguous challenges from a variety of non-state actors and rogue states, and the unity of 2001 quickly evaporated in the hot Iraqi sun.

Moscow's aggression in Ukraine and elsewhere failed to trigger US order-building for the same essential reason: contemporary Russia is insufficiently threatening. Russia's economy is comparable in size to that of South Korea or Canada, and Moscow has typically engaged in covert 'grey zone' tactics and cyber war rather than overt aggression. Russian actions may be especially destructive to the international system because Moscow's 'salami-slicing' tactics cause significant damage to global governance without provoking a commensurate countervailing riposte. A dearth of resources limits Russia's capacity, but it also means that Moscow's aggression does not attract the kind of balancing response that would have occurred during the Cold War.[76] Driving a wedge into US domestic politics through electoral meddling and the propagation of conspiracy theories is especially effective because it turns American against American and impedes the United States from bolstering the system.[77]

Russia is insufficiently threatening

How will the rise of China affect the liberal order? From the perspective of hegemonic-stability theorists, Beijing's economic growth and the shift to bipolarity is an inherent problem because there will no longer be an uncontested Atlas willing and able to hold up the heavens. Alternatively, liberal scholars contend that the future of the liberal order hinges on whether China can be co-opted into the system. The order can adapt to accommodate Beijing, so long as China accepts the underlying rules-based model.[78]

The impact of a growing Chinese threat on the international system may be curvilinear, however. Threat both erodes the order and triggers order-building, and the geopolitical outcome depends on the net effect of construction minus destruction – that is, on whether America places bricks on the wall more quickly than China removes them.

If the Chinese threat turned out to be minimal, the liberal order could continue to erode because the United States might decline to defend the system. In this scenario, the health of the order would require China or other states to step up and provide public goods. A low-to-moderate Chinese threat could inflict the greatest damage on the liberal order. Covert and subtle attacks on the system could cause significant harm without prompting substantial balancing responses from the United States. Indeed, if Beijing's goal were truly to destroy the liberal order, its best approach might be to act with restraint and let American domestic divisions pummel the system from within.

If the Chinese threat were to rise further, however, the net effect could be to strengthen the liberal order. For example, Chinese repression in Hong Kong, bellicosity against India or nationalist fantasies could foster a shared identity among democracies, promote greater US bipartisanship and trust in elites, and motivate the United States to bolster institutions and alliances, and compete with China in the provision of global public goods. The Belt and Road Initiative, China's international investment programme, led the US Congress to pass the Better Utilization of Investments Leading to Development (BUILD) Act in 2018, a multibillion-dollar programme of loan guarantees in the developing world.[79] Of course, at some point, the Chinese threat could be so extreme as to destroy the system entirely.

*   *   *

Again, order needs disorder. Times of peril for the United States, such as the 1940s, triggered the creation of alliances and institutions, whereas periods of safety, such as the 1920s and the post-Cold War era, produced an insular backlash. There are two solutions to this problem. The first is simply for US leaders to understand the cycle of global order, and to act in counter-cyclical ways, tending the garden even when the storm abates. This, however, is easier said than done, and the Obama administration's spotty international performance reflected the pitfalls of order-building without an external peril. The second solution is for US leaders to apprehend the rise of China as a potential impetus to the renewal of global governance. Beijing may be a useful adversary that helps to mobilise American resources for order-building, but deft leadership will be needed in harnessing the positive aspects of danger without spiralling towards another cold war.[80]

Acknowledgements

For valuable research assistance, the author would like to thank Sage Miller and Chloe Sweeney.

Notes

1 See Alana Abramson and Ryan T. Beckwith, 'The Rise and Fall of Rex Tillerson: A Timeline', *Time*, 13 March 2018, https://time.com/5197365/rex-tillerson-fired-timeline/. Some sources add an additional expletive.

2 See Mammo Muchie and Li Xing, 'The Myths and Realities of the Rising Powers: Is China a Threat to the Existing World Order?', in Li Xing (ed.), *The Rise of China and the Capitalist World Order* (Abingdon: Routledge, 2010), p. 52.

3 Hedley Bull, *The Anarchical Society: A Study of Order in World Politics* (London: Macmillan, 1977), p. 8.

4 See Christian Reus-Smit, 'Cultural Diversity and International Order', *International Organization*, vol. 71, no. 4, Fall 2017, pp. 851–85.

5 See G. John Ikenberry, 'The End of Liberal International Order?', *International Affairs*, vol. 94, no. 1, January 2018, pp. 7–23; and Kori Schake, 'The Trump Doctrine Is Winning and the World Is Losing', *New York Times*, 15 June 2018, https://www.nytimes.com/2018/06/15/opinion/sunday/trump-china-america-first.html.

6 See Patrick Porter, *The False Promise of Liberal Order: Nostalgia, Delusion and the Rise of Trump* (Cambridge: Polity Press, 2020).

7 See Jeff D. Colgan, 'Three Visions of International Order', *Washington Quarterly*, vol. 42, no. 2, Summer 2019, pp. 85–98.

8 Daniel Deudney and G. John Ikenberry, 'Liberal World: The Resilient Order', *Foreign Affairs*, vol. 97, no. 4, July/August 2018, p. 25.

9 See Daniel Deudney and G. John Ikenberry, 'The Nature and Sources of Liberal International Order', *Review of International Studies*, vol. 25, no. 2, April 1999, pp. 179–96.

10 See William Nordhaus, 'Climate Clubs: Overcoming Free-riding in International Climate Policy', *American Economic Review*, vol. 105, no. 4, 2015, pp. 1,339–70; and Duncan Snidal, 'Relative Gains and the Pattern of International Cooperation', *American Political Science Review*, vol. 85, no. 3, 1991, pp. 701–26.

11 Charles P. Kindleberger, *The World in Depression, 1929–1939* (Berkeley, CA: University of California Press, 1986), p. 304. See also Stephen D. Krasner, 'State Power and the Structure of International Trade', *World Politics*, vol. 28, no. 3, April 1976, pp. 317–47; and George Modelski, 'The Long Cycle of Global Politics and the Nation-state', *Comparative Studies in Society and History*, vol. 20, no. 2, April 1978, pp. 214–35.

12 See Michael C. Webb and Stephen D. Krasner, 'Hegemonic Stability Theory: An Empirical Assessment', *Review of International Studies*, vol. 15, no. 2, April 1989, pp. 183–98.

13 See Robert Gilpin, *The Political Economy of International Relations* (Princeton, NJ: Princeton University Press, 2016), p. 86.

14 Anne-Marie Slaughter, 'The Return of Anarchy?', *Journal of International Affairs*, vol. 70, March 2017, p. 15.

15 See Ikenberry, 'The End of Liberal International Order?', p. 7; Michael

Mandelbaum, *The Case for Goliath: How America Acts as the World's Government in the Twenty-first Century* (New York: PublicAffairs, 2005); and 'Hundreds of Scholars Have Signed a Statement Defending the International Institutions that Trump Has Attacked', *Washington Post*, 14 August 2018, https://www.washingtonpost.com/news/monkey-cage/wp/2018/08/14/hundreds-of-scholars-have-signed-a-statement-defending-the-international-institutions-that-trump-has-attacked/.

16 Harry S. Truman, 'Address on Foreign Economic Policy, delivered at Baylor University on 6 March 1947. Available from the Harry S. Truman Library Museum, https://www.trumanlibrary.gov/library/public-papers/52/address-foreign-economic-policy-delivered-baylor-university.

17 Secretary of State Madeleine K. Albright, 'Interview on NBC-TV "The Today Show"', 19 February 1998, https://1997-2001.state.gov/statements/1998/980219a.html.

18 See Henry Farrell and Abraham L. Newman, 'Weaponized Interdependence: How Global Economic Networks Shape State Coercion', *International Security*, vol. 44, no. 1, Summer 2019, pp. 42–79.

19 See Gilpin, *The Political Economy of International Relations*; Krasner, 'State Power and the Structure of International Trade'; and Snidal, 'The Limits of Hegemonic Stability Theory'.

20 See Graham Allison, 'The Myth of the Liberal Order: From Historical Accident to Conventional Wisdom', *Foreign Affairs*, vol. 97, no. 4, July/August 2018, pp. 124–33.

21 See Dominic D.P. Johnson and Dominic Tierney, 'Bad World: The Negativity Bias in International Politics', *International Security*, vol. 43, no. 3, Winter 2018/19, pp. 96–140.

22 See Kyle M. Lascurettes, *Orders of Exclusion: Great Powers and the Strategic Source of Foundational Rules in International Relations* (Oxford: Oxford University Press, 2020).

23 See Stephen M. Walt, *The Origins of Alliances* (Ithaca, NY: Cornell University Press, 1987).

24 Fareed Zakaria, *From Wealth to Power: The Unusual Origins of America's World Role* (Princeton, NJ: Princeton University Press, 1999), p. 9.

25 See John R. Hibbing, Kevin B. Smith and John R. Alford, 'Differences in Negativity Bias Underlie Variations in Political Ideology', *Behavioral and Brain Sciences*, vol. 37, no. 3, June 2014, pp. 297–307; and Natalie J. Shook and Russell H. Fazio, 'Political Ideology, Exploration of Novel Stimuli, and Attitude Formation', *Journal of Experimental Social Psychology*, vol. 45, no. 4, July 2009, pp. 995–8.

26 See Dominic Tierney, *How We Fight: Crusades, Quagmires and the American Way of War* (New York: Little, Brown, 2010).

27 Quoted in John Lewis Gaddis, *George F. Kennan: An American Life* (New York: Penguin, 2011), p. 435.

28 See James E. Goodby, 'Groundbreaking Diplomacy: An Interview with George Shultz', *Foreign Service Journal*, December 2016, https://www.afsa.org/groundbreaking-diplomacy-interview-george-shultz.

29 See Ikenberry, 'The End of Liberal International Order?', pp. 8–9.

30 G. John Ikenberry, *Liberal Leviathan: The Origins, Crisis, and Transformation of the American World Order* (Princeton, NJ: Princeton University Press, 2011), p. xii.

31 Quoted in George C. Herring, *From Colony to Superpower: U.S. Foreign Relations Since 1776* (Oxford: Oxford University Press, 2008), p. 307.

32 See David Fromkin, 'Entangling Alliances', *Foreign Affairs*, vol. 48, no. 4, July 1970, pp. 688–700.

33 See Justus D. Doenecke, *Nothing Less Than War: A New History of America's Entry into World War I* (Lexington, KY: University Press of Kentucky, 2011), pp. 2–4; and Ikenberry, 'The End of Liberal International Order?', p. 7.

34 Woodrow Wilson, 'A World League for Peace', speech delivered on 22 January 1917. Available from the Miller Center, University of Virginia, https://millercenter.org/the-presidency/presidential-speeches/january-22-1917-world-league-peace-speech.

35 Quoted in G. John Ikenberry, *After Victory: Institutions, Strategic Restraint, and the Rebuilding of Order After Major Wars* (Princeton, NJ: Princeton University Press, 2019), p. 127.

36 See Lascurettes, *Orders of Exclusion*.

37 *Ibid*.

38 Quoted in David M. Kennedy, *Over Here: The First World War and American Society* (Oxford: Oxford University Press, 2004), p. 105.

39 Woodrow Wilson, *The Bases of Durable Peace As Voiced By President Wilson* (Chicago, IL: Union League Club of Chicago, 1918), p. 21.

40 Quoted in Stuart J. Rochester, *American Liberal Disillusionment: In the Wake of World War I* (University Park, PA: Pennsylvania State University Press, 1977), p. 37.

41 See Ikenberry, *After Victory*, p. 149.

42 'The President Speaks', *New York Times*, 28 September 2018, https://www.nytimes.com/1918/09/28/archives/the-president-speaks.html.

43 See Steven Casey, *When Soldiers Fall: How Americans Have Confronted Combat Losses from World War I to Afghanistan* (Oxford: Oxford University Press, 2014), p. 37.

44 See Ikenberry, *After Victory*, p. 119.

45 See Paul Kennedy, *The Rise and Fall of the Great Powers: Economic Change and Military Conflict from 1500 to 2000* (New York: Random House, 1987), pp. 327–8; Klaus Knorr, *War Potential of Nations* (Princeton, NJ: Princeton University Press, 1956), p. 56; and John A. Thompson, *A Sense of Power: The Roots of America's Global Role* (Ithaca, NY: Cornell University Press, 2015), p. 230.

46 William MacDonald, 'The Madness at Versailles', *Nation*, vol. 108, March 1919, p. 779.

47 Dean Acheson, *Present at the Creation: My Years in the State Department* (New York: W. W. Norton & Company, 1970), p. xvii.

48 See Dale C. Copeland, *The Origins of Major War* (Ithaca, NY: Cornell University Press, 2000).

49 Franklin D. Roosevelt, 'Stab in the Back', speech delivered on 10 June 1940. Available from the Miller Center, University of Virginia, https://millercenter.org/the-presidency/presidential-speeches/june-10-1940-stab-back-speech.

50 Winston Churchill, 'The Sinews of Peace' ('Iron Curtain Speech'),

5 March 1946. Available from the International Churchill Society, https://winstonchurchill.org/resources/speeches/1946-1963-elder-statesman/the-sinews-of-peace/.

51 George Kennan, 'The Long Telegram', in Kenneth M. Jensen (ed.), *Origins of the Cold War: The Novikov, Kennan, and Roberts 'Long Telegrams' of 1946*, Vol. 4 (Washington, DC: United States Institute of Peace, 1993), pp. 17–32.

52 See Ikenberry, *Liberal Leviathan*; and Bruce D. Jones, Carlos Pascual and Stephen John Stedman, *Power and Responsibility: Building International Order in an Era of Transnational Threats* (Washington DC: Brookings Institution Press, 2009), p. 26.

53 See Thompson, *A Sense of Power*, p. 246.

54 Quoted in 'Religion: Man's Hope', *Time*, 8 November 1943.

55 Dwight D. Eisenhower, 'State of the Union, 1955', 6 January 1955. Available from AMDOCS: Documents for the Study of American History, http://www.vlib.us/amdocs/texts/dde1955.htm.

56 Pew Research Center, 'Trust in Government: 1958–2015', 23 November 2015, https://www.people-press.org/2015/11/23/1-trust-in-government-1958-2015/.

57 Elizabeth Borgwardt, *A New Deal for the World* (Cambridge, MA: Harvard University Press, 2007), p. 7.

58 See Thompson, *A Sense of Power*, p. 235.

59 Michael Nelson and Barbara A. Perry (eds), *41: Inside the Presidency of George H.W. Bush* (Ithaca, NY: Cornell University Press, 2014), p. 116.

60 Quoted in Christopher Hemmer, *American Pendulum: Recurring Debates in U.S. Grand Strategy* (Ithaca, NY: Cornell University Press, 2015), p. 116.

61 See Hemmer, *American Pendulum*, p. 116.

62 See Lascurettes, *Orders of Exclusion*.

63 Mira Rapp-Hooper and Rebecca Friedman Lissner, 'The Open World: What America Can Achieve After Trump', *Foreign Affairs*, vol. 98, no. 3, May/June 2019, pp. 18–25.

64 Quoted in John Ydstie, 'As Trump Moves to Renegotiate NAFTA, US Farmers Are Hopeful But Nervous', NPR, 15 October 2017, https://www.npr.org/2017/10/15/555843792/as-trump-moves-to-renegotiate-nafta-u-s-farmers-are-hopeful-but-nervous.

65 Francis Fukuyama, 'US Against the World? Trump's America and the New Global Order', *Financial Times*, 11 November 2016, https://www.ft.com/content/6a43cf54-a75d-11e6-8b69-02899e8bd9d1.

66 Niall McCarthy, 'The Top 15 Countries for Military Expenditure in 2016', *Forbes,* 24 April 2017, https://www.forbes.com/sites/niallmccarthy/2017/04/24/the-top-15-countries-for-military-expenditure-in-2016-infographic/?sh=1d13ea3743f3.

67 Quoted in United States Department of Defense, *Soviet Military Power* (Washington DC: Department of Defense, 1990), p. 21.

68 Deudney and Ikenberry, 'Liberal World: The Resilient Order', p. 22.

69 Quoted in 'Explaining the War', *Wall Street Journal*, 22 February 2005, https://www.wsj.com/articles/SB110904106408260564.

70 See Peter Passell, 'Economic Scene; Russia's Political Turmoil Follows Half Steps, Not Shock Therapy', *New York Times*, 30 December 1993, https://www.nytimes.com/1993/12/30/

business/economic-scene-russia-s-political-turmoil-follows-half-steps-not-shock-therapy.html.

71 Quoted in Stephen Sestanovich, 'Obama's Focus Is on Nation-building at Home', *New York Times*, 20 December 2016, https://www.nytimes.com/roomfordebate/2014/03/11/weakness-or-realism-in-foreign-policy/obamas-focus-is-on-nation-building-at-home.

72 J.E. Rielly, *American Public Opinion and U.S. Foreign Policy* (Chicago, IL: Chicago Council on Foreign Relations, 1999). See also Pew Research Center, 'Public Uncertain, Divided Over America's Place in the World', 5 May 2016, p. 3, https://www.pewresearch.org/politics/wp-content/uploads/sites/4/2016/05/05-05-2016-Foreign-policy-APW-release.pdf.

73 Pew Research Center, 'Trust in Government: 1958–2019'.

74 See Daniel B. Shapiro, 'Saving NATO', *Democracy: A Journal of Ideas*, no. 51, Winter 2019, https://democracyjournal.org/magazine/51/saving-nato/.

75 See John Mueller, 'Is There Still a Terrorist Threat? The Myth of the Omnipresent Enemy', *Foreign Affairs*, vol. 85, no. 5, September/October 2006, pp. 2–8.

76 See Robert Kagan, 'The Twilight of the Liberal World Order', Brookings Institution, 27 January 2017, https://www.brookings.edu/research/the-twilight-of-the-liberal-world-order/.

77 See Lyle K. Morris et al., *Gaining Competitive Advantage in the Gray Zone: Response Options for Coercive Aggression Below the Threshold of Major War* (Santa Monica, CA: RAND National Defense Research Institute, 2019), p. xi.

78 See Ikenberry, *Liberal Leviathan*.

79 See Joshua Busby, 'What International Relations Tells Us about COVID-19', *E-International Relations*, 26 April 2020, https://www.e-ir.info/2020/04/26/what-international-relations-tells-us-about-covid-19.

80 See Thomas J. Christensen, *Useful Adversaries: Grand Strategy, Domestic Mobilization, and Sino-American Conflict, 1947–1958* (Princeton, NJ: Princeton University Press, 1996).

Lifting the Protection Curse: The Rise of New Military Powers in the Middle East

David B. Roberts

Arab militaries tend not to enjoy the strongest of reputations. Lack of spending is not the problem. The Gulf monarchies of Bahrain, Kuwait, Oman, Qatar, Saudi Arabia and the United Arab Emirates (UAE) have invested substantial sums in their military forces, including significant acquisitions of high-end military equipment. Egypt has received over $80 billion in military aid from the United States alone. These states have also had access to superior military training and education, having long sent their cadets and officers to the world's most prestigious military schools and colleges. Weapon-supplying nations – principally France, the United Kingdom and the US – have been intimately involved, for a century in some cases, in the in-country military training and education of Arab forces.

A fundamental reason that so many military forces in the Arab world are not as good as they should be is that they suffer from the protection curse. Under the well-known resource curse, an abundance of natural resources impedes economic and democratic development. Analogously, under the protection curse, a surfeit of de facto international security guarantees inhibits the development of military capability. The greater the guarantees, the more pernicious the curse, and Gulf monarchies are more cosseted by the Pentagon than any other regional grouping. Enjoying effective US security guarantees has permitted the Gulf monarchies to take a fundamentally unserious approach to their militaries. Procurement is often ill-considered

David B. Roberts is an assistant professor in the School of Security Studies at King's College London and adjunct faculty at the Paris School of International Affairs, Sciences Po.

Survival | vol. 63 no. 2 | April–May 2021 | pp. 139–154   https://doi.org/10.1080/00396338.2021.1905997

and whimsical, inefficient training methodologies are not challenged and senior roles are frequently conferred on unqualified royals. These habits undermine any notion of meritocracy, promote the creation of elite fiefdoms, and perpetuate autocratic management approaches that make forces inflexible and unable to execute contemporary manoeuvre-orientated missions that call for delegation. While US and other Western defence contractors have benefitted from a financial bonanza, decades of principally US policies aimed at building local military capabilities in a critical area of the world have broadly failed.

The UAE's exceptional prowess

Despite general military mediocrity in the Arab world, the UAE appears to be escaping the protection curse. Significant Emirati expeditionary deployments in Afghanistan, Libya and Yemen have consistently surprised Western analysts. The UAE has achieved operational successes at distance in challenging circumstances. Several elements of the Emirati military – notably their fast-jet and special-operations forces – have worked cheek by jowl with NATO forces in hostile engagements. No other Arab nation has joined up with NATO forces in this way.

The UAE has developed the Arab world's most effective military expeditionary forces even while enjoying US protection. It has done this thanks to the pressure of a focused and driven leader, Abu Dhabi Crown Prince Mohammed bin Zayed Al Nahyan – known as MbZ – who intuited decades ago that US and UAE threat perceptions might not remain aligned indefinitely. The US would likely retain an enduring interest in protecting the monarchies from an expansionist Iran to maintain the regional status quo. But there was little reason to expect the US to understand or care about emerging sub-state threats if the wider status quo in the Gulf looked secure. This hunch gained validity when the US, in the minds of many Gulf leaders, hastily abandoned its long-standing Egyptian partner Hosni Mubarak during the Arab Spring, and when the American response to anti-regime protests in Bahrain appeared tepid and unreliable.

MbZ had been preparing for an event like the Arab Spring for decades, having long believed that the growth of Islamist groups in the UAE and across the Middle East posed as acute a threat to state stability as the ongoing threat from Iran. Realising that US largesse hardly protected the UAE from this kind of internal peril, from the early 1990s MbZ orchestrated changes to forge national military capabilities sounder and more flexible than the Gulf norm.

American policymakers need to quickly grasp what the growth of increasingly assertive and capable Arab states means for regional security. So far, the UAE remains dependent on the US and its allies for a variety of military functions, from training to logistical support to niche capabilities such as air-to-air refuelling or anti-submarine warfare. Nevertheless, the UAE and Saudi Arabia are becoming increasingly assertive, sometimes to the detriment of US goals in the wider Gulf region. Their blockade of Qatar, in particular, cut against the cohesion of the Gulf monarchies against Iran that the US has long sought to cultivate. As the UAE and Saudi Arabia find they can increasingly do without US support, and reduce their dependence on the US, they are likely to emerge as ever less restrainable regional actors.

Mediocre militaries

Military effectiveness ultimately turns on the efficient translation of resources into military power.[1] Spending alone does not make for an efficient or successful military force, as the US often finds out for itself. But resources remain key to regional assessments of balances of military power. Many Arab states do not lack for raw resources and regularly feature among the world's top arms importers. Over the last six or more decades, the Gulf monarchies have spent at least $1.5 trillion on their militaries, which is almost as much as China has spent.[2] And the wider Middle East region has accounted for nearly a third of all arms imports in the past five years.[3]

Nevertheless, despite escalating spending on defence, Arab military forces and particularly those in the Gulf have long been considered subpar. Norvell De Atkine, a former US Army colonel with decades of experience working with and training Arab military forces, has argued that fundamentally different cultural approaches of Western and Arab military forces make Western training almost futile, and little more than an exercise in 'pounding square pegs into round holes'.[4] Anthony Cordesman, who has written more on this subject than anyone else, is excoriating about the failure of Gulf militaries to perform as they should, observing that procurement is often ruled by a desire for the 'glitter factor' rather than any sensible military rationale.[5] And Kenneth Pollack, one of the field's most prolific authors, has noted the inability of Arab states to develop capable militaries.[6] Surveying the forces of Egypt, Iraq, Jordan, Libya, Saudi Arabia and Syria, he found consistent and debilitating issues of poor tactical and operational leadership, information management, weapons handling and maintenance procedures that significantly undermined military effectiveness.

Pollack's last case study concerned operations *Desert Shield* and *Desert Storm* (1990–91), which presented quintessential examples of Arab military failures. Firstly, the Kuwaiti military provided the lowest of speedbumps for the invading Iraqis, albeit against overwhelming odds. Secondly, having spent immense sums on its own forces, Saudi Arabia still called for protection from over half a million foreign troops, mainly from the United States, despite deep-seated fears of domestic reactions to reliance on Western help.[7] Thirdly, the role of the expensively assembled Gulf forces in the liberation of Kuwait was operationally irrelevant.[8] Fourthly, Iraqi forces – even their battle-tested, well-funded, relatively well kitted-out and much-feared Republican Guard units – were overmatched with humiliating ease.

In the ensuing quarter of a century, despite some notable exceptions, not much changed. The post-Saddam Iraqi army, hollowed out by sectarian misrule by Nouri al-Maliki's Shia-led government, was terrified by a relatively small and ill-equipped group of Islamic State terrorists into fleeing key Sunni cities in 2014 and 2015. This was in spite of assiduous and expensive US-led efforts to train and equip the new Iraqi army. Saudi Arabia was forced into an ignominious stalemate and had to sue for peace in a 2009–10 border conflict with the Houthi militia in Yemen despite an astronomical advantage in relative spending on military forces.[9] Most conspicuously, in its war with Yemen that started in 2015 – admittedly the kind of asymmetrical conflict that is vexing even for highly capable forces such as the US military – Saudi Arabia has not achieved two of its core goals: to stop the Houthis from launching ballistic missiles into Saudi Arabia and to secure the Saudi border from Houthi incursions.

The curse of implicit protection

Explanations for why states fail to translate resources into military power often focus on the role of culture, institutions, foreign input and social structures. But for the Gulf monarchies, the prime factor is the implicit protection afforded by states like the US.

The US has played an increasingly hegemonic role in the Middle East since the Second World War. From the Truman Doctrine to the Carter Doctrine to the liberation of Kuwait to the Iraq War, US policy towards the Gulf became increasingly active and interventionist.[10] Today, with huge and critical US military commands and logistical bases in Bahrain, Kuwait, Qatar and the UAE from which the US conducts operations from Afghanistan to Somalia, the Gulf region remains a core element of the United States' overseas security architecture. While there are no legal defensive agreements in place requiring the US to defend Gulf states, the explicit guarantee to that effect made by Jimmy Carter in 1980 is bolstered by a record of swiftly rescuing Gulf states that have been attacked.[11] The US military does not pre-position brigades, fleets, multiple air wings and special-operations commands in the Gulf because it lacks space for them in the continental US; it does so to guard the status quo in the region from external aggression.

Thus, as with the resource curse, an overabundance of an apparent benefit brings with it a range of detrimental externalities. The pernicious central mechanism at play with both curses is the removal of pressures on leaders to make difficult choices. If leaders do not need to fashion effective domestic armed forces that can protect the state against external enemies because they judge that international allies provide sufficient guarantees of protection, they do not need to carefully match military means to political ends. States so advantaged can procure whatever they want – for prestige alone if they prefer.[12] This is surely why the Gulf monarchies have long purchased the best military aircraft available, but seldom invested seriously in minesweeping capabilities. Warplanes are as eye-catching as military technology gets, visually likening the state that flies them to the advanced powers that manufacture them. Minesweepers, defensive and slow, hardly set pulses racing. Yet maritime security is, justifiably, a strategic fixation of the Gulf monarchies' security establishments. They are critically dependent on seaways for almost all their imports and exports. And the monarchies credibly apprehend Iran as a menacing state in the Gulf that has long threatened to shut down the Strait of Hormuz. Yet the naval forces of the Gulf monarchies – ostensibly critical to securing their national interest – broadly remain under-prioritised and underperforming.

Indeed, it often seems that the monarchies believe in the protection-racket theory of procurement – that a $10bn purchase is more about securing political guarantees from potential adversaries than acquiring actual military capabilities. Qatar's purchase of three exquisitely complex fast jets from France, the UK and the US – something no ordinary procurement manager would ever countenance – seems the apogee of an approach intent on maximising political benefit, not military output.[13]

Several forces around the Arab world also engage in coup-proofing strategies to maximise regime security. They establish praetorian forces to, in effect, protect the regimes from their own regular armed forces. This can be seen in the genesis of the Saudi Arabian National Guard and Iraq's Republican Guard. Sometimes the elites actively undermine the effectiveness of their regular armed forces – for instance, by basing them far from the capital or by restricting ammunition supplies – lest they pose an internal threat. Promotion according to nepotism and loyalty over meritocracy further undercuts the effectiveness of regular forces while reducing the chances of a successful coup. Such calculations have long featured in the deployment and composition of military forces in the Arab world.

Exceptions that test the rule

The protection curse is not universal among Arab militaries. Elements of the Jordanian and Omani forces enjoy a markedly better reputation than many of their Arab counterparts. But with no significant deployments in recent decades, it is difficult to assess their current military effectiveness. In contrast, the 2015 Saudi- and UAE-led war in Yemen provides an up-to-date opportunity to judge the merit of their military forces. The UAE military evidenced a surprising ability to deploy its forces to achieve operational ends. In an especially impressive display, the UAE dispatched special-operations forces to work with local Yemenis to secure a landing zone in Aden for an unprecedented amphibious landing of armour in summer 2015.[14]

American forces were asked to help in this endeavour but refused, arguing that it was beyond Emirati capabilities. Rebuffed, the UAE acquired an ex-US Navy amphibious ship from an Australian company and successfully conducted the operation on its own, which in turn led to wider campaign successes that forced the Houthis out of Aden and its environs. Most NATO nations would have struggled to achieve these outcomes. Switching gears, Emirati forces then moved east, engaging in textbook counter-insurgency operations against al-Qaeda in the Arabian Peninsula (AQAP). While the ultimate success of such operations must be measured in years rather than months, initial signs are positive, as AQAP's grip on towns in eastern Yemen has weakened.

In the Yemen war, the Saudis have superficially improved their military performance. The logistical accomplishment of hosting, supplying and flying eight different fast-jet platforms (American F-15 and F-15C *Eagles*, and F/A-18 *Hornets*; British *Typhoon* Eurofighters and *Tornados*; French *Mirage* 2000s; and Russian *Sukhoi* 24s) from nine different countries (Bahrain, Egypt, Jordan, Kuwait, Morocco, Qatar, Saudi Arabia, Sudan and the UAE) is impressive and valuable. And the Royal Saudi Air Defense Forces are, together with their Emirati counterparts, the most experienced users of the US *Patriot* missile-defence system in the world.

The more substantive story, however, is less positive. One of the central motivating factors for Riyadh in launching the conflict was to eliminate the Houthis' ballistic-missile threat.[15] Continuing missile attacks in Saudi Arabia belie initial claims of success. Although Saudi Arabia and its coalition did manage to push the Houthis back from a position of dominance in the south and central parts of the country, it remains unclear whether Saudi Arabia can secure its long border against Houthi attacks. The Saudi-led air campaign, which sought to kill combatants who easily blended into civilian areas, is also regarded – particularly in the West – as a grim humanitarian and political disaster, causing far too much collateral damage compared to strategic gains.[16] Any such gains have come at an egregiously high cost in terms of accidental civilian deaths, civil-infrastructure destruction and

Saudi forces' loss of credibility. Indeed, the Houthis, a brutal tribe- and clan-based armed movement, have looked increasingly like victims rather than the co-belligerents that they are.

Escaping the protection curse

It is difficult to fathom how change occurs in multifaceted and complex policy environments. The challenges are magnified when dealing with closed and opaque political systems such as those in the Gulf. One theory is that profound shifts are instigated by 'focusing events' – traumatic moments that prompt a fundamental re-evaluation of an issue and galvanise decisive reactions from influential policy entrepreneurs. Shaped by their experience and policy inclinations, these individuals or groups then push through changes in the status quo necessary to transform policy and provide a solution to the newly understood problem.[17]

The monarchies in the Gulf are conducive to policy-entrepreneur scenarios that privilege elite leaders as change drivers or guardians of the status quo. Different leaders evidence idiosyncratic styles and policies that dictate national strategy. Mohammed bin Rashid Al Makhtoum in Dubai is known for economic statecraft. The former Qatari foreign minister Hamad bin Jassim bin Jaber Al Thani – 'a modern-day Metternich' according to the *New York Times* – was famous for cagey negotiation.[18] Iraqi president Saddam Hussein stood for brutal coercion, Oman's Sultan Qaboos bin Said for neutrality and mediation. The principal architect of the UAE's military strategy and the central policy entrepreneur is MbZ, the de facto ruler of the Emirates. He has developed a reputation as a military man who focuses above all on security matters and considers the UAE military as a key tool of state policy.[19]

Leaders across the Gulf were forced to profoundly recalibrate policies when Iraq invaded Kuwait in 1990 – a classic focusing event. Trumping the domestic political cost of being intimately associated with the US because of its support of Israel and being cast as a lackey of Washington was the existential fear of old-fashioned invasion. Emirati leaders, like all Gulf leaders, reacted accordingly and sought greater US interaction.

MbZ, who was soon to emerge as the key security-oriented decision-maker in the UAE according to leaked secret US diplomatic cables, saw another threat for which US protection would be less effective.[20] He feared the slow growth and influence of Islamist movements across the Middle East and in the UAE itself. Leaders in Abu Dhabi, the most powerful emirate, had since the 1980s struggled to curtail the influence of domestic Islamists who received patronage and protection from the leaders of other Emirati federal states.[21] Cables from the mid-1990s discussed MbZ's preoccupation with this threat even though, from the outside, there was little sign of how or why Islamists presented such a dire problem.[22] But with the Arab Spring, and the Muslim Brotherhood's success in Egypt in particular, came proof that Islamists' protestations of an apolitical vocation had been disingenuous. From MbZ's vantage, they had merely waited for their chance to emerge and challenge the old order for political power. An earlier motivating factor for MbZ – and a formative focusing event for all Emiratis – was Iran's forcible seizure of three Emirati islands in the Gulf days before the Emirates' independence from the United Kingdom in 1971.[23]

Energised by the need to prepare for eventualities in which US forces might not be sufficient or suitably inclined to help the UAE, just as departing British forces were of little use for preserving Emirati control of the three islands in 1971, MbZ rammed through the vexing policies required to build a capable military force. They involved the meaningful participation of foreign military personnel to a far greater degree than before. Foreign officers ran training colleges, established a more meritocratic officer-selection process and even took charge of core sections of the armed forces. Empowered as policy entrepreneurs, they slowly imposed Western procedures and standards on the Emirati military.[24] The most obvious example is that of Major-General Mike Hindmarsh, the former chief of the Australian Special Air Service Regiment, who remains the head of the UAE's elite Presidential Guard. For a foreigner to hold such a prestigious position is unique to the UAE in the contemporary Middle East.

MbZ also oversaw a manageable and military-led procurement programme. Compared to the scattershot approach to procurement elsewhere in the Gulf and wider Middle East, the sober and deliberate plans of the UAE make political as well as operational sense. Much of the UAE's military kit comes from either the US or France. This balance avoids UAE dependency on a single supplier without overcomplicating logistical or training chains.

Crucially, MbZ saw to it that Emirati forces were tested under fire, notably alongside NATO International Security Assistance Force troops in Afghanistan for over a decade. Emirati and Australian forces were the only non-NATO ones allowed to provide close-air support for ground troops in Afghanistan. More recently, Emirati special-operations forces worked alongside US counterparts in raids in Yemen. No other Arab state is trusted in this manner, indicating that at least niche elements of the UAE military have developed capabilities compatible with those of the US.[25]

Conditions loosely analogous to those that allowed the UAE to forge its own military capabilities have arisen in Saudi Arabia. Muhammad bin Salman Al Saud (MbS) is one of the most powerful Crown princes in Saudi history – like MbZ, acting far more like a king. MbS is likewise unquestionably in charge of security and defence portfolios. He has instigated multifarious changes across the sociopolitical spectrum in Saudi Arabia, and has the taboo-breaking will to drive through the difficult changes required to forge effective Saudi military power. He too sought to test Saudi forces by launching the war against the Houthis. The Saudi military's failure to achieve key operational goals, however, makes MbS's effort less successful than MbZ's. This very reality, of course, could end up being a focusing event that energises change.

Key differences remain. The UAE is, per capita, vastly richer than Saudi Arabia, and the latter faces a difficult economic environment in the medium term that may curtail wider military plans. Furthermore, MbZ was tightly focused on the military in the 1990s and early 2000s, whereas MbS's attention is, of necessity, dispersed across the social, economic, political and military spheres. MbS is also far younger and less experienced than MbZ, and his sometimes reckless and ruthless disposition may ultimately limit his writ. Nevertheless, the scale of operations led by the UAE and Saudi Arabia in Yemen remains unprecedented for Arab militaries. Given MbS's penchant for iconoclastic policies – such as legalising driving for women and potentially floating part of the national oil company – audacious military reform would not be surprising.

Be careful what you wish for

US relations with the Gulf monarchies have been rocky since the Arab Spring. What use, their leaders wondered, is their economically and politically expensive and multi-decade-long relationship with the US if, when a few riots break out, White House support is only conspicuous by its absence? Furthermore, Gulf royals profoundly misunderstood the pivot to Asia, reading it as if the US were starkly turning away from its allies in the Gulf when in fact it was not. Then, in 2015, the Joint Comprehensive Plan of Action – the Iran nuclear deal – which was loathed in most Arab capitals, seemed to confirm that the US and its Gulf allies were inexorably diverging in their strategic outlook. Donald Trump's courting of the monarchies placated them to a degree, but his transparently transactional diplomacy – encapsulated in the excruciating 2018 White House meeting between Trump and MbS during which the president read the Saudis' military procurement list from a whiteboard – was fleeting by design.

The last card that the US and other Western states have to play in the Middle East is the military one. Only the United States can fulfil its evolved strategic role in the region as a stabiliser, while the UK can provide key niche capabilities such as minesweeping capacity. But for decades Western countries prospered from outsized military contracts with Gulf monarchies, with the risks that the weapons would actually be used staying minimal. Now, however, a more independent and assertive mindset is emerging in Gulf capitals, alongside, in some cases, real signs of growing indigenous military capacity.[26] Add to these factors concerted efforts to develop local arms industries and a wide array of alternative suppliers for military kit, and Western leverage over Gulf Arab states' action appears to be declining.

* * *

Whether monarchies like the UAE and Saudi Arabia are evolving into unrestrainable power centres, heedless of Western states' interests or preferences, remains to be seen. Certainly their initiative and independence have increased in particular circumstances. In 2014, the UAE unilaterally launched airstrikes to help proxy forces in Libya at tremendous distance without requesting or requiring US assistance – a stunning logistical triumph that took observers by surprise.[27] Apparently ongoing Emirati support for its proxies and clients in Libya also challenges Western preferences as well as UN-backed arms embargoes.[28] In 2015, Western states could not dissuade Saudi Arabia and the UAE from undertaking a brutal conflict in Yemen of a magnitude and ambition that is unprecedented in the modern era of the Gulf monarchies.

Diplomatically, the 2017 blockade of Qatar by Bahrain, Egypt, Saudi Arabia and the UAE ranks as one of the most punitive such actions in modern history, and has enervated the Gulf Cooperation Council. That neither the US nor any other state could cajole Saudi Arabia and the UAE to roll back the blockade, despite its running contrary to the interests of key international allies, suggests that the monarchies have already become unreliable partners. Against this backdrop, Oman and Kuwait, both with new leaders taking over from revered predecessors who enjoyed genuine regional respect, are cautiously taking a neutral path.

Farther afield, the UAE has built a miniature version of the Chinese 'string of pearls' by establishing a range of military and supply bases in Eritrea, Somalia and the Arabian Sea. These are the UAE's first foreign military installations and were critical for Emirati operations in Yemen. To what extent the UAE retains these assets after it ceases major operations in Yemen and draws down forces there remains to be seen, though Abu Dhabi seems likely to preserve some strategic presence in the Horn of Africa.[29] Furthermore, the Qatar spat exacerbated internal instability in Somalia, with the capital, Mogadishu, supporting Qatar, and other semi-independent regions like Puntland supporting the UAE. Gulf competition is clearly affecting its near abroad as well as the Middle East itself.

Notes

1   For an overview of the different approaches to understanding military effectiveness, see Stephen Biddle, *Military Power: Explaining Victory and Defeat in Modern Battle* (Princeton, NJ: Princeton University Press, 2010), pp. 19–27, 192–4; Risa Brooks, 'Introduction', in Risa Brooks and Elizabeth Stanley (eds), *Creating Military Power: The Sources of Military*

Effectiveness (Stanford, CA: Stanford University Press, 2007), pp. 2–9; and Caitlin Talmadge, *The Dictator's Army: Battlefield Effectiveness in Authoritarian Regimes* (Ithaca, NY: Cornell University Press, 2015), pp. 238–44.

2   Stockholm International Peace Research Institute, SIPRI Military Expenditure Database, https://www.sipri.org/databases/milex.

3   *Ibid.*

4   Norville B. De Atkine, 'Western Influence on Arab Militaries: Pounding Square Pegs into Round Holes', *Middle East Review of International Affairs*, vol. 17, no. 1, Spring 2013, pp. 1–16; and Norville B. De Atkine, 'Why Arabs Lose Wars', *Middle East Quarterly*, vol. 6, no. 4, December 1999, pp. 17–27. See also Glenn P. Kuffel, 'The Gulf Cooperation Council's Peninsular Shield Force', US Naval War College, 2000, https://apps.dtic.mil/dtic/tr/fulltext/u2/a378521.pdf.

5   See Anthony H. Cordesman, *The Gulf Military Balance: The Conventional and Asymmetric Dimensions* (Lanham, MD: Rowman & Littlefield, 2014), p. 50.

6   See Kenneth M. Pollack, *Arabs at War: Military Effectiveness, 1948–1991* (Lincoln, NE: University of Nebraska Press, 2004), pp. 552–85; Kenneth M. Pollack, *Armies of Sand: The Past, Present and Future of Arab Military Effectiveness* (Oxford: Oxford University Press, 2019); and Kenneth M. Pollack and Michael Eisenstadt, 'Armies of Snow and Sand: The Impact of Soviet Military Doctrine on Arab Militaries', *Middle East Journal*, vol. 55, no. 4, Autumn 2001, pp. 570–6.

7   See Geoffrey F. Gresh, *Gulf Security and the US Military: Regime Survival and the Politics of Basing* (Stanford, CA: Stanford University Press, 2015), chapter six; and Charles A. Kupchan, *The Persian Gulf and the West: The Dilemmas of Security* (Abingdon: Routledge, 1987), chapter six.

8   While some cite the Battle of Khafji in 1991 during the Gulf War as an example of Gulf militaries fighting and contributing to the war efforts, the reality is less impressive. Though they may have fought with bravery, without Western support Gulf forces would have struggled badly in what was a minor skirmish. See James Titus, 'The Battle of Khafji: An Overview and Preliminary Analysis', College of Aerospace Doctrine, Research, and Education, Air University, 1996, https://apps.dtic.mil/sti/pdfs/ADA391794.pdf.

9   See Michael Horton, 'An Unwinnable War: The Houthis, Saudi Arabia and the Future of Yemen', *Jamestown Terrorism Monitor*, vol. 14, no. 22, 11 November 2016.

10 See Salim Yaqub, 'The United States and the Persian Gulf: 1941–Present', in Rosemary A. Kelanic and Charles L. Glaser (eds), *Crude Strategy: Rethinking the US Military Commitment to Defend Persian Gulf Oil* (Washington DC: Georgetown University Press, 2016).

11 See F. Gregory Gause III, *Oil Monarchies: Domestic and Security Challenges in the Arab Gulf States* (New York: Council on Foreign Relations, 1994), pp. 170–95.

12 See Cordesman, *The Gulf Military Balance*, p. 50.

13 See David B. Roberts and Emile Hokayem, 'Friends with Benefits:

The Gulf States and the Perpetual Quest for Alliances', The Century Foundation, 31 January 2018, https://tcf.org/content/report/friends-with-benefits/?agreed=1. For an example of the influence of politics on procurement, see Björn Hagelin and Peter Wallensteen, 'Understanding Swedish Military Expenditures', *Cooperation and Conflict*, vol. 27, no. 4, December 1992, pp. 415–41; and David B. Roberts, 'Securing the Qatari State', Arab Gulf States Institute in Washington, Issue Paper no. 7, 2017, https://agsiw.org/wp-content/uploads/2017/06/Roberts_Qatar_ONLINE.pdf.

14 See David B. Roberts and Emile Hokayem, 'The War in Yemen', *Survival*, vol. 58, no. 6, December 2016–January 2017, pp. 157–86.

15 CSIS updated missile data indicates the scale of ongoing missile strikes and interceptions. See 'Interactive: The Missile War in Yemen', Missile Defense Project, Center for Strategic and International Studies, 13 October 2016 (ongoing), https://missilethreat.csis.org/missile-war-yemen/.

16 See Daniel Byman, 'Yemen's Disastrous War', *Survival*, vol. 60, no. 5, October–November 2018, pp. 141–58; Michael Knights and Alexandre Mello, 'The Saudi–UAE War Effort in Yemen (Part 2): The Air Campaign', Washington Institute for Near East Policy, PolicyWatch 2,465, 11 August 2015, https://www.washingtoninstitute.org/policy-analysis/saudi-uae-war-effort-yemen-part-2-air-campaign; Ralph Shield, 'The Saudi Air War in Yemen: A Case for Coercive Success Through Battlefield Denial',

Journal of Strategic Studies, vol. 41, no. 3, April 2017, pp. 461–89; and Declan Walsh, 'The Tragedy of Saudi Arabia's War', *New York Times*, 26 October 2018, https://www.nytimes.com/interactive/2018/10/26/world/middleeast/saudi-arabia-war-yemen.html.

17 See David B. Roberts, 'Bucking the Trend: The UAE and the Development of Military Capabilities in the Arab World', *Security Studies*, vol. 29, no. 2, February 2020, pp. 301–34.

18 Robert F. Worth, 'Qatar, Playing All Sides, Is a Non Stop Mediator', *New York Times*, 9 July 2008, http://www.nytimes.com/2008/07/09/world/middleeast/09qatar.html.

19 See Ben Hubbard, *MBS: The Rise to Power of Mohammed Bin Salman* (London: William Collins, 2020); and Robert F. Worth, 'Mohammed Bin Zayed's Dark Vision of the Middle East's Future', *New York Times Magazine*, 2 January 2020, https://www.nytimes.com/2020/01/09/magazine/united-arab-emirates-mohammed-bin-zayed.html.

20 See 'Strong Words in Private from Mbz at Idex', 25 February 2009, released by WikiLeaks, Public Library of US Diplomacy, https://wikileaks.org/plusd/cables/09ABUDHABI193_a.html.

21 See David B. Roberts, 'Qatar and the UAE: Exploring Divergent Responses to the Arab Spring', *Middle East Journal*, vol. 71, no. 4, Autumn 2017, pp. 544–62; Lawrence Rubin, *Islam in the Balance: Ideational Threats in Arab Politics* (Stanford, CA: Stanford University Press, 2014), pp. 4–10; and Kristian Coates Ulrichsen, *The United Arab Emirates: Power,*

Politics and Policymaking (Abingdon: Routledge, 2016).

22 See 'UAE Minimizing Influence of Islamic Extremists', 10 November 2004, released by WikiLeaks, Public Library of US Diplomacy, https://wikileaks.org/plusd/cables/04ABUDHABI4061_a.html; 'Scenesetter for Homeland Security and Counterterrorism Advisor Visit to the UAE', 10 April 2006, released by WikiLeaks, Public Library of US Diplomacy, https://wikileaks.org/plusd/cables/06ABUDHABI1401_a.html; 'UAE Dismisses Academics with Presumed Islamist Leanings', 20 September 2007, released by WikiLeaks, Public Library of US Diplomacy, https://wikileaks.org/plusd/cables/07ABUDHABI1567_a.html; and 'Abu Dhabi Crown Prince Stresses Education in Countering Islamic Extremism', 20 May 2008, released by WikiLeaks, Public Library of US Diplomacy, https://wikileaks.org/plusd/cables/08ABUDHABI619_a.html.

23 Coming at a crucial moment of weakness for the UAE, this episode resonates to this day. In 2015, the UAE introduced an annual Martyrs' Day memorial on 30 November, primarily to mark the Emirati losses in Yemeni operations. Not coincidentally, the day also marks the death of Emirati soldier Salem Suhail bin Khamis, the first casualty of Iran's 1971 incursion.

24 See Athol Yates, 'Western Expatriates in the UAE Armed Forces, 1964–2015', *Journal of Arabian Studies*, vol. 6, no. 2, July 2016, pp. 182–200; C.J.B. Copeland, 'Defence Attaché United Arab Emirates Valedictory Report – 1998', Defence Section, Foreign and Commonwealth Office, August 1998; and Patrick Nixon, 'United Arab Emirates: Annual Review 1998', Middle East Department, Foreign and Commonwealth Office, December 1998.

25 See Roberts, 'Bucking the Trend'.

26 See Thomas Juneau, 'The UAE and the War in Yemen: From Surge to Recalibration', *Survival*, vol. 62, no. 4, August–September 2020, pp. 183–208.

27 See David Kirkpatrick and Eric Schmitt, 'Arab Nations Strike in Libya, Surprising U.S.', *New York Times*, 25 August 2014, https://www.nytimes.com/2014/08/26/world/africa/egypt-and-united-arab-emirates-said-to-have-secretly-carried-out-libya-airstrikes.html.

28 See Edith M. Lederer, 'Experts: Libya Rivals UAE, Russia, Turkey Violate UN Embargo', Associated Press, 9 September 2020, https://apnews.com/article/turkey-north-africa-qatar-libya-united-arab-emirates-20a2ad9c585f-40ec291585dbf8e9ed22.

29 See 'Why Are Gulf Countries So Interested in the Horn of Africa?', *The Economist*, 16 January 2019, https://www.economist.com/the-economist-explains/2019/01/16/why-are-gulf-countries-so-interested-in-the-horn-of-africa.

Did the US Intelligence Community Lose Iran?

Ray Takeyh

Claims of an American intelligence failure began even before the triumph of the Iranian Revolution. In November 1978, US president Jimmy Carter complained to his national-security team: 'I am not satisfied with the quality of our political intelligence.'[1] Stansfield Turner, the director of the CIA, followed up with a confession of his own: 'What we didn't forecast was that … a 78-year-old cleric who had been in exile for 15 years would be the catalyst that would bring these forces together, and that we would have one huge volcano – a truly national revolution.'[2] The theme of intelligence mishaps gained more traction after the mullahs' triumph, as Carter and his senior aides looked for someone to blame for the disaster in Iran. Today, it is widely accepted that the CIA missed the Islamist storm that swept away one of America's most consequential allies in the Middle East.

What constitutes an intelligence failure is a question that has often bedevilled historians. Revolutions are a rare historical phenomenon, whose force and ferocity confound all the actors, including those leading it. Four decades after the Iranian Revolution, it is time for a more dispassionate assessment of the intelligence community's performance. The record of the US intelligence services was hardly perfect, but they did get many things right. In the early 1970s, they noticed the rising discontent among key sectors of Iranian society and the importance of religion as an ideology of dissent. As the revolution unfolded, their assessments became sharper and their judgements shrewder.

Ray Takeyh is a Senior Fellow at the Council on Foreign Relations and the author of *The Last Shah: America, Iran, and the Fall of the Pahlavi Dynasty* (Yale University Press, 2021).

Survival | vol. 63 no. 2 | April–May 2021 | pp. 155–170   https://doi.org/10.1080/00396338.2021.1905999

The one thing that the intelligence services got wrong was the belief that the Iranian military was a cohesive force led by capable generals who could handle the situation should the shah falter. Saddled with this misjudgement, the services were too slow to appreciate how quickly the Pahlavi state would crumble. To be fair, even the revolutionaries shared this misapprehension, as they constantly feared the possibility of a coup.

Iran's anxious decade

The Iran of the 1970s was an unusual place, a seemingly dynamic country that no one wanted to live in. Oil money was pouring in, global dignitaries were coming to Tehran and luxury hotels were going up at record speed. And yet, a corrosive spirit of alienation was descending on the country. In many ways, the shah was a victim of his own success in creating a modern middle class and a vast student population. In a system that rewarded a lack of initiative, tolerated corruption and punished ingenuity, there was little room for those who believed in meritocracy. The members of this new urban middle class wanted participatory politics and a voice in their nation's affairs. But the shah was prepared to offer them only financial compensation, which proved fleeting as Iran's economic miracle became a mirage with the global recession of the mid-1970s lowering demand for oil.

Then came the exodus of the shah's best and brightest, even before the initial murmurs of the revolution. Michael Metrinko, one of the more astute political officers in the US Embassy, kept asking well-heeled Iranians why they were leaving the country, only to be told that Iran was an awful place to live.[3] The embassy estimated that in 1976 alone, 6,000 Iranians purchased houses in London. As the revolution unfolded, the best place to find the Pahlavi elite was in Tehran's airport lounge.

These trends were not lost on the intelligence services. In the mid-1970s, no one was suggesting that the shah would be overthrown, as this would have been an unreasonable claim. The shah's power was largely uncontested, and there was little organised opposition beyond some urban terrorist groups. Terrorism was the weapon of the weak, and the guerrillas were soon rounded up by the shah's secret police, the SAVAK. However, both the intelligence community and the embassy were ringing the alarm bells and reporting distressing trends that could portend trouble for the monarchy.

As early as 1973, the embassy noticed the alienation of the middle class, stressing that 'continued economic growth accompanied by broader education and more intimate contact with the West are producing more strident demands by a broad spectrum of Iranian society for political participation in the nation's political system'.[4] Two years later, the CIA station in Tehran echoed this, claiming that 'because all forms of self-expression, such as uncontrolled press, educational forums, and political discussion groups, have been banned or are under tight control, public discontent has no way to vent itself and appears to be building up'.[5] The US State Department's Bureau of Intelligence and Research (INR) picked up these themes, noting 'the professional middle class and those associated with higher education are often not satisfied despite their economic gains'.[6] In 1976, all these analyses were bound together in a National Intelligence Estimate (NIE) that starkly noted: 'The monarchy as an essential feature of Iranian experience is a concept which is likely to be destroyed eventually by more widespread education and by exposure to other political concepts, systems, and customs.'[7]

Meanwhile, beneath the veneer of westernisation, Iran was experiencing a religious revival. Religious books topped bestseller lists, and annual pilgrimages attracted a large segment of the public. Mosques were being built all over the country and a record number of students were entering seminaries. Men with beards and women wearing religious attire became common sights in the universities and even in government offices. Intellectuals such as Ali Shariati began to electrify Iran's lower- and middle-class youth by presenting religion as an ideology of rebellion. Shariati and many young intellectuals were moving beyond Marxism and seeking authenticity in their local culture. In their quest for a revolutionary creed, they sought to refashion the canons of Shi'ism as symbols of protest.

The clerical order featured its own prominent agitator. Ayatollah Ruhollah Khomeini, who had been exiled from Iran in 1964 because of his unbending hostility to the shah and his American patron, was thundering against all aspects of the monarch's rule. His many students and disciples in Iran were busy distributing cassette tapes of his lectures and copies of his published writings. The more esteemed ayatollahs may have kept their distance from all this, but the lower ranks of the clergy were attuned to Khomeini's message of defiance. Iran at the time had approximately 9,000 mosques. No political party could match this resilient national network.

Once more, the signs of religious revival were not missed by US officials. The embassy reported that the 'clergy remain disaffected and religion maintains a still considerable hold over the hearts and minds of the less educated Iranians'.[8] The idea that religion was the opioid of the masses was soon discarded, as another assessment stressed: 'Even the intelligentsia, who in other circumstances would be scornful of the religious establishment, now apparently perceive the religious leaders as sharing common grievances against the present system.'[9] The 1976 NIE also took up the influence of religion, warning: 'The clergy would probably not prefer the elimination of the monarchy but would be happy to see the present Shah go. For them a secular government would be as dangerous as the present Shah, but in the eyes of the religious leaders Mohammad Reza Pahlavi has betrayed an essential element of his role, protection of Islam.'[10]

This was the era in which Richard Nixon and Henry Kissinger had deputised Iran as the linchpin of America's strategy in the Persian Gulf. They ignored all the warnings and kept selling weapons to the shah even though his army could not use them and his economy could not afford them. An America burned by Vietnam was looking for allies and proxies that could patrol critical regions of the world on its behalf, and the shah seemed a safe bet.

Bad moon rising

Iran's problems were not lost on anyone. The shah understood that he had to revive the democratic institutions that he had spent decades hollowing out. He created a national political party whose membership was compulsory for all Iranians, but few took its slogans seriously. He established a variety of commissions to study national ills. And he launched a liberalisation programme that invited criticism of government policies but offered little change.

While this was going on, in summer 1974 the shah was diagnosed with cancer. The finding was kept secret; even his wife was not informed until three years later. The cancer's impact on the shah has been exaggerated. Too many historians have attributed his irresolution during the revolution to his disease. The fact is, the shah had always been an indecisive person who faded from the scene when hard decisions had to be made. Even the infamous 1953 coup that restored his rule was a plot concocted by his generals and the CIA, with limited participation by a monarch who quickly fled Iran when things got tough. The one immediate result of the cancer diagnosis was to focus his mind on succession, as he believed that his teenaged eldest son was not up to the task of managing a system of personalised dictatorship in which a single individual made all the essential decisions. He felt he had to put Iran's affairs in order before handing the country to the Crown prince.

The mid-1970s was an inauspicious time to tinker with the political order. The global recession lessened demand for Iran's oil, causing its production to dip from a high of six million barrels per day to 3.5m by 1976. Inflation reached 24%, and the agricultural sector could not keep up with population growth. Iran had to subsidise foodstuffs and rely on imports to meet its basic needs. The cities continued to lure massive numbers of people from the countryside, causing housing shortages and requiring the average family to spend up to 60% of its income on rents. There was little sign of urban planning, and shanty towns began to grow on the edges of cities.

In the mid-1970s, there were many strands of political opposition but minimal organisation. The riots that broke out in the shrine city of Qom in June 1975 should have served as a warning of the role that religion and Khomeini would play in the politics of Iran. On the anniversary of his expulsion from the country, seminary students took to the streets. The regime had to send troops to put down the riots, eventually arresting some 200 seminarians. The shah dismissed the demonstrations as 'stateless Red and black reactionaries shouting slogans'.[11] He would often return to the theme of Marxist–Islamist collaboration as he could never believe that the clerical order that had traditionally stood with Persian kings would conspire against him.

By 1976, the paradox of Iran would become the concern of a one-time governor of Georgia, with little knowledge of foreign affairs. The shockwaves of the Vietnam War and Watergate led the American people to entrust the presidency to a man who promised not to lie to them. Carter initially hoped to devote his presidency to traditional Cold War concerns: he wanted to transact arms-control agreements with the Soviet Union and complete the normalisation of relations with China that began under Nixon. To the extent that he thought about the Middle East, it was to broker peace between Israel and its Arab neighbours. As a committed Christian and a shrewd politician, Carter saw much promise in bringing peace to the Holy Land.

All the talk of human rights during the campaign did not mean that the new president was going to pressure the shah, who was already liberalising. The Democratic Party's left-wing members were vocal in their denunciations of right-wing dictatorships. The lesson of Vietnam was that such allies can do more harm than good. But Carter was always a pragmatist who blended idealism with practical concerns. Iran was an important American ally in a critical part of the world. As with Nixon, Carter needed Iran to keep an eye on the critical waterways of the Persian Gulf. The shah was as valuable to Carter as he had been to his predecessors.

The newly arrived Carter team received the usual assessments and reviews provided to all administrations when assuming power. The signs out of Iran were not unduly alarming. The CIA commissioned a study that looked ahead, called 'Iran in the 1980s'. One of the deficiencies of this type of intelligence product is that it usually assumes that the incumbent government will remain in power and then proceeds to assess how it will evolve and change. It would have taken a brave and remarkably prescient intelligence analyst to predict that Iran in the 1980s would be governed by an Islamist regime. The CIA report insisted that 'the Shah will be an active participant in Iranian life well into the 1980s'. It went on to conclude that 'we are, then, looking at evolution and not revolution and are identifying trends to watch, not results that can be predicated'.[12]

INR followed up with its own assessment – and would go on to provide many thoughtful analyses during the course of the revolution. Portions of its report have been used by a generation of historians to indict the intelligence community, especially its finding that, 'at age 57, in fine health, and protected by an elaborate security apparatus, the Shah has an excellent chance to rule for a dozen or more years, at which time he has indicated the Crown Prince would assume the throne'.[13] This is indeed a damning conclusion. The shah was not in good health but, as noted, was suffering from cancer. But there is more to the report. INR also observed that

> among the intelligentsia, the professional middle class, and the religious conservatives, dissatisfaction is felt over the Shah's arms purchases and over the effects of a 'top-down' program of modernization on traditional values and on what many think are Iran's most pressing needs. A substantial proportion tacitly withholds ultimate allegiance to the regime, following the age-old Shi'a doctrine of dissimulation in face of superior power.[14]

Both the CIA and INR reports seem to have provided assurances that were not warranted, but that is a retrospective judgement. It is curious that both agencies missed the shah's disease when he was being treated by French doctors who were regularly travelling to Iran. But in 1977, the notion that the shah was in charge despite signs of discontent was a reasonable judgement. The snapshot of Iran provided to the incoming Carter administration was basically on the mark. Senior administration officials had the option of assuring themselves that the shah was in control, or of considering ways to address the widespread alienation in Iran. Even if the latter had been their main concern, the shah had already launched a reform programme that he hoped would revive civic institutions and regenerate public confidence in his rule. To be complacent about Iran at this time was a legitimate reaction.

Iran revolts

The shah launched his ham-fisted liberalisation programme in 1977. Political activists were encouraged to speak out and the newspapers were urged to be more critical. Ever mindful of Western opinion, the shah invited representatives from Amnesty International and the International Commission of Jurists to inspect his prisons and see for themselves that torture had ended. Following their recommendations, he agreed to limit the use of military tribunals and try all political prisoners in civilian courts, where they would have access to their own lawyers.

It is difficult to say with certainty when a revolution really begins, but October 1977 was a significant month in Iran. A series of poetry readings at the Goethe Institute, a German cultural society in Tehran, became an unlikely harbinger of the impending revolution, as thousands came together to listen to poetry readings that soon turned to speeches demanding constitutional rule, the end of censorship and judicial reform. Even more significant were the religious gatherings to mourn Mostafa Khomeini, the ayatollah's son, who died on 23 October.

The outpouring of grief was cleverly exploited by Ruhollah Khomeini and his disciples to enhance his own standing. Khomeini had been away from Iran for 13 years, and before this event no one inside the country was sure of his popularity. Soon, false claims were put forward that Mostafa had been murdered by the shah's secret police, whereas in reality he had died of heart failure. In the aftermath of his son's death, Khomeini came to be seen as a man who had sacrificed dearly for his commitment to principle: first he had been torn away from his homeland, and now the regime had killed his son.

The Shia ritual calendar is ideal for political manipulation given its many commemorative occasions. Roughly 100 days a year can be set aside for some type of religious event, and there is a custom to mourn the dead 40 days after their passing. As the revolution gained traction, all such episodes became platforms for denouncing the regime. Mostafa's 40-day remembrance ceremonies were held throughout the country and drew a large audience. These ceremonies should have provided an indication of Khomeini's continued appeal despite his 13-year absence from Iran.

At every step of the way, Khomeini benefited from his opponents' missteps, and no one did more to empower him than the shah. One of the shah's favourite tactics was to use the state media to attack his opponents. On 7 January 1978, the newspaper *Ettela'at* carried a scurrilous attack on Khomeini's character and background. In response, the country exploded with demonstrations engulfing all the major cities. More important, clerical elders were forced to come to Khomeini's defence and even accede to his authority. Young seminarians stood outside the homes of senior ayatollahs, calling on them to act and shaming them into supporting one of their own. They all issued statements defending Khomeini and denouncing the monarchy.

All this did not escape the notice of US intelligence services. INR reported:

> The recent incidents of violence in Iran are the most serious of their kind in a decade. Though they are not an immediate threat to the Shah's regime, they may have put his traditionalist Islamic opponents in their strongest position since 1963. If he crushes the dissidents, he will damage Iran's relations with the US; if he does not, they will be encouraged to step up their actions against him. So far, the shah has demonstrated considerable uncertainty about how to face the challenge.[15]

The report did not get Iran wrong, but did misapprehend Carter's reaction. Despite his self-professed regard for human rights, his administration stood firmly behind the shah.

All revolutions ebb and flow. At the start of summer 1978 there was hope that perhaps the crisis had passed. The cycle of protests had simmered down and the attempt in June to commemorate Khomeini's expulsion had largely fizzled. Iranian liberals appeared intrigued by the shah's reformist moves. Demonstrations still occurred in various cities, but the protest movement seemed to have stalled. At the palace, the shah and his coterie still thought liberalisation would succeed. The monarch spoke with unusual confidence in insisting: 'Nobody can overthrow me. I have the support of 700,000 troops, all the workers and most of the people. I have the power.'[16] In a more discreet move, the shah began negotiating with moderate elements of the opposition such as Ayatollah Mohammad Kazem Shariatmadari and Mehdi Bazargan, the head of the Freedom Movement. The talks seemed to be going well as both parties were interested in crafting a new national compact that preserved the monarchy but imposed constitutional limits on its powers.

The nature of events in Iran led Stansfield Turner, the director of the CIA, to commission an NIE, the most prized and comprehensive of the agency's assessments, which takes months to develop. A number of background studies and papers were written, but ultimately, given how fast events were moving, Turner decided to shelve the NIE. Many of the studies compiled for the report have remained classified, but a few documents have surfaced and duly been used by the agency's critics to castigate it.

One report in particular has caught the eye of historians. The report is titled 'Iran after the Shah' and is dated August 1978. Its preface includes the much-touted phrase: 'Iran is not in a revolutionary or even a "pre-revolutionary" situation.'[17] It is important to note, however, that this report was an updated version of the one completed in August 1977. The phrase in question seems to have been retained from the previous report. This was not the agency's final judgement or product, but one of many papers that analysts wrote as they compiled the background material for the NIE.

Even if we take the report at face value, it is doubtful that anyone would have categorically said in summer 1978 that the monarchy would collapse. As we have seen, at that time, the shah seemed to have reasserted control over the country. Key opposition figures were negotiating with the palace. Khomeini and the radicals seemed isolated as they could not muster sufficient street muscle to disrupt the talks. It would have been reasonable at that time to conclude that the shah's liberalisation strategy was working. He was skilfully using both carrots and sticks. His army was formidable, and the opposition seemed fragmented. The judgement that Iran was not even in a 'pre-revolutionary stage' was certainly imprudent, but the notion that the monarchy could survive the latest crisis was not indefensible.

Moreover, by focusing on this one document, historians have neglected other reports that were written at the same time. One draft of the NIE offered important forewarnings: 'The period up to mid-1979 is likely to prove critical in determining the ability of the Shah to preserve the powers of the Pahlavi dynasty and Iran's existing political system in even a weakened form functioning as they have in the past.'[18] In a more pointed passage, the draft report took a cautionary view of the shah's liberalisation plan. 'Even sweeping concessions will not ensure continued calm,' it says, 'for there is an almost universal tendency among Iranians, and certainly among the political and religious opposition, to interpret any concession as a sign of weakness that should be exploited rather than as a positive element of a political settlement.'[19]

In the end, the agency decided to shelve the product. In a memorandum, Turner criticised the report for 'the almost totally non-quantitative nature of the discussion' and 'the tone of categorical pronouncements rather than comparison and evaluation of pros and cons'.[20] In an unusual move, it was decided that the State Department's INR would take over and formulate a report that took into consideration the judgement of the entire intelligence community.

Farewell to the shah

Acts of terrorism can change the trajectory of history. The burning of the Rex Cinema was one such event. Khomeini and the militants wanted a spectacular act of violence to galvanise the population and derail the talks between the shah and leading oppositionists. On 19 August 1978, the doors of the Rex Cinema in Abadan, which was packed with people, were barred and a fire deliberately lit. It took the fire department more than an hour to respond to the emergency, by which time more than 400 people had died. This was the most egregious act of arson in Iran's modern history – meticulously planned and designed to provoke national outrage. The subsequent investigation revealed the perpetrators to have been Islamists.

The bewildered Pahlavi state, however, found itself blamed for the tragedy. The palace issued its condemnations, but no one from the royal family went to Abadan to mourn the victims. Khomeini and his aides cleverly insisted that the shah's secret police were responsible, a charge that stuck. The Rex Cinema fire was to completely overshadow the shah's promises of liberalisation. The sense of outrage transformed the protest movement. Up to this point, only hardcore opponents of the shah had participated in the demonstrations. Now, many fence-sitters began tilting toward the opposition. The size of the marches grew by thousands, and the talks between the shah and the moderate opposition faltered. The shah now had a full-scale popular revolt on his hands.

By autumn 1978, things were falling apart in Iran. Demonstrations engulfed the streets and strikes brought the economy to a standstill. The shah seemed paralysed by indecision. He deployed his army to the streets but avoided bloodshed. He loosened censorship laws and then complained about poor press coverage. He persisted with his liberalisation policy at a time when the street dictated the course of events. He appointed a succession of prime ministers who seemed as bewildered as the monarch they served.

All the while, the opposition was lining up behind Khomeini, drowning out moderate voices.

In Washington, the mayhem in Iran finally forced Carter and his aides to focus closely on that country. Soon, the administration fractured. The patrician secretary of state, Cyrus Vance, pressed for a coalition government with the shah and his opponents sharing power. Zbigniew Brzezinski, the national security advisor, favoured a crackdown. Carter often sided with Brzezinski and grew frustrated with the pleadings of his chief diplomat. They all looked to the intelligence community for an affirmation of their perspective.

In the latter stages of the revolution, the intelligence community made three key judgements. It began to appreciate that the shah was not able to handle the situation. It rejected the notion of a coalition government that had gained popularity in the State Department. But it did not discount the idea of a military takeover, even without the shah. The available record does not indicate that the intelligence community assessed the viability of a crackdown, suggesting it simply assumed that the armed forces could discharge that task if necessary. This key misjudgement led Carter and Brzezinski to believe that they had more time than they actually did, and that an iron-fist strategy remained a possibility.

In autumn 1978, the State Department's INR was tasked with crafting an assessment that reflected the judgement of the entire intelligence community. The report, produced in late September, stated that there was a question 'of [the shah's] ability to survive in power over the next 18 to 24 months'.[21] In a separate paper reflecting just its own views, INR was even starker, observing that the shah's 'reversion to the moods of depression and vacillation he displayed in the early 1950s make it doubtful that he can move to salvage what remains of national unity, unless others intervene on his behalf'.[22] Even this report has to be considered optimistic as it was unclear who could intervene on behalf of an absolute monarch who had lost his footing.

A month later, the CIA followed up with its own assessment. The intelligence community showed little confidence that the shah could handle the situation, through either the use of force or a negotiated solution. The

CIA noted that 'military rule according to the Shah, would only bring more bloodshed and would not be a long-lived solution'.[23] But it is unclear whether the agency concurred with the shah's perspective. This left unanswered the question of whether the shah's generals could restore order. As for a negotiated solution, 'if Khomeini continues to refuse to go along, the Shah would persist in his effort to isolate the religious extremists and work with the moderate opposition. Prospects for success of efforts to isolate Khomeini are dim, however.'[24] For Washington, the shah had become the problem.

The monarch's last act was to appoint Shapour Bakhtiar as prime minister. Bakhtiar was a rarity in Iran, a liberal with guts. A former member of Mohammad Mossadegh's cabinet and a leading member of the National Front party, he was the Iranian that the White House hoped would salvage the situation. By this time, everyone was eager for the shah to leave. The new premier did not think he could save Iran with an indecisive monarch on the

Bakhtiar was a liberal with guts

scene. Vance, too, believed that the shah's presence was an obstacle to creating a power-sharing arrangement between the army and the opposition. Brzezinski felt that the shah's vacillation was hamstringing the military, and that once he was gone, Bakhtiar and the generals could restore order. In the end, the person most eager for the shah to leave was the monarch himself. On 16 January 1979, Mohammad Reza Pahlavi left Iran for the last time.

The departure of the shah failed to calm the situation. Khomeini returned from exile determined to put an end to the monarchical order. Paradoxically, the warring camps in Washington were only fortified in their views. Vance and the State Department continued to believe that it was possible to negotiate with the opposition. On this point, the intelligence community was firm. Turner stressed in his report: 'I emphasize that we have seen no indication of willingness to compromise on … [Khomeini's] part and that optimism that an arrangement might be worked out [is] unjustified.'[25] INR similarly reported that 'Khomeini is likely to continue to ignore entreaties from lesser religious leaders and moderate politicians that steps be taken to prevent the disintegration of the Iranian polity.'[26] In championing a negotiated solution, Vance chose to ignore his own analysts.

The intelligence community failed to account for the disintegration of the Iranian armed forces. There is no indication that American analysts appreciated that the shah's generals were as tentative as the monarch himself. Carter and Brzezinski never lost confidence in the military, and assumed that, free of the shah's vacillations, the generals could restore order. The administration dispatched General Robert Huyser to Iran in January to ready the generals for a military takeover. All this came to naught on 11 February, when the armed forces declared their neutrality. Bakhtiar fled the country. Khomeini established the Islamic Republic that would go on to haunt America and its allies for the next four decades.

*   *   *

Allegations of US intelligence failures in the run-up to the Iranian Revolution should not ignore the fact that Carter and his aides frequently ignored the judgements of their own spy agencies. They had views of their own, and those views were seldom altered by countervailing assessments. Vance never lost hope in a compromise with Khomeini even though both the CIA and INR rejected that possibility. Carter and Brzezinski were on slightly firmer ground in believing that an iron-fist strategy could work, because the intelligence community did not disabuse them of that notion. Had they done so, would these two very confident policymakers have heeded their warnings? Most likely, Carter would still have dispatched Huyser to Tehran in hope of keeping the military intact and ready for action.

The intelligence community is often asked to do the impossible – to predict the future. When it falters, it is castigated as incompetent. Indeed, it has proven a convenient punching bag for politicians of all stripes. The fact that the most esteemed academics and journalists in Iran failed to predict the revolution has not provoked a proportionate share of condemnations. The record of the US intelligence services was not perfect, but nor was it one of incompetence. The CIA got many things right, and some things wrong. Revolution is a phenomenon that is essentially impossible to predict and difficult to understand as it rapidly unfolds. In the end, America's intelligence agencies did a reasonable job in an impossible situation.

Notes

1   Chris Whipple, *The Spymasters: How the CIA Directors Shaped History and the Future* (New York: Scribner, 2020), p. 100.

2   Quoted in 'CIA Inaccurate on Iran, Director Concedes', *Los Angeles Times*, 5 February 1979.

3   See Michael Metrinko, oral history transcript, Oral History Archives, Foundation of Iranian Studies, 14 June 1988, p. 55.

4   US Department of State, Office of the Historian, *Foreign Relations of the United States 1969–1976*, vol. 27: *Iran; Iraq, 1973–1976* (Washington DC: United States Government Printing Office, 2012), p. 4.

5   *Ibid.*, p. 344.

6   *Ibid.*, p. 438.

7   *Ibid.*, p. 487.

8   *Ibid.*, p. 5.

9   *Ibid.*, p. 532.

10 *Ibid.*, p. 487.

11 Eric Pace, 'Iranian Riots Reported as Militants Fight Changes', *New York Times*, 11 June 1975.

12 CIA, 'Iran in the 1980s', August 1977, available from the CIA Reading Room, https://www.cia.gov/library/reading-room/docs/Iran in the 1980s.

13 US Department of State, Bureau of Intelligence and Research, 'The Future of Iran: Implications for the US', Report No. 704, 28 January 1977, p. 1.

14 *Ibid.*, p. 3.

15 Michael Donovan, 'National Intelligence and the Iranian Revolution', *Intelligence and National Security*, Winter 1977, p. 144.

16 Barry Rubin, *Paved with Good Intentions: The American Experience and Iran* (New York: Penguin, 1980), p. 206.

17 CIA, 'Iran After the Shah', 31 August 1978, available from the CIA Reading Room, CIA-RDP80T00634A00900100001-6.

18 *Ibid.*

19 CIA, 'Draft of the NIE', September 1978, available from the CIA Reading Room, CIA-RDP80T00634A000900100002-7.

20 Director of Central Intelligence, 'Memorandum for the Deputy Director for National Intelligence Foreign Assessment', 8 August 1978, available from the CIA Reading Room, CIA-RDP8155R003400050063-5, https://www.cia.gov/library/readingroom/docs/Memorandum for the Deputy Director for National Intelligence Foreign Assessment.

21 US Department of State, Bureau of Intelligence and Research, 'The Evolution of the U.S.–Iranian Relationship: A Brief Survey of U.S.–Iranian Relations, 1941–1979', 28 September 1979, available from the Digital National Security Archive, https://nsarchive.gwu.edu/digital-national-security-archive.

22 *Ibid.*

23 Director of National Foreign Assessment Center, 'Memorandum for Director of Central Intelligence', 6 November 1978, available from the CIA Reading Room, CIA-RDP81B00401R0020000120001-9.

24 *Ibid.*

25 CIA, 'Morning Meeting', 29 January 1979, available from the CIA Reading Room, CIA-RDP81B00493R000100070002-4.

26 *Ibid.*

Rebel with a Cause

Russell Crandall

Ten Days in Harlem: Fidel Castro and the Making of the 1960s
Simon Hall. London: Faber, 2020. £17.99. 276 pp.

Fidel Castro's first trip to New York was on honeymoon. Together with his new wife, Mirta Díaz-Balart, he spent almost three months in the Big Apple, staying in the leafy Upper West Side of Manhattan.[1] Castro used his extended stay to study English, read *Das Kapital* and, in a decidedly capitalist manner, motor around New York in a Lincoln convertible. Seduced by the city's steak dinners and gleaming skyscrapers, the charismatic Cuban thought about applying to study law at Columbia University. In the end, he decided to return to Cuba, where he earned his degree in 1950. For a time he worked as a lawyer with a special devotion to the downtrodden and the overlooked.

Inspired in no small part by fellow Cuban José Martí, known as the 'apostle of Cuban independence' against colonial Spain, Castro would soon commit himself to eradicating what he believed was the endemic corruption, humiliation and subjugation of Cuban society. In 1952, he threw his hat into the electoral ring, hoping to win a seat in Cuba's national assembly

Russell Crandall is a professor of American foreign policy and international politics at Davidson College in North Carolina, and a contributing editor to *Survival*. His latest book is *Drugs and Thugs: The History and Future of America's War on Drugs* (Yale University Press, 2020).

Survival | vol. 63 no. 2 | April–May 2021 | pp. 171–180   https://doi.org/10.1080/00396338.2021.1906002

This article was originally published with errors, which have now been corrected in the online version. Please see Correction (http://dx.doi.org/10.1080/00396338.2021.1912975)

as a member of the leftist Partido Ortodoxo. The election did not go ahead, however, because of a coup led by Fulgencio Batista, who suspended the voting along with the country's constitution.

In signature fashion, Castro took the matter into his own hands. On 26 July 1953, he launched an attack on the Moncada Barracks in the provincial city of Santiago de Cuba, hoping to spark a widespread anti-Batista insurrection. The scheme failed and Castro was sentenced to 15 years in prison. In 1955, Batista foolishly released his nemesis, who then made his way to Mexico to plot revenge, vowing 'one does not return, or if one does, it is with tyranny beheaded at our feet'.[2]

In November 1956, Castro made his move. Together with 80-odd *barbudos* (bearded ones), he set sail in the barely seaworthy *Granma* yacht to invade

Cuba. Against all odds, he succeeded. By January 1959, the Castro-led '26th of July Movement' (so called to commemorate the Moncada attack) had forced Batista into exile and taken power in Havana.

Fidelmania

Among the earliest goals of Castro's revolutionary regime was to tackle the endemic anti-black racism in Cuban society, the legacy of almost three centuries of Spanish colonial rule and slave trading (not abolished until 1886), which was largely focused on Cuba's sugar plantations. Now all races would be equal – at least in theory. Historians have found little evidence that Castro's policies delivered on their promises, which may have been an exercise in public relations. Even so, the first year or so after the revolution was a heady time for the anti-racism movement in Cuba, which attracted the admiration of black activists and political figures in nearby *yanqui-landia*, where the Jim Crow laws still held sway in much of the South. Adam Clayton Powell, Jr – one of just two African Americans serving in the US House of Representatives – arrived in Cuba in early 1959 and joined Castro at a massive rally in Havana, where the congressman sang the praises of El Comandante's new policies. Noted activist Julian Mayfield entreated his black American comrades to 'take a closer look at the Cuban Revolution', arguing that the revolution showed 'that it doesn't take decades of gentle persuasion to deal a death blow to white supremacy' (p. 82). Robert F. Williams, an organiser for the National Association for the Advancement of Colored People (NAACP), made two visits to Cuba in the mid-1960s and was taken aback by the absence of 'white only' signs and segregation in schools and public offices. When asked by American reporters whether Castro's Cuba was 'going red', he rejoined that if this were communism, he'd take it (p. 83).

Three months into his world-rattling revolution, Castro, seeking to gin up positive press coverage, paid an informal 11-day visit to the United States. There he was to meet with a mixed reception. President Dwight Eisenhower found the time to go golfing when Castro visited Washington DC on 19 April, but vice president Richard Nixon, a noted anti-communist, spent a couple of hours with the 'somewhat nervous and tense' Cuban leader (p. 72).

After the meeting, Nixon wrote a memo to Eisenhower, secretary of state Christian Herter and CIA director Allen Dulles in which he observed that Castro 'has those undefinable qualities which make him a leader of men', and that 'whatever we may think of him he is going to be a great factor in the development of Cuba and very possibly in Latin American affairs generally'. Nixon assessed that Castro was 'either incredibly naïve about Communism or under Communist discipline – my guess is the former'. For now, Nixon concluded, Washington had 'no choice but at least to try and orient him in the right direction' (p. 72).

Two days later, Castro, attired in his trademark olive-green fatigues, arrived in New York for four frenetic days, during which time his charisma and personal story proved irresistible to many Americans.[3] The Cuban leader walked the floor of the New York Stock Exchange, ate hot dogs and ice cream, lobbed peanuts to elephants at the Bronx Zoo, met black baseball legend Jackie Robinson and told tens of thousands of Cuban Americans in a Central Park speech that the revolution was 'Bread with Liberty' (p. 21).

Arthur Schlesinger, Jr, who would later play a role in the Kennedy administration's handling of the Cuban Missile Crisis, watched as Castro gave a 90-minute address to thousands of awed students and Bostonians at Harvard's football stadium on 25 April 1959. Schlesinger noted Castro's ability to connect with idealistic, liberal, middle-class students and citizens: 'The [Harvard] undergraduates saw in him, I think, the hipster who in the era of the Organization Man had joyfully defied the system, summoned a dozen good friends and overturned a government of wicked old men' (pp. 113–14).

Things fall apart

If April 1959 was a second US honeymoon for Castro, the relationship quickly soured. Fierce debates continue as to which side was responsible for the breakdown, though it is safe to say that there is enough blame to go around. The Cuban government's sweeping land reform, enacted in the middle of 1959, had targeted large estates – a move that unsurprisingly infuriated legions of American-based owners. One irate Texan fired off a letter to the White House demanding that Eisenhower take 'immediate action to avenge the barbaric thievery practiced by Fidel Castro' (p. 23).

More directly worrisome for US policymakers was Castro's closer ties with the Soviet Union. In February 1960, Castro inked a deal for 'oil, goods, and technical assistance for sugar' with Moscow. Havana then nationalised US oil refineries after they refused to refine Soviet crude. In retaliation, Eisenhower cut sugar quotas (p. 72).

With only a year left before their two-term tenure at the White House would be over, Eisenhower and Nixon elected to give up on Castro's revolutionary government, which itself had effectively done the same in reverse. Eisenhower's senior advisers convened classified meetings to, as Dulles put it, figure out if 'covert contingency planning to accomplish the fall of the Castro government might be in order' (p. 72).

British prime minister Harold Macmillan tried both empathy and admonishment in a letter to his American counterpart on 25 July 1960: 'We fully share your concern at the way in which Castro has allowed his country to become even more open to communist and Soviet influence', he wrote, conceding that a communist Cuba would represent an 'obvious menace'. But he also warned that if the US applied too much pressure, 'many Cubans who might otherwise have gradually drifted into opposition to Castro will instead be inclined to regard him – and themselves – as martyrs' (p. 71).

A better path forward, according to Macmillan, would simply be to 'let the yeast rise of its own accord'. It would also 'help if we had a rather clearer understanding of your purpose – the unseating of Castro and his replacement by a more suitable regime – but I am not very clear how you really mean to achieve this aim'. He finished by raising the still sensitive topic of London's failed 1956 gambit to remove Egypt's Gamal Abdel Nasser. 'We have been through it all ourselves and know the difficulties and dangers' (p. 71).

Soviet premier Nikita Khrushchev himself was explicit about what those dangers might be. He had initially been doubtful of Castro's bona fides, but by July 1960 Khrushchev was publicly threatening that if 'aggressive forces in the Pentagon' dared to launch an intervention against Cuba, then 'Soviet artillerymen' would back the Cuban nation 'with rocket fire' (p. 129).

Setting British caution and Soviet threats aside, Eisenhower eventually gave the green light for regime change. His plan was inherited and endorsed by his fresh-faced Democratic successor, John F. Kennedy, and was put into action in April 1961 in what would become known as the Bay of Pigs invasion. Before that happened, however, Castro visited New York one more time.

A not-so-United Nations

A sense of revolutionary change was very much in the air in September 1960 as the 15th UN General Assembly opened in New York City. The preceding months had been exceptionally tense in the aftermath of the diplomatic crisis that had arisen after the Soviets shot down an American U-2 spy plane on a 'photographic-reconnaissance mission' deep within Soviet territory on 1 May. Worse, pilot Francis Gary Powers had been taken captive – a development that forced Eisenhower to admit that the CIA had been running the covert mission for a good while.[4]

Khrushchev used the U-2 incident as proof of American perfidy, and turned up the heat on the divided city of Berlin, which he viewed as a 'fishbone in his throat' (p. 5). A 'brain drain' of Germans fleeing the German Democratic Republic (GDR) for the safety of West Berlin (and onward to other parts of the Western world) was for East German leaders not just a daily reminder of the West's relative wealth and success, but a threat to the

GDR's very survival. Meanwhile, the United States was on the verge of its own tectonic social change as the Civil Rights Movement gathered pace.

Joining the long list of heads of state, prime ministers and foreign ministers who were converging on New York in 1960 was Castro. As Leeds University historian Simon Hall explains in his *Ten Days in Harlem: Fidel Castro and the Making of the 1960s*, the Americans didn't exactly roll out the red carpet for this UN-sponsored guest. Indeed, the mood in New York was overtly hostile, although African-American activists still backed Castro for his stated goal of tackling racial inequality in Cuba (p. 1). US officials tasked with providing security for Castro's visit reckoned that 200,000 Americans would assassinate him 'if given half a chance' (p. 33). Staten Island residents burned the Cuban leader in effigy. To further spite the visiting dignitary, secretary of state Herter ordered that Castro not be allowed to venture anywhere off Manhattan Island. Said CBS journalist Robert Taber in the run-up to Castro's arrival: 'When he descends from the plane at the international airport in New York ... Fidel will enter an atmosphere more poisonous than that which the Cubans breathed in the hellish Havana of the days of Batista' (p. 30).

For their first night in the city, Castro and his sizeable Cuban delegation booked a block of rooms at the Shelburne Hotel on Lexington Avenue at a cost of $20 a night ($180 in today's money). In less than 24 hours, rumours had begun to circulate that the cigar-chomping (and ash-dropping) guests were roasting chickens in their suites. Hotel owner Edward Spatz, who had displayed an American flag over the building's entrance and refused to accept a Cuban bond to cover the security deposit ('It looked wrong'), lost all patience with Castro, declaring 'I hate him' (p. 35).

After other guests moaned about the unruly Cubans, Spatz banned the delegation from the hotel's cafeteria. The affronted Cubans duly avowed that they were done with Spatz's 'climate of hostility', and even suggested they might camp in Central Park. When a news reporter asked if they were worried about becoming the victims of crime in that iconic setting, Castro wondered aloud: 'How can there be thieves in this country? Don't the workers earn decent salaries? Aren't there salaries for everyone here?' (p. 46).

The next day, Castro and company switched to the Hotel Theresa at Seventh Avenue and 125th Street in Harlem – the 'unofficial capital of black

America' – which was technically still on Manhattan even if it was, in social and economic terms, light years away from the UN's Turtle Bay locale. From their new base at what some called the 'Waldorf of Harlem', the Cubans were introduced to an entirely different side of American society (p. 84).

Here the Cubans met with a markedly warmer reception than the one they had received in Midtown, as throngs of Harlemistas turned out to cheer for their hero. As the community-run *New York Citizen-Call* reported: 'To Harlem's oppressed ghetto dwellers, Castro was that bearded revolutionary who had thrown his nation's rascals out and who had then told white America to go to hell' (p. 52). Placards held by exuberant fans outside the hotel declared: 'Fidel is Welcome in Harlem Anytime! Cuba Practices Real Democracy. No Race Discrimination' and 'U.S. Jim Crows Fidel Just Like U.S. Jim Crows Us Negroes' (p. 76). One spectator, a 30-something Maya Angelou, would later recall 'hover[ing] with my friends on the edges of the crowd, enjoying the Spanish songs, the screams of "Viva Castro" and the sounds of conga drums being played nearby in the damp air' (p. 53).

Harlemistas turned out to cheer

Within hours, Castro received civil-rights activist Malcolm X, with whom he smoked cigars and discussed the problem of racism. Castro's take was that African Americans had 'more political consciousness, more vision than anyone else', while X praised the Cuban leader for 'denounc[ing] racial discrimination in Cuba', adding that 'usually when one sees a man whom the United States is against, there is something good in that man'. Castro rejoined that 'only the people in power in the United States are against him [X], not the masses' (p. 59).

Next to visit was Khrushchev, who, like Castro, had initially been met with a hostile reception when 'anti-communist longshoremen' shouted expletives at his ship, the *Baltika*, as it docked in the East River.[5] The Soviet premier was taken aback when he walked into the Theresa, recounting that the 'air was heavy and stale. Apparently the furniture and bedclothes had not been aired out sufficiently, and perhaps they were not, as we say, of the first degree of freshness – or even the second' (p. 67). The pair embraced in what was immediately labelled a 'bear hug' – a physical and metaphorical sign of communist solidarity.[6]

Their impromptu chat lasted less than a half hour, but the significance of the event was immense. Hall reminds us that, for Khrushchev, meeting his Cuban comrade, in the heart of black Harlem, in a nation rife with racial tensions, was a chance to stick it to the Americans in the midst of an international contest for 'hearts and minds' (p. 66).

Once again, fawning crowds gathered to greet the two leaders as they exited their meeting. Here is how *Izvestia* reporters painted the scene for Soviet readers:

> The head of a great state had cast aside the conventions of diplomatic etiquette and had come to Harlem to call on the national hero of Cuba, a man whom capitalist America treated without ceremony … Never before had anything like this happened in Harlem. (p. 69)

Speaking before the press, the Soviet premier heaped acclaim upon Castro, calling him a 'heroic man' who had fearlessly freed his country from 'the tyranny of Batista' and 'provided a better life for his people' (p. 70). Privately, however, Khrushchev observed that 'Castro is like a young horse that hasn't been broken' (p. 70).

The meeting was a major publicity coup for Castro. Eisenhower may have snubbed him the year before, but now the Soviet premier was coming to him. 'Thanks to the Cuban revolution,' Havana's *El Mundo* reported, 'our little country is the center of world attention today because it is expressing the desire and hopes of all small and weak countries' (p. 68).

Needless to say, US policymakers saw things differently. The White House was embarrassed and irritated by the leaders' meeting, and Eisenhower made it clear that the cold-shoulder approach was to continue. After speaking at the United Nations on 22 September, he hosted a lunch for 18 Latin American heads of state at the Waldorf Astoria. Castro was not invited.

Unmoved, Castro declared that 'we are not sad. We are going to take it easy. We wish them a good appetite.' Shrewdly, he hosted a rival lunch at the Theresa's ballroom, saying that he was 'honored to lunch with the poor and humble people of Harlem' (p. 107). The event was another propaganda coup for Havana. The regime-controlled *Revolución* newspaper reported that while 'the shark and the sardines [ate] together' at the Waldorf Astoria, their chief dined with 'negroes' in a slum (p. 107).

The General Assembly itself was no less eventful. After promising to be brief, Castro's address ran to four and a half hours – still a record. Khrushchev's own address was also markedly idiosyncratic, with the Soviet premier taking off his shoe and waving it 'menacingly' at speaker Lorenzo Sumulong of the Philippines, who had just mentioned Soviet machinations behind the Iron Curtain.[7]

*   *   *

Overall, Professor Hall's reasonable take is that Castro's time in New York elevated the Global South to become part of the Cold War agenda. Equally significant is that the fast relationship that developed between Castro and Khrushchev all but guaranteed a 'decisive and fateful rupture' between Washington and Havana (p. 2). The disastrous Bay of Pigs invasion would only tighten the Castro–Khrushchev bear hug.

Few at that time could have imagined how quickly the romance would evaporate, but the October 1962 Cuban Missile Crisis changed everything. Castro learned that his Soviet comrade had cut a deal with Kennedy behind his back, leaving the Cuban leader apoplectic. Even so, the military, economic and cultural ties between the Soviet Union and Cuba would persist until the end of the Cold War.

As for Castro's Harlem stay, Hall reveals that it wasn't just the anti-communists in the White House who grew weary of Castro. Some in Harlem also grew resentful at being, as they saw it, co-opted into the Cuban's ideological battles. Still, Hall declares Castro's visit a 'turning point' in both Cold War history and 'what we think of as "the Sixties"' (p. 2). Castro melded the 'rebelliousness of a James Dean' with social and political reforms that seemed to transcend orthodox communism, making him the 'ideal revolutionary for a generation that was changing against the drab consensus of the 1950s' (p. 118). The eminent Marxist historian Eric Hobsbawm similarly concluded years later that 'the Cuban Revolution had everything: romance, heroism in the mountains, ex-student leaders with the selfless generosity of youth – the eldest was barely past thirty – a jubilant people, in a tropical tourist paradise pulsing with rumba rhythms' (p. 114). Heady times indeed.

As the prodigious list of primary sources in Hall's bibliography indicates, the story of Castro's 1960 jaunt to Harlem has been amply documented, and little new ground is broken here. But Hall's storytelling helps bring this episode in Cold War history to life. It is a story that in some ways has yet to end: the US–Cuba antagonism on display for ten days in 1960 persists to this day. Even though Castro is long gone, the legacy of Harlem lives on.

Notes

[1] See Tony Perrottet, 'Fidel Castro's Secret Love Affair with NYC', BBC, 26 September 2019, http://www.bbc.com/travel/story/20190924-fidel-castros-secret-love-affair-with-nyc.

[2] Nick Miroff, 'New Fidel Castro Memoir Recalls Rebel's Life in Mexico', GlobalPost, 24 February 2012, https://www.pri.org/stories/2012-02-24/new-fidel-castro-memoir-recalls-rebel-s-life-mexico.

[3] See '60 Years Ago, "Fidelmania" Took New York City by Storm', NPR, 20 April 2019, https://www.npr.org/2019/04/20/715393922/60-years-ago-fidelmania-took-new-york-city-by-storm; and Evan Andrews, 'Fidel Castro's Wild New York Visit', History, 31 August 2018, https://www.history.com/news/fidel-castros-wild-new-york-visit-55-years-ago.

[4] See National Archives, 'U-2 Spy Plane Incident', https://www.eisenhowerlibrary.gov/research/online-documents/u-2-spy-plane-incident; Kateryna Oliynyk and Stuart Greer, 'Powers Down: The 60th Anniversary of the U-2 Spy Plane Incident', 1 May 2020, https://www.rferl.org/a/sixty-years-ago-the-soviet-union-shot-down-u-s-spy-plane/30585501.html; and Office of the Historian, 'U-2 Overflights and the Capture of Francis Gary Powers, 1960', https://history.state.gov/milestones/1953-1960/u2-incident.

[5] See Eric Pace, 'Recalling the Year of the Banging Shoe', *New York Times*, 5 December 1988, https://www.nytimes.com/1988/12/05/world/recalling-year-of-the-banging-shoe.html.

[6] See James G. Hershberg, 'New Russian Evidence on Soviet–Cuban Relations, 1960–61: When Nikita Met Fidel, the Bay of Pigs, and Assassination Plotting', Wilson Center, February 2019, https://www.wilsoncenter.org/publication/new-russian-evidence-soviet-cuban-relations-1960-61-when-nikita-met-fidel-the-bay-pigs.

[7] Pace, 'Recalling the Year of the Banging Shoe'.

Book Reviews

Environment and Resources
Jeffrey Mazo

Hope in Hell: A Decade to Confront the Climate Emergency
Jonathon Porritt. London: Simon & Schuster, 2020. £16.99.
384 pp.

Few contemporary observers have been warning of, and advocating solutions for, climate change for longer than Jonathon Porritt. As an early chair of what later became the United Kingdom's Green Party, director of Friends of the Earth for six years in the run-up to the Rio Earth Summit and a co-founder of the non-governmental Forum for the Future, he has been a prominent voice for sustainability and environmental issues for nearly half a century. *Hope in Hell* is his surprisingly optimistic and unsurprisingly eloquent prescription for deflecting the 'hell' of runaway warming. Refreshingly self-aware of his own ideological biases, assumptions and preferences, he advocates radical but necessary solutions – solutions that might have been less extreme if they had not been left until the last possible minute.

There has been some steady, incremental progress, Porritt concedes, but continued over the next decade, let alone the next three, 'means only one thing: *it will by then be too late*' (p. 304, emphasis original). He takes issue with those on both sides – catastrophists and denialists – who claim that it is already too late. The available solutions, which he examines in detail, fall into three areas: 'radical decarbonisation of the economy through technology', 'radical recarbonisation of the natural world' and 'radical political disruption through civil disobedience' (p. 10). The first two are, Porritt argues, conditional on the third. To the extent we know what must be done, we already know how to do it; the key is getting vested interests and politicians to agree on what must be done in

Survival | vol. 63 no. 2 | April–May 2021 | pp. 181–187   https://doi.org/10.1080/00396338.2021.1906003

the first place. With time running out, he concludes 'we have no alternative ... The case for civil disobedience is now overwhelming' (p. 304).

The economic and social mobilisation needed to confront the climate emergency is daunting, but Porritt makes it abundantly clear that the status quo is not an option. And the scale of mobilisation required is not unprecedented; it is less, in fact, than that drawn on by the UK or the United States in the Second World War. Despite the similarities in scope and scale, Porritt rejects the framing of emergency climate action as going on a war footing, deeming this tempting but counterproductive. He instead favours the 'Green New Deal' analogy to the 1930s and the Great Depression. This is ideologically driven and not entirely persuasive in terms of either tactics or accuracy, especially as a case can be made that it was mobilisation for war and not the New Deal that ended the Depression.

In his introduction, written in early April 2020, Porritt discusses how the COVID-19 pandemic, which drove climate activists off the streets and climate advocacy out of the news, is paradoxically another reason to be cheerful. Beyond the breathing space afforded by the drop in emissions due to lockdowns and the potential for a green recovery, the response to this acute crisis has demonstrated that the spirit of community, solidarity and empathy are still powerful forces. And the shock of COVID-19 may galvanise governments into more forward-looking responses to the chronic climate threat. The new US administration's renewed and reinvigorated approach to climate is an early sign that this hope may be justified.

**The Power of Deserts: Climate Change, the Middle East,
and the Promise of a Post-oil Era**
Dan Rabinowitz. Stanford, CA: Stanford University Press, 2020.
$14.00. 184 pp.

Only in the last few years has our understanding of the regional impacts of global warming, on the one hand, and the interaction of climate with social, economic and political conditions, on the other, advanced to the point that a book like *The Power of Deserts* is possible. In this short volume, Israeli sociologist and anthropologist Dan Rabinowitz examines how the Middle East and North Africa will be peculiarly affected by climate change, and how the region's unique qualities might offer great opportunities to its people in uncertain times.

Long-predicted impacts of climate change on human and national security have already begun to emerge in the Middle East and adjacent parts of Africa, earlier than anywhere else in the world. And this is only the start: projected temperature rises are double the global average (with even greater increases in the Gulf) and precipitation is likely to fall significantly, especially in the northern parts of the region. Cities in Iran, Saudi Arabia and the United Arab Emirates may be unfit for human habitation by 2060 due to changes in temperature and humidity.

What makes Rabinowitz's approach particularly valuable is his detailed dissection of the intra-regional variations both in projected climate change and in factors such as social and economic inequality, patterns of ethnicity, wealth, agriculture, infrastructure and political stability. The Middle East writ large comprises about 7% of the global population and accounts for about 8% of global greenhouse-gas emissions. But it contains the highest per capita emitting nation (Kuwait) and six of the top ten, along with the lowest (Sudan). The degree of inequality within regional states also varies significantly, and higher inequality means higher emissions, other things being equal.

The role of oil in the Middle East is particularly salient. Just as the region contains a disproportionate share of global hydrocarbons, it contains a disproportionate share of land suitable for large-scale solar-energy production. Countries in the region that do not rely on oil production are focusing on renewables, but Rabinowitz points out that the trend is extending to oil states such as Iraq and Iran. The six Gulf Cooperation Council (GCC) states may be late to the party but they too are beginning to change, with some more progressive than others. Yet these states are, according to the author, particularly suitable for large-scale solar projects by virtue not only of their abundant sunshine and otherwise unproductive land (traits they share with poorer countries in the Maghreb, for example) but also of their financial-liquidity and civil-infrastructure track records – both legacies of their petro-state status.

This raises an intriguing possibility. Rabinowitz argues that a switch by the GCC states from oil to solar could trigger an eclipse of fossil fuels worldwide. This requires that GCC leaders be convinced of the urgency of decarbonisation both domestically and globally. Regional-development strategies already pay at least lip service to this imperative, and to the need to diversify Middle Eastern domestic economies in general. Moreover, these states are among the most vulnerable to climate change, even if they are also well placed to adapt. Rabinowitz notes that it may be over-optimistic for GCC leaders to take a 'mammoth leap of faith' and abandon oil as a source of wealth (p. 115). Yet there are compelling reasons for them to do so that are in their own self-interest. As Rabinowitz puts it, 200 men could save the planet.

Climate Change and the Nation State: The Realist Case
Anatol Lieven. London: Allen Lane, 2020. £20.00. 240 pp.

This book is the extended cut of Anatol Lieven's insightful article 'Climate Change and the State: A Case for Environmental Realism' published in this journal last year (April–May 2020, pp. 7–26). As such, it covers the same key messages: in the context of a climate crisis that will soon underlie and overshadow all other issues of international relations, the West should shift from the expansion to the defence of liberal democracy and from civilisational to civic nationalism, concentrating on strengthening domestic systems and institutions, and taking the lead internationally on climate change. Only strong nation-states acting in their own self-interest can avert climate catastrophe, practically and politically, and the language and framing of national security are important tools to this end.

Much of *Climate Change and the Nation State* can be seen as the detailed report of which Lieven's article was a sort of executive summary, especially with regard to climate threats to states individually and conceptually (chapter two), and the evolving nature of nationalism (chapter three). But perhaps a third of the book presents additional arguments and insights into the evolving tensions and balance between unfettered capitalism and competing social-welfare models in the face of climate-change impacts and solutions. Lieven argues that 'Green New Deals' are essential not only to meet specific climate threats, but also to generate the kind of national unity that is essential for Western democracies to survive.

It is not clear how the author sees this working. Multiple policy packages have been floated under the Green New Deal label across various countries, and within the United States in particular. Many of the individual policies have been around for ages. Lieven appears to imply that, just as with the original New Deal in the 1930s, it is the overall label rather than the sum of the individual policies and programmes that will give the Green New Deal its unifying force. Yet he criticises the most formal version – introduced in the US Congress by progressive representatives in 2019 – as politically divisive and alienating. Most Democratic presidential candidates supported a Green New Deal during the 2020 campaign, but with the benefit of hindsight (the book was published in March 2020) we see that the winner, Joe Biden, ran on most of the policies but explicitly rejected the label.

Despite this quibble, Lieven's analysis of the political barriers (national and international) to effective climate action and the ways in which these can be overcome is astute. He has identified both a key dilemma and its solution: most of the impetus behind climate action so far has come from activists with transnational viewpoints and agendas, but this same perspective has limited their effectiveness. The answer, Lieven implies, is 'to think globally, act nationally' (p. xxii).

Oilcraft: The Myths of Scarcity and Security that Haunt U.S. Energy Policy
Robert Vitalis. Stanford, CA: Stanford University Press, 2020. $24.00. 240 pp.

In his provocative and engaging *Oilcraft*, Robert Vitalis takes on the 'myth' that 'oil as a lifeblood or weapon or prize is different or unique or exceptional' (p. 7). 'Popular and scholarly beliefs about oil-as-power', he argues, 'have no basis in fact' (p. 122). These beliefs are instead a pernicious form of magical thinking akin to witchcraft, rather than the statecraft they purport to inform, and their consequences include a perverse statecraft that justifies – in fact, requires – striking Devil's bargains with states such as Saudi Arabia.

Setting aside the fact that oil is quite literally the single most important source of power in today's world, there are some serious flaws in Vitalis's thesis. In arguing that the views of academics and public intellectuals are incorrect, he quotes policymakers who reject those views, while elsewhere claiming that these views are the basis of US policy. He conflates the simplistic slogans and throwaway lines of protesters and pundits with serious scholarly analysis, to the detriment of the latter. By adducing the views of academics and pundits with contrarian views, he in fact demonstrates that the purported consensus against which he rails does not really exist. In fact, it is not at all clear that anyone believes oil is *sui generis*, nor must it be for resource insecurity in general to be a real thing. Taken to the extreme, his argument requires an entirely implausible decoupling of economics and security across the board. In his detailed dissection of US–Saudi relations, Vitalis also reduces the complex international politics of the Middle East to simple transactional relationships, then claims that these relationships are based on unfounded or incorrect assumptions.

Oilcraft, then, is a jeremiad less against a particular framing than against multiple academic disciplines. As such, it requires much stronger evidence and analytical clarity than Vitalis provides. If his premises are right, he is asking us to throw out entire fields of study based on a handful of disputed data points. If they are wrong, there is no case to answer. This makes his often self-important tone all the more jarring.

It is always worth challenging the conventional wisdom and revisiting assumptions. But the conventional wisdom usually exists for good reason; the bar is high for those who want to overturn it, and Vitalis fails to reach that bar. The ultimate value of *Oilcraft* is that it offers scholars, analysts and policymakers concerned with resource scarcity, security and geopolitics an opportunity to reflect on their own assumptions, logic and conclusions. The net result, though, is more likely reinforcement than revolution.

A Question of Power: Electricity and the Wealth of Nations
Robert Bryce. New York: PublicAffairs, 2020. $28.00. 352 pp.

Fossil fuels may be the primary energy source globally, but it is electricity, converted from fossil fuels or other sources, that defines the modern world. It has transformed the lives of billions, and determined the fate of nations and peoples – yet billions more remain stuck in the dark. With global electricity demand likely to double between now and the late 2030s, how we choose to meet that demand will have profound implications for equality, human rights, women's rights and climate change.

This, in a nutshell, is Robert Bryce's argument in *A Question of Power*. He traces the history of rapid electrification in the United States as part of the New Deal (in 1930, only one in ten households were wired; in 1950, only one in ten were not) and contends that it helped secure America's superpower status after the Second World War. US electrical production grew another order of magnitude by 1970. Electricity freed women from household drudgery: 'the washing machine may be the single most important device that can help raise the status of women and girls' (p. 65).

Yet the average person on the planet today uses less electricity than the average American 50 years ago. Bryce offers a staggering detail: 3.3 billion people live in countries where the per capita electrical consumption is lower than that of his kitchen refrigerator. A billion of these use no electricity at all. The author calls these 3.3bn the 'Unplugged'. The 'Low-Watt' countries, with per capita consumption up to four times this refrigerator standard, comprise another 2.7bn. Above around 4,000 kilowatt-hours per year, the top of the Low-Watt range, increasing consumption no longer tracks increasing standards of living as measured by the Human Development Index.

Based on case studies in Iceland, India, Iraq, Lebanon, Puerto Rico and the United States, Bryce concludes that successful electricity grids, of whatever size, rely on three things: integrity (including a robust civil society and rule of law), capital and fuel. The first two are major barriers to development in the Unplugged and Low-Watt nations, while the latter is fraught in terms of its impact on global warming. Meanwhile, the information economy, cryptocurrencies, cannabis cultivation and, paradoxically, the quest for decarbonisation are all increasing electricity demand in the already High-Watt nations. Furthermore, in High-Watt nations electrical grids are still vulnerable to natural disasters, cyber and physical attacks, and even squirrels. Even here the integrity of supply is at risk.

How do we add the six terawatts of new generation capacity needed in the next 20 years, while at the same time bringing net carbon emissions down to near zero? Bryce argues that it is simply not possible to meet both goals with renewable electricity: 'Let me be clear about where I stand … If you are anti-carbon dioxide and antinuclear, you are pro-blackout' (p. 247). Even worse, he concludes that 'we will need all the available fuels around the world – coal, nuclear, oil, natural gas, hydro, solar, wind and geothermal – to meet the Terawatt Challenge' (p. 244). And he is cavalier about the environmental risks of nuclear and fossil fuels compared with his critiques of wind and solar energy. But his conclusion is based on the observation that poor governance and corruption are the greatest obstacles to new capacity. The capital is there; if the problem of integrity can be overcome, we do not need to compromise on the question of fuel. If it cannot, the Unplugged are likely to remain so anyway. *A Question of Power* is ultimately a pessimistic book, but leaves room for hope.

Middle East
Ray Takeyh

Black Wave: Saudi Arabia, Iran, and the Forty-year Rivalry
that Unraveled Culture, Religion, and Collective Memory
in the Middle East
Kim Ghattas. New York: Henry Holt and Co., 2020. $30.00.
400 pp.

Black Wave is an impressive and thoughtful account of the past four decades of Middle Eastern history. Author Kim Ghattas brings a reporter's eye and a poet's stylistic elegance to her narrative, which begins in 1979, the year that everything went wrong. This was the year in which the Iranian Revolution triumphed, Islamist insurgents laid siege to the Great Mosque in Mecca and the Soviet Union invaded Afghanistan. A generation of jihadists would go on to make a name for themselves expelling the Russian army, while triumphant mullahs waged war against the established order in the Middle East. Saudi rulers might have needed the help of French troops to reclaim the Great Mosque, but they soon reaffirmed their own commitment to Islam – a commitment that, together with Iran's Shia imperialism, created havoc in the Middle East, according to Ghattas. The events of 1979 continue to reverberate throughout the region.

Though it may be difficult to believe today, there was a time when Middle Eastern politics was the domain of secular politicians – when military officers, monarchs and intellectuals sought to define the future of the region. This was a time when coups were more common than invasions. Various ideologies were invoked, but most were poorly understood. Politics was about power, not refashioning societies. The defeat of Egyptian president Gamal Abdel Nasser, the most important of the Arab rulers, in the 1967 war against Israel is considered to have presaged the rise of Islamism as an alternative to pan-Arabism.

Historians and analysts are today revisiting the 1970s, a decade that has been neglected despite its significance. Placing the region's transformative moment squarely in 1979, Ghattas is unsparing toward Iranian revolutionary leader Ayatollah Ruhollah Khomeini, justifiably depicting him as a monster. The author also describes how Saudi rulers tried to compete with his message of defiance by subsidising Islamist actors of dubious character. This competition can be blamed for the broken politics of Lebanon, Iran, Iraq, Syria and even Saudi Arabia itself.

As important as the competition between Iran and Saudi Arabia may be, the principal security dilemma for the United States from 1990 to 2013 was Iraq. It was Saddam Hussein's invasions of Iran and Kuwait that brought American

Survival | vol. 63 no. 2 | April–May 2021 | pp. 188–193   https://doi.org/10.1080/00396338.2021.1906004

troops to the Middle East on a scale never seen before. The US invaded Iraq not because of the machinations of Iranian mullahs or Saudi monarchs, but because of its exaggerated fears of a tyrannical secular leader. This was a grave error. It can be argued that the Middle East has never recovered from that invasion. And then came the Arab Spring, whose dashed hopes have served as a reminder of how difficult it can be to liberalise the region's political culture.

Black Wave is a rewarding must-read for anyone who wants to better understand the turbulent politics of the Middle East, offering insightful vignettes and valuable lessons.

Oil Powers: A History of the U.S.–Saudi Alliance
Victor McFarland. New York: Columbia University Press, 2020.
£27.00/$35.00. 376 pp.

US ties with Saudi Arabia have long puzzled both historians and casual observers. There is little to unite these two nations: one is a vibrant democracy that bends toward secularism, the other a traditional monarchy that rests its legitimacy on an austere interpretation of Islam. Oil may have lubricated the alliance, and anti-communism may have provided its strategic rationale, but as the author of this impressive and important book cogently argues, the relationship ultimately serves the interests of each nation's elites. Yet both sides have denied the depth of the relationship.

The House of Saud has been rightly criticised for its profligacy, corruption and sponsorship of Islamist radicalism. Yet the monarchy is also responsible for creating the modern Saudi state, transforming vast areas of desert into urban centres with an intricate infrastructure and establishing a reliable welfare system. Riyadh fought the good fight during the Cold War, standing with the US through various crises and crusades. This risked attracting the ire of preachers and other domestic critics, who often decried the West and its 'decadent' ways. Saudi Arabia needed its relationship with the United States, but often denied that this was the case.

As Victor McFarland demonstrates, American elites have harboured similar concerns. They recognised that the retrogressive monarchy, which proscribed slavery only in the 1960s and insists on gender segregation, was distasteful to most Americans. But there was money to be made and communists to contain, so such sensibilities were put aside as a succession of US presidents and secretaries of state devoted themselves to 'managing' the Saudi–US relationship. While they have acknowledged the significant differences between the two countries, they have also emphasised that no ally is perfect. The depth of this imperfection was to become more evident after 9/11, when Saudi complicity in nurturing toxic Islamism was exposed. And yet the relationship has endured, because there is still oil to pump, and now Iranian mullahs to contain.

Saudi Arabia is today undergoing an important attempt to refashion its antiquated national compact as Crown Prince Muhammad bin Salman (often referred to as 'MBS') seeks to rein in subsidies and encourage Saudi employment. He has even looked to mend fences with Israel. Efforts by authoritarian rulers to reform their polities can be fraught with risk, and the elite understanding that has underpinned the US–Saudi alliance may now be facing its most consequential test.

When Reagan Sent In the Marines: The Invasion of Lebanon
Patrick J. Sloyan. New York: Thomas Dunne Books, 2019.
$29.99. 240 pp.

Lebanon has usually been thought of as the graveyard of empires, its politics too messy and its sectarian divisions too toxic to be sorted out by external powers. France established the country's territorial demarcations; Syria tried to impose order through occupation; and Israel attempted to refashion its politics. None of these efforts were successful as Lebanon proved too slippery for foreigners. Only Iran has had success in this troubled land, which it achieved by creating its own lethal auxiliary force in the form of Hizbullah. This may have helped to empower the long-neglected Shia majority, but even in this case the costs have outweighed the actual benefits.

Patrick Sloyan's focus in this polemical but interesting book is limited to Ronald Reagan's presidency. Reagan's adventurous secretary of state, Alexander Haig, made common cause with Israeli General Ariel Sharon not just to expel Yassir Arafat's Palestinian Liberation Organization (PLO) from Lebanon but to create a Christian rump state that would make peace with Israel and break with the Arab states. Lebanon's Christian politicians proved mendacious and unreliable, however. The Lebanese Civil War, which pitted the country's various sects against each other, was further inflamed by Israel's misguided invasion in 1982. The following year, Reagan decided to dispatch a contingent of marines to escort the PLO out of Lebanon and then presumably separate the country's feuding factions just as the country appeared to be coming apart.

Sloyan's account is filled with villains but very few heroes. Reagan is dismissed as ignorant; Haig as impetuous; Sharon as reckless; Lebanese Christians as duplicitous; and the Pentagon's top brass as feckless. The true heroes of this tragic tale were the marine commanders who were unsure of their mission and who warned of a tragedy that in retrospect seems all but inevitable. Both the US Embassy and the marine encampment at Beirut's international airport were vulnerable targets, and yet measures to ensure their safety did not materialise until it was too late. On 23 October 1983, a suicide bomber drove a truck loaded with explosives into the barracks, killing 241 American servicemen.

The evidence obtained at the time clearly implicated Tehran in the terrorist plot. Hizbullah carried out the attack, but Iran ordered it. This was not the Islamic Republic's first crime against America, and it would not be its last. The mullahs had already held US diplomats hostage for 444 days. This time, however, their intervention proved lethal. The Pentagon contemplated various retaliatory measures, but in the end opted to withdraw from Lebanon. Iran remained unrepentant, and would go on to attack other American targets and personnel, most importantly in Iraq two decades later. The lesson that America's adversaries in Tehran learned is that there are certain crimes, no matter how egregious, that they can get away with.

Syrian Requiem: The Civil War and Its Aftermath
Itamar Rabinovich and Carmit Valensi. Princeton, NJ: Princeton University Press, 2021. £25.00/$29.95. 288 pp.

Syrian Requiem is an important and impressive book. It is a primer for Syria's civil war, a conflict that needs a dispassionate reassessment. Today the war is effectively over, having been won by Bashar al-Assad. A despot with an unusual thirst for violence has proved an essential lesson of history: victory often goes to the merciless. But Assad is the master of a shell of a country, his dynasty dependent on unsavoury allies such as Russia and Iran, which have their own competing and at times conflicting agendas. Syria will remain divided, its population dispossessed, its refugees unclaimed and its economy ruined.

It all stared out well, with Syrians coming together to demand freedom and democracy. This was not a sectarian uprising in a nation that was thought to be divided along religious and ethnic lines. In the heady days of the Arab Spring, anything seemed possible. But this discounted Assad's cunning and cruelty. He unleashed his army on the protesters with a vengeance. The conflict soon took on a sectarian tinge as Assad's Alawite regime was joined by Christians and Druze minorities, as well as elements of the Sunni business class who had benefited from his largess. Islamists from across the region joined the fray, which reinforced the regime's narrative that it was resisting radical jihadists and not democratic activists. The fact that the Syrian Democratic Forces were initially relative moderates with a dream of an inclusive nation was forgotten in the fog of war. They stood little chance in a civil war that soon spiralled out of control.

In the end, Assad benefited not only from his own regime's inherit strengths but from the fragmentation of the opposition into an array of rebels and radicals pressing their own agendas. He was the beneficiary of steady support from both Iran and Russia. The Islamic Republic furnished Assad with technical support, military advisers and an expeditionary force that it cobbled together from its various militias. Russia's airpower proved just as decisive as its aircraft pummelled the opposition.

On the other side of the conflict, the Obama administration could not decide how to approach a war that it did not want but could not entirely ignore because of domestic political considerations. President Barack Obama insisted that Assad must go but failed to make plans to bring this about. He then drew red lines about the use of chemical weapons that he refused to enforce. When administrations are at a loss, they often take refuge in grand diplomatic conclaves, and secretary of state John Kerry duly shuttled between various capitals proposing power-sharing arrangements that no one took seriously. Would a more determined American intervention have turned the tide? It is impossible to answer this question with precision, but it seems clear that Washington would have needed to deploy a sizeable contingent of troops and make a prolonged commitment to the reconstruction of a shattered country to displace Assad. The American political class was unwilling to engage in such an enterprise after the war in Iraq.

Syrian Requiem is an indispensable book for anyone wishing to understand one of the most tragic civil wars in the Middle East – a war that will continue to shape the contours of the region.

Vision or Mirage: Saudi Arabia at the Crossroads
David Rundell. London: I.B. Tauris, 2021. £20.00. 336 pp.

Saudi Arabia is claiming its share of attention in both scholarly and journalistic circles. The attention may be unwelcome in Riyadh as it appears to be causing Americans to question the value of the alliance. The opacity of the Kingdom lends itself to misapprehensions on all sides. Is the Saudi state a reliable ally unwisely maligned by the progressive left? Or is it just another reactionary monarchy doomed to failure given its corruption, unwise foreign-policy choices and inability to reform its outdated national compact? The parallels with the erstwhile shah of Iran are too blatant to ignore.

Into this contested terrain steps a seasoned and thoughtful observer of the Kingdom, David Rundell. A former diplomat who spent decades in Saudi Arabia, Rundell approaches his subject without the hysteria that is too often present in other books. His mission is to explain the subtle ways of the monarchy and how it has overcome a variety of challenges. Each of the book's five sections focuses on a different issue. It is often forgotten that Saudi Arabia is a relatively new nation that has managed to flourish against all odds. Oil helped, but the Kingdom has had its share of prudent custodians too. Rundell assesses the country's complicated tribal structure and its ever-shifting caste of elites. Saudi Arabia is as much a nation of princes as uncompromising clerics, thoughtful technocrats and merchants. Religious orthodoxy and petrodollars papered over various mistakes, but as sources of legitimacy they are beginning to weaken.

The future of the Kingdom seems up for grabs as past verities and assumptions become questions. The transactional national compact, whereby the princely class purchased political quiescence, is coming to an end. The complexion of energy markets is changing, and although Saudi oil remains an essential commodity, it is losing its centrality to alternative energies and even nuclear power. The modern middle class wants a say in how it is governed, while the country's conservatives are growing alarmed at all the talk of change. Saudi Arabia's American ally seems less reliable as the newly installed Democratic administration raises questions about the Kingdom's enmities that the Trump White House chose to neglect. Opposition to Iran can no longer shield Saudi Arabia from criticism of its disastrous war in Yemen.

In the midst of all this stands a ruler who may be too controversial to serve as a steady guide for a nation undergoing important transformations. MBS may have made a splash at the outset of his rule with his embrace of Western development paradigms purchased from various high-priced consultancies, but he is no longer welcome in many Western capitals, including Washington, since the murder of dissident journalist Jamal Khashoggi. Given all these changes, a thoughtful and incisive assessment of the country is needed. Rundell has performed an important service by illuminating the murky corners of this unusual country.

United States

David C. Unger

Four Threats: The Recurring Crises of American Democracy
Suzanne Mettler and Robert C. Lieberman. New York: St.
Martin's Press, 2020. $28.99. 304 pp.

This timely and readable book by two leading US political scientists situates Donald Trump's presidency in the context of two and a quarter centuries of American history. It might seem comforting to imagine that before the most recent hyper-partisan decades, American politics was characterised by civil discourse and bipartisan adherence to democratic norms. Suzanne Mettler and Robert Lieberman remind us how often this was not the case.

The authors guide us through the venomous political warfare of the 1790s between the Federalist Party of John Adams and Alexander Hamilton, and the Democratic-Republican Party of Thomas Jefferson and James Madison; the violent nineteenth-century clashes over slavery and Reconstruction; the political and industrial battles ignited by the extreme wealth inequalities of the Gilded Age; and the incremental undermining of constitutional checks and balances by the steady growth of executive powers over the past century.

In this way, Mettler and Lieberman provide essential background for evaluating the dangers to democracy in the age of Trump. Their message is anything but a reassuring 'relax, this has happened before'. Instead, they argue that the Trump era was uniquely dangerous. They identify four key threats to democratic survival: polarised partisan politics; conflict over which categories of people are – or are not – legitimate members of the political community; severe and worsening economic inequality; and overreaching executive power. They contend that the greater number of these threats that are simultaneously in play, the graver the threat to the survival of American democracy. Today, they say, all four are present for the first time in American history. Partisan polarisation is intense, economic inequalities have returned to Gilded Age levels, and conflicts over immigration and race were deliberately stoked by a president wielding executive powers engorged by decades of constitutional overreach.

Mettler, who teaches at Cornell, and Lieberman, who teaches at Johns Hopkins, sometimes seem to load the argument, giving us a kind of Whig history in reverse, in which all the democracy-threatening trends in American history have built inexorably toward a cataclysmic Trumpian conclusion. Maybe they are right, but the Trump moment is just too recent to judge with scholarly objectivity. Their questionable conclusion aside, there is no disputing, especially after the 6 January mob assault on the US Capitol, that American democracy is today

Survival | vol. 63 no. 2 | April–May 2021 | pp. 194–202   https://doi.org/10.1080/00396338.2021.1906005

profoundly threatened. In the book's conclusion, Mettler and Lieberman call on readers to draw sobering lessons from the history they have recounted and to take proactive steps to extricate American democracy from its current crisis. Their chief recommendation is to develop a political culture of 'putting democracy first', by judging every candidacy, policy or structural reform according to whether it helps entrench or dilute democratic values such as 'free and fair elections, the rule of law, the legitimacy of competition and the integrity of rights' (pp. 253, 256).

That may be easier for people to agree on in principle than in practice. Americans across the political spectrum say they strongly believe in the importance of honest elections. The authors, writing before the 2020 US presidential election, make a strong case that the Republican Party has broken faith with that value by enacting discriminatory voter restrictions and redistricting maps. Still, in the wake of Trump's refusal to accept defeat in his re-election bid, millions of Republican voters sincerely believe (albeit without evidence) that the 2020 election was stolen. Under those conditions, how can Americans make free and fair elections a unifying, rather than a divisive, issue?

Tomorrow, the World: The Birth of U.S. Global Supremacy
Stephen Wertheim. Cambridge, MA: The Belknap Press of
Harvard University Press, 2020. £23.95/$29.95. 272 pp.

Plenty of revisionist histories have been written about the origins of the Cold War, but challenges to the conventional wisdom about the period immediately preceding it are relatively rare. Conventional wisdom holds that the US Senate's rejection of Woodrow Wilson's League of Nations ushered in two decades of myopic isolationism, during which America wallowed in the comforting but costly illusion that it could safely sit on the sidelines of world politics, even in an age of aggressive dictators. As the story goes, it took the fall of France, the Battle of Britain, the far-sighted interventionism of Franklin Roosevelt and, finally, the Japanese attack on Pearl Harbor to rudely awaken America to its real international situation and corresponding responsibilities.

In *Tomorrow, the World*, Stephen Wertheim tells a very different story, based mainly on new research into policy documents and debates from the Council on Foreign Relations in the early 1940s, many of which were produced in knowing coordination with Roosevelt's State Department. Rather than a debate between isolationism and internationalism, these materials portray a debate between two very different forms of internationalism. The older, more traditionally American form envisioned an idealist and exceptionalist United States leading the Old World away from its destructive pattern of great-power struggles for mastery toward a new, peaceful coexistence of sovereign equals (reminiscent of the rhetoric of Wilson's Fourteen Points). A newer, more aggressively realist form, also dating to Wilson, summoned the United States to use its economic and military power to impose a new American-based world order (a world 'made safe for democracy', as Wilson proclaimed). Two of the more prominent proponents of the older form were legal scholar Edwin Borchard and historian James Shotwell, although Shotwell later converted to the newer version.

By the early 1940s, the newer version of American internationalism became the dominant one. Its adherents pinned the label of isolationism onto the older form and thereby succeeded in foreclosing further debate. After Pearl Harbor, there was obviously no space for isolationism in mainstream American discourse. But, Wertheim argues, there were no real isolationists in that debate – just what he calls 'imaginary isolationists', imagined into history as handy foils for the arguments of the new-style interventionists before, during and after American entry into the Second World War.

Critics might counter that this is just an argument about semantics and that, from today's vantage point, the older version of internationalism can justly be called isolationism, with Wertheim himself doing the relabelling. But to accept that premise, we would have to label Woodrow Wilson as an isolationist, which he clearly was not. Critics might also accuse Wertheim of chronological sleight of hand by focusing on the documents and debates of the early 1940s rather than the 1930s, the decade in which the Nye Committee was established and the Neutrality Acts were passed. But while Wertheim focuses on evidence from the early 1940s, he also builds a historical argument reaching back to the Founding era to show that American exceptionalism always included robust international ambitions. Some might point out that if 'real isolationists' were to be found in the early 1940s, it would not be at the Council on Foreign Relations, an organisation founded to promote international engagement. What Wertheim did find, however, was an earlier strain of American internationalism that has almost been airbrushed, Kremlin-style, from conventional accounts of these years.

The book confines itself to these historical debates. But Wertheim, who is director of the Grand Strategy Program at the realist Quincy Institute for Responsible Statecraft, is presumably interested in illuminating more recent US foreign-policy choices as well, specifically Washington's fateful post-war strategy choice of global hegemony rather than the offshore balancing favoured by Britain during the nineteenth-century Pax Britannica. Offshore balancing is not isolationism, its advocates insist, but an overdue return to strategic solvency. It would also mark a return to a more traditional American version of internationalism, this book suggests.

States of Exception in American History
Gary Gerstle and Joel Isaac, eds. Chicago, IL: University of
Chicago Press, 2020. $30.00. 364 pp.

This collection of essays, edited by historians Gary Gerstle of the University of Cambridge and Joel Isaac of the University of Chicago, makes timely reading as America looks to repair its democracy from the constitutional ravages of the Trump era. This book is useful not just for gauging how far Trump may have strayed from the United States' professed legal norms, but also for situating the past four years in a longer-term historical perspective. Throughout the book, 'states of exception' are defined as situations in which formal constitutional guarantees are suspended or otherwise unavailable to all or part of the population. As several contributors remind us, Americans have lived through states of exception before: nationwide during the Civil War and the First World War; regionally for African Americans in the Jim Crow South and for residents of unincorporated colonial territories under the American flag; and selectively and arbitrarily for non-citizen resident aliens.

Most of the contributors are willing to concede that there can be situations that may require even the most rigorously constitutional and liberal regimes to resort to actions beyond their explicit constitutional authority. Unsurprisingly, then, the arguments of the twentieth-century German political theorist Carl Schmitt are key reference points for many of these essays. Schmitt's insistence that liberal-constitutional theories could provide no adequate answers for real-world emergencies was used to justify Nazi dictatorship. For the most part, the contributors reject Schmitt's conclusion that such emergencies require the illiberal exercise of absolute sovereign power by a Führer-like leader. Instead, most argue that there are both liberal and illiberal ways of taking on and laying aside emergency powers, as well as ways to condition the exercise of necessary powers that will leave liberal cultures and institutions intact so that, once a crisis is overcome, regular constitutional norms can be restored.

The contributors cite a variety of historical precedents. The Roman Republic, for example, provided for the temporary appointment of an official dictator to meet specific dangers. During the American Civil War, Abraham Lincoln suspended habeas corpus and then unilaterally proclaimed the emancipation of slaves in the Confederate states. During Reconstruction, federal military governments exercised power in defeated Southern states. More recently, the George W. Bush administration, until it was partially reined in by the Supreme Court, used the American naval base at Guantanamo Bay to operate a detention regime outside the Constitution. A less obvious example also explored in this volume is the century-long growth of a federal administrative state, built up through the delegation of many powers, which the Constitution had carefully vested in an electorally accountable legislature, into the hands of a vast and only indirectly accountable executive-branch bureaucracy.

The essays range widely. Some focus on the intellectual efforts of major American theorists who have grappled with problems of exception, such as John Dewey, Charles E. Merriam and Clinton Rossiter. Others creatively rework the concept of 'states of exception', or what Elisabeth S. Clemens calls 'spaces of exception', to shine new light on episodes that are more or less familiar. Mariah Zeisberg, for example, examines Frederick Douglass's impressive efforts to call into being a theory of the American Constitution that left no space for slavery, even in the face of the Dred Scott decision and the Fugitive Slave Law. Though not always easy reading, many of these essays are richly rewarding.

The Great Demographic Illusion: Majority, Minority, and the Expanding American Mainstream
Richard Alba. Princeton, NJ: Princeton University Press, 2020.
£25.00/$29.95. 336 pp.

The premise of this book is that conservative white Americans have become alarmed by what is really a statistical illusion. News media and politicians tell them that the US Census Bureau now predicts that the United States will become 'majority-minority' by 2040 – in other words, that their children and grandchildren will by then be minority-group members. The Census Bureau has in fact issued such predictions. But Richard Alba argues that these forecasts are distorted because they count the rapidly growing number of Americans with mixed-race backgrounds as 'minority'. This is a counting method generally favoured by African-American, Hispanic and other minority-advocacy organisations concerned that the size of minority communities would otherwise be understated when federal funds are apportioned. Ironically, this counting method also perpetuates the white-supremacist ideology of the old Jim Crow South, where 'one drop' of non-white blood was sufficient to categorise a person as non-white.

Alba's central argument is that the Census Bureau's categorisation system does not accurately reflect twenty-first-century American realities, which are characterised by rapidly growing numbers of children of mixed-race partnerships who identify in a variety of ways with their mixed ancestry. If we were to subtract or reallocate multiracial Americans (or at least those who identify with the majority element of their ancestry) from the bureau's count of minorities – as Alba believes we should – the timeline for a majority-minority America would be pushed back by decades, or might not arrive at all, since the categorisations by both individuals and society of mixed-race and non-mixed-race Americans are constantly changing, and since many of the people in question have not yet been born. Alba, a sociologist at the City University of New York, points to the historical examples of Italians, Jews and other ethnic groups who are now considered – and consider themselves – fully part of the white majority, but who, as recently as the early twentieth century, were considered outside the American ethnic mainstream.

Does the Census Bureau's count or non-count of mixed-race Americans matter as much as Alba thinks it does? Are conservative white people worried about an illusion, or a reality? Whatever categories the Census Bureau employs, conservative white Americans accurately perceive an increasingly diverse population, workforce and political leadership, one in which being white no longer guarantees the status and privileges it used to. Would this group not be just as anxious about an ethnically changing society if a different counting method pushed the majority-minority threshold back by a few decades? And might greater awareness of the rapid, recent growth in mixed-race families make them feel more threatened, rather than less?

After analysing the available demographic data, Alba explores some of the relevant theoretical literature. The two main strands of analysis he considers are 'race theory', with its historic model of white supremacy and rigid hierarchies separating and defining white and other races worldwide, and 'assimilation theory', which also posits hierarchies but with more subtle gradations and more fluid boundaries. Alba believes that race theory can explain some of the persistent barriers to social mixing and mobility faced by mixed-race Americans with one African-American parent, but that assimilation theory is a better fit for others, especially those who have one white parent and one who is Hispanic, Asian American or Native American. Here, he foresees something similar to the assimilation experience that transformed American perceptions of Jews, Italians and other European ethnic groups after the Second World War.

Similar, but not identical. Alba recognises two key differences. Firstly, postwar assimilation did not much change the perception of what 'mainstream' meant, just who was entitled to be considered part of it. Today, assimilation is viewed as a process of changing the nature of the mainstream, not just joining it. The second difference seems more challenging. The strong, prolonged economic expansion after the Second World War enabled what Alba describes as a non-zero-sum assimilation, in which the status gains of minority groups were not perceived as coming at the economic expense of traditional mainstream groups, who also made gains during these years. Under today's conditions of stagnant growth and limited mobility, this is not the case. Alba proposes instead what he calls 'zero-sum demographics', whereby traditional groups are ageing out of the labour force while younger (and often better-educated) people from today's expanding mixed-race and minority groups are stepping into middle- and upper-echelon positions in their place. In some technical sense this may not be zero-sum, but it may not appear that way to those who used to feel exclusively entitled to those positions by virtue of their whiteness.

The survey data on the ethnic and racial perceptions of mixed-race Americans, with which this book abounds, does not make clear the ethnic and racial perceptions of the traditionally defined white mainstream. A clearer picture might come from analysing exit polls and surveys of the 2020 presidential electorate.

Disrupt, Discredit, and Divide: How the New FBI Damages Democracy
Mike German. New York: The New Press, 2019. $27.99. 352 pp.

Mike German was a special agent for the FBI for 16 years. He then went to work for the Washington legislative office of the American Civil Liberties Union (ACLU). *In Disrupt, Discredit, and Divide*, he draws on his experiences in both jobs to portray the FBI as an underperforming, badly led counter-intelligence agency hobbled by racial, ethnic and ideological prejudices harking back to the J. Edgar Hoover era, which supposedly ended a half-century ago.

German contends that the bureau's recent directors, in particular Robert Mueller and James Comey, failed to deliver on repeated promises of promoting diversity in the ranks, increasing transparency and public accountability, and refocusing the FBI on professional law enforcement. He faults these two directors for letting post-9/11 presidents from both parties turn the bureau into a more politicised and less law-abiding federal police force. German portrays an FBI that devotes more energy to harassing its own whistle-blowers and citizens engaged in lawful political protests than to tracking down dangerous terrorists.

In the wake of the Watergate scandal, congressional investigators documented decades of FBI lawlessness. Yet the bureau has avoided the enactment of a strong legislative charter that could permit effective congressional oversight. Instead, the only check on FBI overreach comes from in-house Justice Department guidelines, which have been watered down by successive attorneys general, especially since 9/11. This has effectively left the FBI with the power to set and enforce its own rules. By German's account, neither Mueller nor Comey rose to this basic challenge.

German tells story after story of FBI officers harassed and driven from the ranks largely because they were naturalised citizens, Muslims, or members of racial or ethnic minorities, or because they filed whistle-blower complaints –

even when they did so through the authorised chain of command. We learn about these episodes from the former agents' viewpoint, meaning there may be other unreported factors in at least some of these cases. But cumulatively they reveal a disturbing pattern, one that conforms to similar stories of bureaucratic harassment in other US intelligence agencies, such as the CIA. This kind of profiling and harassment has deleterious consequences that reach beyond the individual injustices. Effective counter-intelligence and undercover work requires foreign-language skills, familiarity with other cultures and patient efforts to earn the trust of minority communities. Yet these were the very attributes that attracted profiling and harassment in German's case studies.

The author also recounts cases of people subjected to FBI surveillance, searches and armed raids as a result of peaceful protest activity on behalf of causes and groups the bureau does not politically approve of, such as an activist for the Council on American–Islamic Relations (CAIR); protesters against the Dakota Access Pipeline; and Midwestern labour and peace activists organising demonstrations near the 2008 Republican National Convention in Minneapolis–Saint Paul, Minnesota. Again, we read only the activists' side of these stories, but again a disturbing pattern emerges, this time of politicised policing and misallocated investigative resources. During the post-9/11 period German writes about, the FBI rated the supposed threat from 'ecological terrorism' as more pressing and dangerous than, say, that of white-supremacist violence or far-right terrorism.

A big part of the problem, German argues, is the FBI's over-reliance on 'radicalisation theory'. This theory holds that people go through stages of radicalisation, marked by a set of non-criminal activities that, the bureau believes, inexorably lead to criminal terrorism. The problem is the 'inexorably' part. Just because people who actually do become terrorists may have become more conspicuously religious or political along the way, does not mean that all people who become more conspicuously religious or political will eventually become terrorists. To assume that they will is to turn peaceful and legal religious and political activity into 'pre-crimes'. Furthermore, German contends, the FBI refuses to acknowledge that terrorists can be motivated by political grievances. Acknowledging this motivation does not 'legitimate' any terrorist acts so motivated, but does make would-be terrorists easier to find, deter or thwart before violent acts are committed. Effective undercover counter-intelligence requires picking up on subtle signs, not wielding a law-enforcement meat axe against constitutionally protected activities.

German calls on Congress to ban racial and ethnic profiling, and to exercise more effective oversight. He asks local law-enforcement agencies to think about withholding their participation from misdirected FBI Joint Terrorism Task Forces. He encourages ordinary citizens to pressure the FBI from below to reform its ways, by working through civil-society organisations, such as the ACLU, CAIR and the Electronic Frontier Foundation.

It will be up to the newly confirmed attorney general, Merrick Garland, to set and enforce tighter law-enforcement guidelines, and up to Congress to enact a clear legislative charter and effective whistle-blower protection. These were once bipartisan causes. There is no obvious reason why they cannot become so again.

Closing Argument

Is Putin Doomed to Run in 2024?

Nigel Gould-Davies

I

Russia's 2024 presidential election, though still three years away, now dominates the country's political landscape. Two things are already clear. Firstly, the election will take place in difficult conditions. Russia's economy is more stagnant, its politics more repressive and its relationship with the West more adversarial than at any time since President Vladimir Putin took office. Secondly, the 'administrative resources' of the Russian state can nonetheless manage and manipulate the election to deliver another handsome victory. But will Putin run? The answer reveals much about Russia, the political dynamics of the wider region, and the relative strengths and weaknesses of authoritarianism and democracy.

At first sight it seems likely that Putin will seek an assured re-election. He has won all four presidential elections he has contested. His last victory in 2018, with 76.7% of the vote according to official results, was the most emphatic yet. In 2020, he amended the constitution to give himself the option to run again. Unlike many post-Soviet leaders, he did not abolish the existing prohibition on serving two consecutive terms, but 'reset to zero' the number of terms he had already served. This unexpected manoeuvre broke the spirit, but not the letter, of carefully worded

Nigel Gould-Davies is IISS Senior Fellow for Russia and Eurasia and Editor of *Strategic Survey*. From 2000–10, he served in the UK Foreign and Commonwealth Office, including as ambassador to Belarus. He later held senior government-relations roles in the energy industry. He is author of *Tectonic Politics: Global Political Risk in an Age of Transformation* (Brookings, 2019).

Survival | vol. 63 no. 2 | April–May 2021 | pp. 203–212   https://doi.org/10.1080/00396338.2021.1906007

assurances that he would abide by the constitutional limits on presidential rule.[1] He is now eligible to run in 2024 and 2030, and remain in power until he is 83 in 2036. For many, a looming 'post-Putin' era has abruptly given way to a 'forever Putin' scenario.

But Putin has refused to confirm whether he will stay on. Instead, he has justified the amendment as a way to instil a healthy uncertainty among elites and officials. In his words, if he were unable to run again, then 'in a couple of years … instead of a normal work routine, people at many levels of authority will start looking around in search of possible successors'.[2] His intention, which he must declare by January 2024, has been the subject of speculation and gossip, but little sustained analysis. Two matters will decide this. Firstly, does Putin wish to stay in office? Secondly, if he would prefer to stand down, can he do so? The first is personal, the second systemic.

By 2024, Putin will have spent over 40% of his adult life ruling Russia. At 68, he is now the same age that his predecessor, Boris Yeltsin, was when he stepped down in favour of Putin. For nearly a decade, rumours have circulated about Putin's wish to spend more time on private pursuits. More recently, many have noted his partial withdrawal from day-to-day official duties, shorter working day and inclination to spend more time outside Moscow. There has been speculation, too, about his health. Retirement would free him from a demanding job to enjoy his remaining time and accumulated wealth. But power itself can also be a pleasure, even an addiction. The longer most leaders enjoy it, the harder it becomes for them to give it up. So imperatives may pull in different directions. Putin has a psychological equation to solve.

No one can look into the inner life of another person – especially that of a former KGB officer practised in concealing intentions – and divine a reliable answer. But the January 2021 video released by Alexei Navalny revealing the details of Putin's palace complex in Gelendzhik casts new light. Although guarded by the Presidential Security Service and Federal Security Service, the palace is not an official residence or state property. Putin's entourage has gone to great lengths to conceal both its ownership and the financial flows that paid for it. The palace is for Putin's personal use. But presidential duties and the palace's location – over 1,200 kilometres from Moscow on the Black Sea coast – limit his enjoyment of it. Retirement would allow him to spend far more time in the luxury of its aqua-disco, casino, amphitheatre, ice-hockey stadium, spas and vineyards.

Even if Putin would now rather enjoy his wealth in Gelendzhik than wield power from the Kremlin, can he safely do so? Like other authoritarian states, Russia lacks a stable and orderly mechanism for transferring power from one leader to the next. Since the prize is rule with few constraints, the stakes are high. Winning means control of the material and symbolic resources of the state. Losing means the absence of these things and the potential loss of security, liberty or even life. At its worst, authoritarian succession may trigger a Hobbesian struggle for a Leviathan state. Even if a new leader accommodates rather than punishes rivals, the latter know they remain dependent on the favours that he (it is nearly always a he) bestows. In matters large and small, erosion of fortune, position and rank remain a permanent possibility. To protect themselves and their interests, elites must submit to the perpetual intrigue and manoeuvre of court politics.

This is especially true when an authoritarian regime is also autocratic – that is, when a leader dominates with few or no formal constraints. It is striking that no post-Soviet regime, however authoritarian, has been ruled by an institutionalised party as the Soviet Union was.[3] After Stalin's death in 1953, the Communist Party, terrorised by him as everything else was, re-emerged as the main instrument of power. This served to protect elites whose very lives had until then been in permanent jeopardy. Successive general secretaries now ruled through the party, not over it as Stalin had. Nikita Khrushchev set the tone by demoting rather than liquidating his defeated rivals: Georgy Malenkov to run a power station in Kazakhstan, Viacheslav Molotov to head the embassy in Mongolia, Lazar Kaganovich to manage a potash factory in the Urals. Despite bearing responsibility for the deaths of millions, and then losing in a power struggle, all three lived peacefully until their deaths at the age of 86, 96 and 97 respectively.[4]

Khrushchev, for his part, lived out his days as a heavily surveilled pensioner after his ouster in 1964. During the long tenure of Leonid Brezhnev that followed, collective leadership and *partiinost'* (party-mindedness)

reached their zenith. While Communist Party rule remained highly authoritarian, and was especially ruthless towards dissidents, its members and
officials were largely secure not only from arbitrary dismissal or worse but,
increasingly, from performance accountability. 'Stability of cadres' degen-
erated into stagnant gerontocracy. The minutes of one Politburo meeting
illustrate this: 'On Comrade Zasyadko. They say he's stopped drinking.
Then shall we make him minister to Ukraine?'[5]

II

In post-Soviet autocracies, by contrast, elites cannot rely on the reassuring structures and solidary ethos of a ruling party. Instead, they are, as
one well-connected figure told me, 'like spiders in a jar'. Even the powerful walk with an anxious swagger. Since each succession brings a new
ruling personality, uncertainty shifts from chronic to acute. With both the
ancient solution of hereditary monarchy and the modern one of collective
party rule unavailable, there is no settled way to decide succession.[6] The
outcome matters to elites and can be influenced by them. The result can be
sudden instability, even regime change. As Henry Hale has shown, most
post-Soviet regime changes have taken place against the background of
looming succession.[7]

For democracies, successions are not generally stress points because
elites are not vulnerable. Democracies decide who will govern next
through regular, competitive elections. However fiercely contested these
are, all sides accept the rules of the game that define their conduct and
limit their consequences. The stakes are restricted to temporary occupation of political office circumscribed by the rule of law. The defeated may
be bitterly disappointed, but they need not be afraid. Democracy stabilises
succession by making it safe for the powerful to lose.[8]

This is an under-appreciated strength. Democracy's advantage is
usually defined as accountability of the powerful few to the ordinary
many. But no less important, it reassures the powerful to one another.
Winners may not persecute losers. Equally, losers must go quietly. To
reject an outcome without good reason is to call into question the legitimacy of political authority. The most acute recent threat to a Western

democracy has come not from an 'imperial presidency' or 'elective dictatorship' but a defeated incumbent. Donald Trump the 2020 loser is more
dangerous to democracy than Trump the 2016 winner.

If it is not safe to lose in an authoritarian succession, it may not be
safe to trigger one by giving up power. For this reason, few authoritarian leaders anywhere have ever resigned voluntarily. Instead, their rule
nearly always ends in forced removal (in a coup, revolt or revolution) or
the ultimate term limit of mortality. A leader who wishes to spend his or
her last years freed from the pressures of office may judge it unsafe to do
so. Hence the authoritarian paradox: leaders are captive of the system they
rule. Retirement is not an option.

Some countries that are not liberal democracies have experimented
with living leadership succession. Under the elite bargain of post-Mao
China, the president would serve ten years and then stand down while
remaining a respected and influential senior figure. But Xi Jinping has
torn up this convention and appears set to remain general secretary of the
Chinese Communist Party until 2035. In 1990, Singapore's first leadership
transition since independence saw Lee Kuan Yew resign as prime minister
after 31 years to become senior minister and, in 2004, 'minister mentor'. He
retained enormous influence until the end of his life.

Kazakhstan, closer to Russia in every way, offers a more recent and
resonant example. In 2019, Nursultan Nazarbayev resigned from the
presidency he had held since independence in favour of Kassym-Jomart
Tokayev. The comparison with Lee was widely noted. Nazarbayev himself
had hinted years earlier that he might follow the Singapore example. As
Lee did, he has retained considerable influence as chairman of the Security
Council and enjoys unique prestige as *elbasy* (father of the nation).

The Nazarbayev–Tokayev leadership arrangement, unprecedented in
the post-Soviet world, is evolving and remains uncertain. There are signs
of jockeying for position as boundaries are tested and prerogatives shift.
It is too early to tell how stable and effective it will prove. Putin's January
2020 constitutional amendments suggested he might adopt the Kazakhstan
solution in 2024, until he amended the amendments two months later to
allow himself to run again.

Nor has Putin shown any interest in repeating a home-grown experiment, the 'tandem' by which he steered round the two-term problem when it first arose in 2008 by swapping places with prime minister Dmitry Medvedev. Although tensions occasionally surfaced between Putin and Medvedev, everyone understood that power followed the man rather than the office: Putin still ran the show. But nothing strained this arrangement like its dissolution. The casual insouciance with which the two men agreed to switch back to their old jobs sparked, in 2011–12, the biggest demonstrations of the Putin era. This is not an experience Putin wishes to repeat. No Kazakh model, no tandem: he is ruling out alternatives to running or retiring.

What could he, or any strongman, do to resolve the authoritarian paradox and retire securely? He could amend the constitution to grant himself lifetime immunity. Putin did so in 2020, though parliament can overrule this provision. He could also try to ensure that his successor – and occupants of other key positions, such as security-service heads – are loyalists who will never turn against him. While Putin has not designated a successor, he has greatly strengthened the role and influence of *siloviki*, officials with a security-service background like his own. The *siloviki* not only share a similar professional worldview but are personally indebted to Putin for their elevation.

Yet uncertainty will always remain. Even trusted allies and protégés can change once they are in power, and constitutional safeguards can be dismantled. But while Putin cannot foresee Russia's future, he can reflect on lessons of its past.

The leadership transition Putin knows best is his own ascent to the presidency following Yeltsin's resignation. As the only voluntary resignation of a leader in Russian history, this is also the obvious precedent. But it is an ambiguous one. On the one hand, Putin has not touched the personal or family interests of his predecessor. The recent revelation that Yeltsin's son-in-law and former chief of staff, Valentin Yumashev, still serves as a Kremlin advisor confirms this.[9] On the other hand, Putin has taken the country in a fundamentally different direction than Yeltsin did. He has stifled civic freedoms for which Yeltsin once risked his life, re-established a strong state role in the economy that Yeltsin rolled back, and revived Soviet practices that Yeltsin helped to dismantle. Putin has also cowed, exiled and imprisoned oligarchs who had been influential and close to Yeltsin. No one foresaw this rapid and profound change of course. Putin knows from his own actions how a new leader can confound the expectations of those who gave him power.

III

Putin might also pay attention to precedents from Russia's post-Soviet neighbours, whose culture and political and legal systems still bear the imprint of their common origins. Since the break-up of the Soviet Union in 1991, these 15 successor states have charted divergent paths from the wreckage of state socialism. A range of systems, from highly autocratic to fully democratic, has emerged. The three Baltic states forged early transitions to stable democracy, with its orderly management of leadership change. In many of the remaining 12 states, severe political conflicts unfolded in the 1990s. These encompassed struggles for ultimate political authority (as with Russia's executive–legislative showdown in 1992–93) and major armed violence, including civil wars and separatism. By the end of the decade, the region had stabilised as monopolies of power secured control in each country (with the exception of five – after Adjaria's 2004 reintegration into Georgia, four – 'frozen conflicts'). But while power was no longer continuously contested, it was periodically challenged at elections (even imperfect ones) and through popular revolts (usually abetted by a section of the elite).[10] What fates have befallen leaders as a consequence?

Since 2000, nine of the 12 non-Baltic successor states of the Soviet Union have undergone leadership change. Only Belarus, Russia and Tajikistan have not done so. Among these nine, there have been 19 changes of leadership (excluding acting or stand-in arrangements). Two of these – the successions of Gurbanguly Berdymukhamedov in Turkmenistan in 2007 and Shavkat Mirziyoyev in Uzbekistan in 2016 – were triggered by the non-violent deaths of the long-ruling incumbents, Saparmurat Niyazov and Islam Karimov. A third such transition took place in Azerbaijan in preparation for the incumbent's imminent demise: in October 2003, Heydar Aliev handed the presidency to his son, Ilham, and died two months later.

In the remaining six countries, there have been 16 changes of leader since 2000. Eight of these – that is, 50% – faced prosecution after leaving or losing power: Armenia's Robert Kocharian and Serzh Sargsian; Kyrgyzstan's Askar Akayev, Kurmanbek Bakiyev and Almazbek Atambayev; Moldova's Vlad Filat; and Ukraine's Victor Yanukovych and Petro Poroshenko. In some cases, charges brought against former leaders have appeared to be politically motivated. In others, there is evidence of genuine crimes or abuses. But in all cases, leaders became vulnerable only after stepping down from, or being forced out of, office.[11]

These are not good odds for Putin, or any other leader in the region, contemplating life after politics. Three further facts might give him greater pause. Firstly, even if former leaders feel secure on leaving office, they can face trouble years later – as the 2018 arrest of Kocharian, who had stepped down from the Armenian presidency ten years earlier, shows.

Secondly, former leaders are more likely to face trouble in relatively pluralistic systems, whose development is shaped by a wider, less predictable range of political forces. Erstwhile leaders of Armenia, Kyrgyzstan and Ukraine – countries at the more politically open end of the post-Soviet spectrum – have all had charges brought against them.

Thirdly, leaders who voluntarily leave office, as well as those forced out by unhappy elites or popular uprising, can encounter such difficulties. The most striking case is also one of the most recent: in June 2020 former Ukrainian president Poroshenko, who had lost his re-election bid the previous year and left office peacefully, was charged with abuse of office. Ruslan Riaboshapka, the reforming prosecutor-general who had been removed shortly before, described the charges as 'legal trash'.[12]

The wider post-Soviet record thus offers a sobering lesson for Putin, as for other leaders in the region. Leaving high office carries a significant risk of prosecution. The implication is that it is safer to stay in power. If Putin nonetheless decides to retire, he may conclude that the best way to protect himself is to make the system he has fashioned even more *silovik-*

dominated and less pluralistic. Either way, Russia faces more difficult times ahead.

Notes

1   See Harriet Agerholm, 'Vladimir Putin Says He Will Step Down as President in 2024', *Independent*, 26 May 2018, https://www.independent.co.uk/news/world/europe/vladimir-putin-russia-step-down-president-2024-a8370361.html.

2   'Putin Did Not Rule Out that He Will Run for a New Term', TASS, 21 June 2020, https://tass.ru/politika/8782125.

3   Some post-Soviet presidents also head political parties – notably United Russia, Yeni Azerbaijan and, in Kazakhstan, Nur Otan. But the president's power does not arise from this status. The parties themselves fulfil few important functions and play no role in implementing policy as the Communist Party of the Soviet Union did.

4   The last senior figure to be executed was Lavrentiy Beria, head of the secret police, in December 1953.

5   Cited in Yegor Gaidar, *Collapse of an Empire: Lessons for Modern Russia* (Washington DC: Brookings Institution Press, 2007), p. 131.

6   Even hereditary monarchy was not foolproof. Disputed successions and rival claims to legitimacy could lead to severe disorder and even civil war. But inherited rule still pops up. It has been fused into Communist Party rule in North Korea. Azerbaijan's 2003 leadership transition was primogenital. There are signs that leaders of Turkmenistan and even Belarus may be contemplating blood succession, too.

7   See Henry E. Hale, *Patronal Politics: Eurasian Regime Dynamics in Comparative Perspective* (Cambridge: Cambridge University Press, 2015).

8   Reassuring elites is also key to managing a stable and permanent transition from authoritarianism to democracy. See, for example, Giuseppe di Palma, *To Craft Democracies: An Essay on Democratic Transitions* (Berkeley, CA: University of California Press, 1990).

9   See 'Putin Appoints Yeltsin's Old Chief of Staff to Serve as an Adviser, But the Kremlin Says He's Been Helping Out for 18 Years', *Meduza*, 22 June 2018, https://meduza.io/en/news/2018/06/22/putin-appoints-yeltsin-s-old-chief-of-staff-to-serve-as-an-adviser-but-the-kremlin-says-he-s-been-helping-out-for-18-years.

10 See Hale, *Patronal Politics*.

11 As former French president Nicolas Sarkozy recently learned, democracies can imprison ex-leaders too. But, governed by due process, such outcomes are a result of legal prosecution rather than political persecution.

12 Quoted in International Institute for Strategic Studies, 'Zelensky's First Year as Ukrainian President', *Strategic Survey: The Annual Assessment of Geopolitics* (Abingdon: Routledge, 2020), p. 246.